CREATIVE BREAKTHROUGHS IN THERAPY

CREATIVE BREAKTHROUGHS IN THERAPY

TALES OF TRANSFORMATION AND ASTONISHMENT

JEFFREY A. KOTTLER
AND
JON CARLSON

WILEY

JOHN WILEY & SONS, INC.

This book is printed on acid-free paper. ♾

Published by John Wiley & Sons, Inc., Hoboken, New Jersey.

Published simultaneously in Canada.

For general information on our other products and services please contact our Customer Care Department within the U.S. at (800) 762-2974, outside the United States at (317) 572-3993 or fax (317) 572-4002.

Wiley also publishes its books in a variety of electronic formats. Some content that appears in print may not be available in electronic books. For more information about Wiley products, visit our website at www.wiley.com.

LIBRARY OF CONGRESS CATALOGING-IN-PUBLICATION DATA:

Kottler, Jeffrey A.
Creative breakthroughs in therapy : tales of transformation and astonishment / Jeffrey A. Kottler, Jon Carlson.
p. cm.
Includes bibliographical references and index.
Summary: "In Creative Breakthroughs in Therapy, well-known authors Kottler and Carlson have invited some of the world's most creative therapists and researchers to share stories that have resulted in transformative breakthrough and behavioral change. Questions are directed to each contributor about how they achieved breakthrough so that readers gain insight into the creative process. Professionals in the field of psychology, counseling, social work and human services, graduate students, and general readers alike will be moved to discover their own creative paths as a result of reading this unique collection of inspiring narratives"—Provided by publisher.
ISBN 978-0-470-36240-2
1. Psychotherapy. I. Carlson, Jon. II. Title.
RC480.R668 2009
616.89'14—dc22

2009024943

Printed in the United States of America

10 9 8 7 6 5 4 3 2 1

CONTENTS

Preface *vii*

1 • A Personal Introduction to Creativity in Therapy *1*

2 • Stephen Lankton: Ambiguity, Relevance, and the Creeping Devils *13*

3 • Bradford Keeney: Creating Nonsense through Connections of Love *31*

4 • Sam Gladding: Being Unstuck without Becoming Unglued *51*

5 • Stephen Madigan: Therapy as Community Connections *65*

6 • Michael Yapko: You Don't Learn This Stuff in Graduate School *81*

7 • Scott Miller: I Have Creative Clients *101*

8 • Jeff Zeig: A White, Fluffy Cloud and a Dissociative Moment *117*

9 • Judy Jordan: What about Love? *133*

10 • Robert Neimeyer: A Little Hug from Heaven *143*

11 • Laura Brown: Working in a Box *163*

12 • Bill O'Hanlon: Falling on Your Face *175*

13 • Cloé Madanes: A Trilogy of Courage *189*

14 • Len Sperry: Accessing the Creative Self *205*

15 • Fred Bemak: Getting People Up Off the Floor *217*

16 • Nancy McWilliams: The Wisdom of Not Knowing *231*

17 • Nick Cummings: A Narrative History of Creativity in Action *237*

18 • Alfonso Montuori: Creative Inquiry and Discovering the Unforeseen *245*

19 • Some Creative Themes *257*

20 • Clinical Applications *271*

References *295*

PREFACE

Whereas the experience of being a therapist can often seem routine—dealing with similar issues, telling well-worn stories, using standard skills, applying favored methods—occasionally there are moments, even whole sessions, that appear miraculous in their innovation. During such creative breakthroughs, therapists find themselves saying or doing things that have never been done before. They have crossed a threshold from the familiar into completely unknown territory, a place where it feels as if a new voice has been discovered.

In theory, therapists are supposed to treat each client as a unique individual. Each session is supposed to be a novel experience in which the strategy formulated, and the means to carry out that treatment, is custom-tailored to fit the requirements of the situation and particular needs of the client at that moment in time.

Unfortunately, after years of practice, clinicians sometimes slip into familiar patterns, doing what has essentially been done before, albeit in slightly new formulations. Yet there are also those rare circumstances when we are faced with situations we haven't seen before, or when we have already exhausted everything we already know how to do—all without noticeable effect. We may feel frustrated and confused, at a loss as to what to do next.

It would be nice under such circumstances if there were a supervisory team on the other side of a one-way mirror, always available to offer brilliant new ideas for us to introduce. But, alas, we are on our own, feeling stuck and discouraged.

All therapists have had the experience, admittedly rare, when everything we already know how to do has failed us, and worse, failed the client. We can hear the voices in our heads of all our previous and current supervisors giving advice. We take inventory of our repertoire of interventions and find the stores are now empty. Yet the client waits. For something. For relief. For deliverance.

It is then that we are faced with opportunities to create something wholly new, to cross into another whole realm of possibilities. We are no longer following a familiar path, imitating a mentor, or repeating what we have seen or done previously. We have become our own guide.

The best therapy we have ever done, and will ever do, is like creating a work of art, if not a masterpiece. We weave together disparate themes that begin to form patterns. We create new ways of explaining things. We invent alternative ways to make a difference. We speak in ways so powerful that we can hardly believe that the voice is our own.

And it is not just our clients who experience breakthroughs that alter their reality forever after, but we are different as well—not just in the ways that we work, but also in the ways we relate to the world.

In this volume, we have recruited many of the world's most accomplished theoreticians and practitioners in the field, especially those who are known for their creative innovations in theory or technique. We have selected them based on the breadth and depth of their clinical experience and the influence of their published work, as well as their diversity in approach, style, and personal characteristics. We invited psychiatrists, psychologists, counselors, social workers, and family therapists to participate. We selected therapists representing many of the major schools of thought, including Adlerian, existential, narrative, feminist, cognitive-behavioral, relational-cultural, Ericksonian, constructivist, psychoanalytic, solution-focused, and person-centered. Some still work exclusively as clinicians, while others now spend the majority of their time as supervisors, academics, researchers, authors, and consultants. They represent different ages, generations, cultures, genders, sexual orientations, geographical regions, clinical settings, and perspectives. What they all have in common is a commitment to pushing the edge of their work, devising new, more creative ways to make a difference in people's lives.

We have asked them to tell us a story of their most creative breakthrough. Each was asked to talk to us about a baffling case that led to a breakthrough for them, as well as for their clients. These stories demonstrate out-of-the-box thinking that frees people to create alternative ways of meeting their needs.

This book is all about how to be creative and a constructive risk taker, going to places where others have not gone before. Each chapter explores some of the following questions:

- How and why did the situation call for such a radical, innovative approach to a problem?
- How do extraordinarily talented and creative therapists give themselves permission to experiment as change agents?
- How did their clients respond to their unusual interventions?
- What adjustments were made to customize the approach to the client?
- Where did the germ of this novel idea originate? How did the creative process unfold?
- What is the best understanding for how and why this approach actually worked (if it did)?
- What were some of the concerns, apprehensions, reservations, feelings, and thoughts after attempting this intervention that crossed the usual boundaries of what is expected or acceptable?

- How does this particular case example instruct and inform others to be more creative in their own change efforts or to promote them in others?

After presenting the 18 stories that we have written, based on interviews with the participants, we then discuss the universal themes that emerged, as well as the implications for professionals wishing to infuse greater creativity in their lives and work. We hope you will agree that the cases in this book are not only interesting and entertaining, but that they inspire and encourage each of us to promote more creative breakthroughs.

ACKNOWLEDGMENTS

We are most grateful to Lisa Gebo, our original editor and friend, who helped craft the idea for this project in collaboration with our agent, Claire Gerus. Special thanks to Peggy Alexander and Marquita Flemming at Wiley, who have worked with us to complete the project.

Debbie Nelson and Suzanne Lindner were instrumental in this project, typing all the transcripts based on interviews with some very fast talkers. Finally, we are grateful to all our contributors, who were so generous and open in sharing their stories of creative innovation.

Jeffrey Kottler
Huntington Beach, California

Jon Carlson
Lake Geneva, Wisconsin

CONTRIBUTORS

Fred Bemak, Ph.D., is a professor in the Graduate School of Education and the director and cofounder of the Diversity Research and Action Center at George Mason University. Bemak has done extensive consultation, training, and supervision with mental health professionals and organizations throughout the United States and internationally in more than 30 countries. He is a past Fulbright scholar, World Rehabilitation Fund Fellow, Kellogg International Fellow, and American Psychological Association Visiting Psychologist. He has published more than 80 book chapters and professional journal articles and coauthored four books.

Laura Brown, Ph.D., is a clinical and forensic psychologist specializing in culturally competent work with survivors of trauma. In addition to her many publications, she is featured in three APA psychotherapy videos. She is the founder and director of the Fremont Community Therapy Project, a low-fee training clinic in Seattle, where she lives with her partner and her canine cotherapist, and is moving slowly through the belts of aikido.

Nicholas A. Cummings, Ph.D., Sc.D., a past president of the American Psychological Association, is known for predicting the future of psychology practice during the past 60 years and also for helping to create it. Cummings not only designed and implemented the nation's first prepaid psychotherapy insurance, but also launched the professional school movement with the four campuses of the California School of Professional Psychology (now Alliant University). He founded American Biodyne, the first and only managed behavioral health organization completely managed by psychologists. He is now Distinguished Professor at the University of Nevada, Reno, and president of the Cummings Foundation for Behavioral Health. He is the author or coauthor of 46 books and has published more than 450 refereed journal articles.

Samuel T. Gladding, Ph.D., is chair and professor in the Department of Counseling at Wake Forest University in Winston-Salem, North Carolina. His leadership in the field of counseling includes service as president of the American Counseling Association (ACA), Association for Counselor Education and Supervision (ACES), the Association for Specialists in Group Work (ASGW), and Chi Sigma Iota. He is the former editor of the *Journal for Specialists in Group Work* and the author of more than 100 professional publications, including 29 books.

Judith V. Jordan, Ph.D., is the director of the Jean Baker Miller Training Institute and Founding Scholar of the Stone Center at Wellesley College, where she and her colleagues have been developing Relational-Cultural Theory (RCT) since the late 1970s. She is an assistant professor of psychology at Harvard Medical School, served as the director of Psychology Training at Mclean Hospital, and was the founding director of the Women's Treatment Program there. Jordan coauthored *Women's Growth in Connection* and edited *Women's Growth in Diversity* and *The Complexity of Connection*. She is committed to shifting the prevailing paradigm in psychology from one that reveres separation and "the separate self" to one that appreciates the centrality of connection in people's lives.

Bradford Keeney, Ph.D., has followed an academic career as a systems theorist and psychotherapist. He spent over a decade traveling the globe, living with spiritual teachers, shamans, healers, and medicine people to study and describe their experiences. The result of Keeney's work is one of the broadest and most intense field studies of healing and shamanism, chronicled in the book series *Profiles of Healing*, an 11-volume encyclopedia of the world's healing practices. Keeney presently conducts his clinical work at the Center for Children and Families, Monroe, Louisiana. He also serves as professor of Transformative Studies, California Institute of Integral Studies, San Francisco; Honorary Senior Research Fellow, Rock Art Research Institute, University of Witwatersrand, Johannesburg, South Africa; and founding director of the *Bushman (San) N/om-Kxaosi Ethnographic Project*, Institute for Religion and Health, Texas Medical Center, Houston.

Stephen R. Lankton, M.S.W., DAHB, is a licensed clinical social worker in Phoenix, Arizona. He is editor of the *American Journal of Clinical Hypnosis* and executive director of the Phoenix Institute of Ericksonian Therapy. Lankton is faculty associate at Arizona State University, Diplomate in Clinical Hypnosis, past president of the American Hypnosis Board for Clinical Social Work, and a Fellow and Approved Consultant of the American Society of Clinical Hypnosis. He is author of 17 books, with translations in several languages, regarding techniques of hypnosis, family therapy, and brief therapy. He has a clinical practice in Phoenix and trains professionals internationally.

Cloé Madanes is a world-renowned innovator and teacher of family and brief therapy and one of the originators of the strategic approach to family therapy. She has authored five books, including *Strategic Family Therapy; Behind the One-Way Mirror; Sex, Love, and Violence; The Secret Meaning of Money*; and *The Violence of Men.* She has won several awards for distinguished contributions to psychology and has counseled outstanding individuals from all walks of life. Her books have been translated into more than 10 languages.

Stephen Madigan, M.S.W., Ph.D., opened Yaletown Family Therapy in Vancouver, Canada, as the first narrative therapy clinic and training site in the Northern Hemisphere. In June 2007, the American Family Therapy Academy (AFTA) honored Madigan with its Distinguished Award for Innovative Practice in Family Therapy Theory and Practice. He has worked with the American Psychological Association (APA) to write the "primer" for narrative therapy and to produce a seven-part DVD featuring his "live" narrative therapy work. Madigan designs and produces the Therapeutic Conversations conferences and teaches narrative therapy training workshops worldwide on a regular basis.

Nancy McWilliams, Ph.D., teaches at Rutgers University's Graduate School of Applied & Professional Psychology and has a private practice in Flemington, New Jersey. She is author of *Psychoanalytic Diagnosis*, *Psychoanalytic Case Formulation*, and *Psychoanalytic Psychotherapy* and is associate editor of the *Psychodynamic Diagnostic Manual*. She is president of Division 39 (Psychoanalysis) of the American Psychological Association and is on the editorial boards of *Psychoanalytic Psychology* and *The Psychoanalytic Review*.

Scott D. Miller, Ph.D., is a cofounder of the Institute for the Study of Therapeutic Change, a private group of clinicians and researchers dedicated to studying what works in mental health and substance abuse treatment. Miller, the author of numerous articles, is also coauthor of several books, including *Working with the Problem Drinker: A Solution-Focused Approach*; *Escape from Babel: Toward a Unifying Language for Psychotherapy Practice*; *The Heart and Soul of Change: What Works in*

Therapy; and *The Heroic Client: A Revolutionary Way to Improve Effectiveness through Client-Directed, Outcome-Informed Therapy.*

Alfonso Montuori, Ph.D., is professor and department chair of the graduate programs in transformative studies and leadership at California Institute of Integral Studies. He was a Distinguished Professor in the School of Fine Arts at Miami University in Oxford, Ohio, and taught at the Central South University in Hunan, China. A former professional musician, he is the author of several books and numerous articles on creativity and complexity. Montuori is principal of Evolutionary Strategies, a consulting firm focusing on creativity and executive development. He lives in San Francisco.

Robert A. Neimeyer, Ph.D., is a professor and director of psychotherapy research in the Department of Psychology, University of Memphis, where he also maintains an active clinical practice. Neimeyer has published 20 books, including *Meaning Reconstruction and the Experience of Loss*; *Lessons of Loss: A Guide to Coping*; and *Rainbow in the Stone,* a book of contemporary poetry. The author of more than 300 articles and book chapters, he is currently working to advance a more adequate theory of grieving as a meaning-making process, both in his published work and through his frequent professional workshops for national and international audiences.

Bill O'Hanlon, M.S., LMFT, has authored or coauthored 29 books, the latest being *A Guide to Trance Land*; *Write Is a Verb*; *Pathways to Spirituality*; *Change 101: A Practical Guide to Creating Change*; and *Thriving Through Crisis.* O'Hanlon is a Licensed Mental Health Professional, Certified Professional Counselor, and a Licensed Marriage and Family Therapist. He is known for his storytelling, irreverent humor, clear and accessible style, and his boundless enthusiasm for whatever he is doing.

Len Sperry, M.D., Ph.D., who has practiced, taught, and researched psychotherapy for nearly 40 years, is a professor of mental health counseling at Florida Atlantic University and a clinical professor of psychiatry at the Medical College of Wisconsin. Sperry is a Distinguished Fellow of the American Psychiatric Association, a Fellow in the American Psychological Association, and board-certified in both psychiatry and clinical psychology. He serves on the editorial boards of 10 professional journals and has published some 500 articles and books.

Michael D. Yapko, Ph.D., a clinical psychologist and marriage and family therapist in Fallbrook, California, is the author of numerous books, book chapters, and articles on the subjects of hypnosis and the use of strategic psychotherapies in treating depression. Internationally recognized for his work in outcome-focused psychotherapy, Yapko routinely teaches professional audiences all over the world. He is the recipient of numerous awards honoring his lifetime contributions to the fields of clinical hypnosis and psychotherapy.

Jeffrey K. Zeig, Ph.D., is the founder and director of the Milton H. Erickson Foundation. He has edited, coedited, authored, or coauthored more than 20 books on psychotherapy that appear in 11 foreign languages. Zeig is the architect of The Evolution of Psychotherapy Conferences, which are considered the most important conferences in the history of psychotherapy. He organizes the Brief Therapy Conferences, the Couples Conferences, and the International Congresses on Ericksonian Approaches to Hypnosis and Psychotherapy. A psychologist in private practice in Phoenix, Arizona, he conducts workshops internationally (40 countries). He is president of Zeig, Tucker & Theisen, Inc., publishers in the behavioral sciences.

CHAPTER 1

A Personal Introduction to Creativity in Therapy

I (Jeffrey) was waiting to appear onstage, ready to deliver a speech at a conference. I was restless with nervous energy, ready to do my thing so I could relax and enjoy some unscheduled time. But I still had a few hours to go.

I looked up from a couch where I'd been reviewing my notes and organizing slides. I didn't really need to rehearse what I was going to say, but I wanted to be as prepared as I could be because I knew it was going to be a tough audience: They'd be tired after lunch.

I noticed the organizer of the conference pacing back and forth and talking into a phone. She looked panic-stricken. How did I know this? Based on my superior therapeutic skills I deduced many symptoms of extreme anxiety. Besides, she was screaming loudly enough for me to hear: "What the hell do you mean you're not coming?!"

When the conference organizer finished the call, I observed that she looked like she was about to burst into tears. My perception was confirmed when she muttered to herself, loud enough for me to hear: "I just want to cry."

"Something the matter?" I said to her with real concern. I liked this person a lot and appreciated all she had done to bring this conference together.

She just shook her head, unable to speak, so I waited.

"I've heard 'em all," she said, shaking her head in disbelief, "this takes the cake."

"What's the matter?" I asked again.

"Oh, no big deal. It's just that there's a program set to start in fifteen minutes—just over there." She gestured with her arm in the direction of a room where people were filing in.

"Yeah? So, what's the problem? Looks like a good crowd to me."

She nodded her head. "Would you believe that the presenter just called me?" She looked down at the phone she was still holding in her hand, squeezing it tightly, practically strangling it for bringing her unwanted news. "She said she won't be able to make it here."

"You mean the person who's supposed to be doing this program isn't showing up?"

"Exactly. So I've got a roomful of people sitting in there waiting for a workshop, and the person they came to see is a no-show."

"What's it called?" I asked her, not sure what else to say.

"Art therapy. It's a workshop on art therapy. Now what the hell am I going to do? These people are going to be bloody upset and I don't blame them."

I don't know what made me do it. But before I could stop myself, I heard a voice come out of my mouth, as if someone else were inside my body: "Well, if you need someone to bail you out, I can do the workshop for you." As soon as I said the words I had this sickly smile on my face, feeling both amused and horrified at what I had just volunteered to do.

The woman looked at me with stunned surprise. "You mean you can do a workshop on art therapy? I didn't know you knew anything about that."

As a matter of fact, I hadn't a clue what the topic was about. I can honestly say that in my whole life I'd never even done a single minute of art therapy, unless I count the time I stopped a kid from drawing on the wall of my waiting room.

"Well, sure, I can take the group for you. I'm sure we can come up with something that we could do together, but . . ."

Before I could finish the thought, the organizer had raced off to the room and was making an announcement that they were going to have a special treat. She was telling them that the keynote speaker was going to do a special session for them and he'd be right in.

I took a deep breath and started walking toward the room. Immediately, I had a flashback to another time in my life, at the very beginning of my career. I had been added as the fifth presenter to a program at my very first national conference. I was a lowly student at the time, just starting my classes. My adviser, who was quite well known, decided to add me to his program as an afterthought. Along with a friend of his, who had just authored a best-selling book, and two doctoral students, we were going to present together. This was to be my first public presentation, and my role was going to be fairly limited with all these big guns to carry the weight.

As it turned out, the famous author never showed up at the conference. My adviser had been out drinking all night, so when I went to his room to get him out of bed, he refused to answer the door. That left me and the two doctoral students. Since they were both experienced counselors and supervisors, and one of them was even a champion athlete who had won a gold medal in the Olympics, I still wasn't that worried: I would follow their lead.

When we showed up at the room, there was a crowd packed into the space. It was not just standing room only, but people were literally sitting in the aisles—hundreds of them had come to catch a glimpse of the famous author and my adviser. I peeked in the room, feeling my heart pounding, wondering what the heck we were going to do. I skipped over a few bodies blocking the door, nudged my way through the crowd, and fought my way to the front of the room. There were dirty looks all along the way, since nobody could imagine that someone as young and innocent looking as me (I was only 23) could possibly be one of the presenters.

When I turned around to face the audience, I saw only one of my partners standing next to me. It seems that one of the doctoral students, the Olympic champion, absolutely freaked out when he saw the huge audience: He fled, leaving just the two of us to handle things. We stood before these hundreds of people, all of whom were expecting someone quite different, and looked at one another with a shrug. Somehow we would get through this.

I had exactly this same feeling as I now approached the roomful of expectant people at this international conference 25 years later. They wanted a program on art therapy and I didn't have any idea about what that involved; I couldn't even begin to fake it. I reviewed every option within my extensive repertoire and still came up utterly blank. Instead, I asked the group, now growing restless, what it would be like to participate in a workshop without a name. "What if you could be part of an experience that addressed something you'd always wanted to study?"

"I thought we were here to do art therapy," someone called out from the audience.

"I already explained that to you," I said as patiently as I could. Damn, I knew this wouldn't work! Then I said, a little more forcefully than I intended: "I know that is what you came for, but that isn't going to happen. After all, being a therapist is about being flexible, isn't it? It's about going with whatever clients bring us, no matter what we've prepared. It's about improvisation and creativity, that is, devising solutions to problems that had previously seemed unsolvable. It's about letting go of things outside of your control and going with the flow. And that's what we're going to do today."

"You mean we aren't doing art therapy?" the voice asked again.

I counted slowly to myself. "That's right. No art therapy. So, what do you want to do instead?"

We spent the next few hours talking to one another about what we needed most, and what was getting in the way of reaching those goals. I had no idea where things were going or where we would proceed next. I just listened carefully, not only to the people speaking, but to the voice inside my head that had gotten me into this situation. Or perhaps I should say that differently: This was the voice helping me to find my way in a situation without markers or signs, without even a trail. But then, that is often what it feels like to me when I do therapy in the beginning stages, and especially when the client and I are venturing into new territory. That is what makes the process so exciting and such an adventure. We may have encountered what appears to be a familiar situation, and yet the best work that we do takes place during creative breakthroughs when we go far beyond the boundaries of where we have trod before.

I wouldn't say that the presentation I did at that conference was the best program I'd ever done. How could it be, without a minute's preparation, no structure, and an audience that had some rather highly defined expectations about what they'd come for? Still, I think it was one of the most satisfying workshops I'd ever done. I don't think many of the participants left disappointed, at least those who were willing to surrender their initial expectations and go with what unfolded.

In many ways, I did the perfect "anti-workshop" workshop. It was a program completely without structure, without an agenda, without handouts or slides, without any defined goals or outcomes. It was just an opportunity for a group of professionals to let go of their expectations and embrace what was available.

This experience was a major breakthrough for me, not only as a presenter, but as a therapist, supervisor, and author. I had finally found my voice and had learned to trust my own ability to be helpful without needing to plan so intentionally what I was going to do next. Just as I somehow managed to take care of business in my very first professional presentation 25 years earlier, this time I was able to do a workshop on art therapy without knowing a single thing about the subject. Instead, we examined how we could all be more creative in our work, and what was blocking us from being even more innovative.

Healing a Broken Heart

When Jeffrey shared this story, it reminded me (Jon) of all the ways we have to push beyond the boundaries of what we already know, and can already do, in order to reach new levels of creative effectiveness. This doesn't happen every day, and perhaps not every week, but these breakthroughs represent the most exciting and challenging aspects of our work when we are operating without a map, or even a compass, in explored territory.

Frank was severely depressed and suicidal, so much so that he required almost daily sessions for a period of time in order to keep from hurting himself. Even with this unusual level of support, as well as antidepressant medication, his condition was worsening. And no wonder: His grief was literally eating him alive. Just a few months earlier, his eight-year-old son had been run over by the school bus right in front of their home. Understandably, this devastated the family, Frank perhaps worst of all, who felt somehow responsible for the accident.

Everything I tried, everything I knew how to do, failed to have much of an impact on Frank. After referring him for medication without success, I tried hypnosis, meditation, cognitive therapy, spiritual interventions, and every other therapy I could think of, all without noticeable effect. As one of the world's leading experts in Adlerian therapy, I introduced every action method within my repertoire—again with no observable impact. If anything, Frank sank deeper and deeper into his depression.

I came to dread our sessions as an exercise in futility, imagining that things couldn't possibly be worse. I was wrong: Frank suffered a life-threatening heart attack. He almost died, quite literally, of a broken heart.

I not only felt sorry for Frank, but also for myself. I felt inept. His hopelessness and despair were beginning to seep into my own soul, leading me to question what I do and how I do it. Yet I couldn't just give up on him; I had to do something. So I went to the local sporting goods store and purchased a pair of running shoes in Frank's size, asking that they be delivered to his hospital room.

A couple of weeks later, Frank had been released from the hospital and was back in my office. He said he was feeling physically better but was desperately afraid that his broken heart would collapse once again. "By the way," he mentioned as the session was about to end, "how come you sent me those shoes? I mean I appreciate it and all, but you could have sent flowers." For a second, he almost smiled—not quite, but the left upper lip moved upward just a little.

I smiled back at him. "Because we are going to start training for a marathon."

"Are you drugs on or something? For Christ's sake, I just had a heart attack and almost died!"

"I know that you almost died, but I also know that your heart is a muscle that can be strengthened through exercise. So I plan to be at your house each morning at 7:00 a.m. to go for a walk. Each week we will go a little farther, and eventually we'll be able to do the local 26.2-mile run." Frank knew that I had a history of being a competitive distance runner and had frequently honked at me when he drove by in his car.

Frank was more than reluctant about this plan, and to tell you the truth, so was I. There are rules about how therapy should be conducted, strict ethical guidelines that enforce clear boundaries regarding time, place, and the kind of relationship that can take place. By taking the therapy outside of the office and onto the streets, I was realigning the nature of our alliance. Yet with his life at stake and all conventional methods proving ineffective, I knew I had to try something radical and unusual to get through to him. I certainly felt misgivings, but I could justify that what I was doing was for my client's best interests.

The next morning I showed up at his door at 7:00 a.m. as promised. We walked one block, painfully slowly, before Frank said he'd had enough and wanted to go home. He complained the whole time about how stupid this was, how tired he felt, how cold it was, how I was going too fast for him, and how he was crazy to trust a therapist who couldn't even help him. Nobody could help him. His heart was broken and that's just the way it was.

Our routine continued for the next several weeks. We would walk a few blocks with Frank complaining and grumbling the whole time and then insisting we go home. Yet we both persevered, and eventually he could walk several miles (but still complaining). I began to notice some improvement in his mood. Occasionally he would smile, or even laugh at jokes I would tell him. His gait had more bounce in it. He appeared more alive.

A month later, we were up to a slow jog, going five miles or longer. Frank began to lose weight and gain confidence. He returned to work. He stopped taking the antidepressants, as he felt they weren't needed any longer. Six months after that, he was ready for his first marathon. We got special permission from the organizers to start three hours before the official beginning, knowing that he would need extra time to complete the 26-mile course. Indeed, it took him seven hours to finish, with me at his side the whole way, offering encouragement and support. We both had tears in our eyes when we finally crossed the finish line.

Soon after this, our "therapy" ended, although we agreed to meet each year for our annual marathon, which continued for the next nine years.

As I reflect on this case, I learned, or actually relearned, that doing the same thing (talk therapy) over and over again and expecting a different result is pretty crazy. You can't solve a problem with the same thinking that created it. It was necessary to let go of the logical and rational in favor of the novel and creative.

I guess it isn't so creative these days to suggest exercise for depression, but 20 years ago it was not at all well accepted. It was also one thing to tell a client to go and exercise but a much different prospect to be knocking on his door at 7:00 a.m. in my shorts and running shoes.

All of my previous therapy experiences had been done in the safety of my office with a set 45-minute time limit. I frequently found myself worrying, "What if he has another heart attack? Maybe I am pushing him too hard? What are other people saying about our helping relationship outside the boundaries of my office?

I know that it wasn't just the running that helped Frank. He was deeply moved that I cared enough about him to invest this kind of time and effort to help him through the most critical time in his life. He felt my caring, my compassion, and my confidence that he could rejuvenate himself. Although at one point I myself had started to lose hope, it was this creative breakthrough that helped me find my own faith in his self-healing powers.

This case became the first of many instances afterward when I learned to trust my own intuition and my own wisdom. Certainly, these creative hunches evolved from long experience, but until this point in my work, I had been imitating my mentors, doing what I imagined they would do in similar circumstances. Finally, I gave myself permission to write my own textbook instead of following those written by others.

Since that first experience with Frank many years ago, I have worked with delinquent teens, getting them outside of my office and volunteering to work with handicapped children. Since the prognosis for addictions is so poor in traditional therapy, I have used meditation retreats in lieu of a traditional rehab program. I have suggested that some conflicted couples stop coming to therapy and instead volunteer their time on behalf of a social justice project they both value.

The Difference between Being Lost and Found

Each of these nontraditional activities described is a valid treatment suggestion that resulted in a successful outcome. As a friend of ours, Frank Pittman, mentioned in a previous book we wrote about failures in therapy (Kottler & Carlson, 2002), you can't do good therapy unless you do bad therapy, meaning you have to take risks, to invent new methods that perhaps were never tried before. Sometimes it works out, sometimes it doesn't. Yet if you have developed a solid enough relationship with clients, then they will be patient enough to stick around long enough for you to collaborate together on a satisfactory outcome.

The clients we see are all so different that each one requires an individualized approach, one that has been customized for his or her unique needs, complaints, and preferences. This is one of the aspects of our work that makes it so exciting and creative, yet those feelings are acknowledged only after the problems are resolved. Doing therapy is among the hardest, most bewildering, most challenging jobs on the planet (at least among those that can be conducted in an office). We are constantly being tested, never sure what is real and what is not. Our own issues are just on the edge of the conversations, gently (sometimes forcibly) pushed aside. We enter such intimate, personal relationships, yet must continuously guard against any self-indulgence. We are expected to care deeply about our clients, but not so much that we lose perspective or control.

Crossing creative boundaries often occurs during periods of our work in which we feel most lost. Yet the state of being—or feeling—lost is not as easy to define as one might imagine. Scientists who study lost behavior variously describe the state of "lostness" as

(1) not knowing where you are, (2) not being able to locate your position in relation to your destination, (3) spending more than 30 minutes without a known location, (4) being the subject of a search. Although they are referring to being lost in a wilderness area, this is still a familiar condition to most therapists a good portion of the time.

The first step to being "unlost," or "found," is admitting that you don't know where you are going in the first place. In the examples mentioned earlier, Jeffrey freely admitted that he didn't know the first thing about the subject of the workshop, and then invited participants to co-create with him a new experience. Jon surrendered to his feelings of being stuck with Frank, and that made it possible for him to invent a new way of being a therapist, one who crosses boundaries that had previously seemed impermeable.

Many stubborn wanderers have literally walked off cliffs because they refused to acknowledge that they had no accurate mental map of their location. When they don't recognize familiar landmarks, the natural tendency is to speed up one's pace, to hurry up and find the correct path that may be just over the next ridge. Therapists, as well, persist in doing what they are already doing, even though it is clear that it may not be working very well.

In studies of lost behavior in the wilderness, there are distinct stages of disorientation, beginning with denial there is a problem. During those times, when people don't know where they are going, or where they are in relation to where they hope to be, they try to make the terrain fit their imperfect mental image. This is similar to therapists insisting that their clients fit their theories in spite of compelling evidence that the situation and context don't appear to apply to them.

Panic sets in next. The urgency to find familiar landmarks leads to a sense of bewilderment and acute stress. Most of us became therapists in the first place because we enjoy the illusion of making sense of things, of finding (or creating) meaning in circumstances beyond our control, of acting as confident guides through a chaotic world. As apprehension grows, so does the capacity for clear, rational thought. Those who are lost at sea or in mountains, clouds, or woods, start making poor decisions that become progressively more rigid, unproductive, and dangerous. Their range of options appears increasingly more limited. They persist in doing what is clearly already unhelpful.

In a state of frustration and disordered thinking, people (and therapists) who feel lost make poor decisions. They follow a path of convenience rather than one that leads home. Eventually, it feels like all viable strategies have been tried and there is nothing left to be done. Clients are sometimes "fired" at this point, or helped to discover alternative resources ("Let me give you a referral").

Creative breakthroughs take place when, during these lost experiences, clinicians are required to invent new ways of navigating through a wilderness in which they have had no previous experience. Everything they know has failed them. All their route-finding skills, all their internal resources, all their technical equipment, all their strength and conditioning cannot save them. They wander in circles—or walk off cliffs. In the language of orienteering, they are "bending the map," trying to make reality conform to expectations.

The stories that follow represent seminal cases in which boundaries were crossed. The most eminent theorists in therapy and related fields share some of the creative breakthroughs that led them to find their own unique voices as clinicians and writers and inspirational figures. We hope their experiences will inspire you to discover your own creative path.

CHAPTER 2

STEPHEN LANKTON: AMBIGUITY, RELEVANCE, AND THE CREEPING DEVILS

There is something altogether contrived about asking a creative professional not only to tell us about a story, but to show us what he or she does, to demonstrate innovation in action. Steve Lankton was our very first interviewee for the project, and we hadn't yet worked the bugs out. Thus, after spending well over an hour hearing the most remarkable story of a case, we discovered to our horror that the recorder hadn't been functioning: All was lost to posterity.

It was with considerable hesitation that Lankton agreed to talk to us again, not because of any disappointment with the lost dialogue, but because we insisted that he tell us the same story again. It had been so perfect for the intent of this project that we couldn't imagine anything better. The problem was that for Lankton creativity is a spontaneous moment, one that can never be repeated in the same way. Rather than trying to re-create a conversation that already took place, Lankton preferred to begin anew with whatever seemed present at the time. That is, after all, what good therapy involves: honoring whatever is going on in the moment.

The Balance between Ambiguity and Relevance

Creativity, to Steve Lankton, is doing something outside the norm of the way you typically operate or what is expected of you by others. It is based on discovering new resources, both within yourself—and your client. He isn't just referring to intellectual or emotional factors, but also bodily sensations that become present and lead to an epiphany. It all begins with increased awareness and focused concentration.

Lankton remembered a case from several years ago that occurred during a demonstration in front of an audience of a thousand people. The client had been dealing with chronic pain for many years and had volunteered to come onstage because she heard that Lankton might be able to hypnotize her to make the pain go away.

"I was sitting there," Lankton remembered, "watching her sitting down and being strapped into the microphone and I was thinking, oh my god, what if I can't hypnotize her? What if I can't get rid of her pain in front of all these witnesses?"

Those feelings of doubt, accompanied by mild tremors within his body, signaled to Lankton that if he wanted something useful, if not wonderful, to result from this encounter, he had better concentrate on letting go of everything else except the moment.

"I felt all the details and distractions fade away to a softer focus, which included increased awareness, a wider peripheral vision. I sat in the chair up onstage and reminded myself that I can't make anybody go into a trance and I can't make anyone's pain go away. It is all about indirect suggestion, binds, confusion, and metaphors—tools that I've learned to use really well. That's all I can do; the rest is up to her. And that often is enough for most people . . . maybe for her. If not, I've done all I know to do."

Lankton could feel his anxiety and fear of performance melt away. Maybe this would work for her, maybe not. But he remembers that moment as a landmark related to performing under pressure, and he has never felt such anxiety again in those circumstances. "Instead I feel tremendous relaxed alertness that is as much a physical sensation as it is a sense of confidence in what I do. It allows me to pay a great deal of attention to the client and trust what might unfold between us that might be useful. This goes hand in hand with creativity in that I can shift more readily into new resources."

Rather than going back into the far past for an example of a creative breakthrough, Lankton mentioned a client that he had seen this very day. Brian's brother had died when he had been a boy, and he had been talking about how he never felt any closure because his parents didn't take him to the hospital to see his brother before he died. All he remembered is that he was dressed up one day and taken to the funeral to say goodbye. At the time, he wasn't even clear about what a funeral was except that it was a sad place where everyone cried.

"My parents never told me what was going on," Brian related. "They never sat me down and explained that my brother was dead. They never told me how they felt about it. They never asked me how I felt. They never reassured me it wasn't my fault. They never said a damn thing. They just left me in my room alone."

Lankton pointed out that it wasn't the first time his parents had neglected him. "They were experts at neglect, weren't they?"

Brian talked about how he had felt ignored throughout much of his childhood, a predicament that somehow left him feeling he had earned and deserved punishment. Ever since, he had chosen women to date who would be certain to censure and berate him for everything he did and make it seem wrong—living out the familiar pattern that had been established when he was young.

"You know," Brian admitted in the session, "after that trance we did last week when you were talking about me letting go of images that were bothersome. I thought we were just talking about my ex-girlfriend that I just broke up with. But later that night I woke up flooded with all these memories of my brother's death and I was sobbing and crying and something came to me." He stopped to catch his breath.

"What's that?" Lankton prompted him gently. "What came to you?"

"I was just remembering how the last time I ever spoke to my brother he was talking to me while we each lay in our beds. Rather than listening to him I just told him I was tired and wanted to go to sleep." Brian broke down in tears. "That's the last thing I ever said to him. He was dead the next day. And I just wish . . . I wish . . ."

"You wish you could have listened that one time," Lankton finished.

Brian could only nod, still crying as he relived this painful memory, still feeling somehow responsible for his brother's death.

"Let me ask you something," Lankton said as gently as he could. "I notice that you tend to remember only those things you've done that you regret. I wonder if you can think of any moments when you absolutely *knew* you had done something right, something you were confident was correct?"

Brian thought for a moment, seemingly confused, if not stumped by the question. "Well," he said, "there was this one time I went to Spain. . . . No, maybe not. That didn't work out so well." He hesitated for another minute, trying to think of a time he did something right, without second-guessing himself.

"Just give yourself some time to think about this question. It's important."

"There was this time in college. . ."

"Go on."

"Well, I didn't have very good grades. I wasn't a good student or. . ."

"Remember, this is an exercise in remembering something you did well. Here you go again remembering how you screwed up."

"Right. So anyway, I talked the admissions counselor into letting me in to the college. I just knew that I had done the right thing. I was positive."

"You look very confident as you say that."

Brian smiled, "Yeah, I guess so."

"Okay, I want you to hold onto that image in two ways. First I want you to visualize it, make it come alive. Can you do that?"

Brian closed his eyes for a moment as he had been taught to do during trances. Finally he nodded.

"Good. Make the image of confidence as vibrant as you can. Then I want you to hold it between your palms like you're holding a large grapefruit. Hold out your hands and support the confidence and let it come into you through your hands and arms so you can feel its substance."

Brian extended his arms as directed, palms outward as if holding the weight of an orb in his hands. Within a minute or two, his arms started to shake, then his whole body as he began sobbing. "Oh my God," he said. "I can do this! I can really do this! I can feel the confidence. I can feel it in my body."

Lankton let Brian revel in the sensation of being confident, enjoying the moment, weeping for joy. It reminded Lankton of something that Milton Erickson had once said about how people will work to succeed at something that they want so badly and then rather than holding onto that feeling of success, they just hurry off to do the next thing they have to do. People build up all those feelings of success that they have never really used and integrated into their self-image. It makes far more sense to undertake a task with the feeling of success right from the beginning rather than to wait until the end. Brian had never savored his successes in the past, and that was part of his problem. He punished himself over and over by recalling how he had told his brother that he didn't want to listen to him but just to go to sleep, and it only reinforced the idea that his parents ignored him because he did something wrong.

"What would it be like," Lankton asked, "if you had that same sense of confidence that what you said to your brother in that last conversation was also right? After all, you were eight years old. It was late. You were tired. You were not mean or hostile. You didn't know your brother was going to die."

Brian thought about that for a moment, then slowly nodded his head. "Wow."

"What?"

"You know, it's not survivor's guilt that I feel now."

"It's not?"

"No. It's the realization that any decision I made at that time, or any other time, is right. It's okay that I didn't want to talk to my brother when I was tired. There were plenty of times he told me to shut up. It's all right to sometimes take care of myself."

Lankton nodded.

"That's why I was with my last girlfriend so long. I let her beat me up and criticize me over and over; I guess I felt I deserved it."

For the rest of the session, Brian brought up more and more examples of this, taking the idea and running with it. He became more animated as he talked, emphasizing his strengths. Lankton observed that this represented Brian's attempt to bring resources from one context to assist him in others, a type of metaphoric translation.

Whether in the case of a client like Brian or in the therapist's own resourcefulness, Lankton believes that the essence of creativity comes from a place of "not knowing." It is within this experience of ambiguity that opportunities are offered to create something new. If the therapist can offer suggestions to clients that are ambiguous enough that they have enough room to operate, and yet relevant enough to their situations that they can find or create a connection, this technique often leads to transformative experiences. "A suggestion must be offered that appears strongly related to the client's issues, but also quite ambiguous," Lankton summarized the essence of the process. "It can't be too ambiguous or it loses its relevance. There has to be a balance between the two—that is what cranks out new meaning and understanding for the person. When interventions meet that criteria, they have long-lasting impact and are long remembered."

An Unexpected Assignment

We wondered where and how Steve Lankton learned to trust his creative intuition. How did he develop the confidence to throw out, as he is known to do, suggestions to clients that appear quite nonsensical at first, or to create elaborate metaphorical stories that seem to be woven from thin air?

Naturally, the question reminds Lankton of a story. In fact, it is one of the seminal stories of his life, one that remains the focal point of developing his own creative resourcefulness.

Lankton was participating in a training seminar with Milton Erickson, part of his third weeklong visit. Each previous time he attended the session, Erickson would ask people what they wanted to learn or what they wanted to work on. Why were they there?

Each time Lankton was asked the question, he said the same thing: "I want to learn how to undo client experiences that seemed like posthypnotic behavior that had been created in their family of origin. How do you get people to stop doing things they've learned under those circumstances?"

Erickson just stared at Lankton and smiled, but didn't say a word.

In his nervousness, Lankton continued saying what he wanted. "You know, it's kind of like when you lead a horse to water and the horse says there's no water there."

Again Erickson nodded but didn't speak.

Lankton explained further, "It's like when someone comes out of a posthypnotic suggestion, and you tell him to go get that red book on the shelf that they were instructed to not notice—they don't see a red book! And the person goes over to the bookshelf and says there's no red book. You insist it's there, and the person still can't find it and just gets irritated. So, you know . . . this is similar to the behavior of clients who are operating within their dictated life-script."

Erickson cleared his throat. "Each time you see me," Erickson said, "you ask me the same thing."

Lankton didn't know what to say to that, so he just sat there, frozen.

"If you want to continue to train with me, you're going to have to do something different."

"Sure," Lankton replied, "what do you want me to do?"

Erickson continued. "You're going to have to find the boojum tree."

"The what?"

"The boojum tree," Erickson repeated. "You can find it at the botanical gardens, but don't go there. . . . Some of my students have seen it growing north of Squaw Peak in the desert. Go there and find it."

Lankton wracked his brain. What the hell was a boojum tree? Could there really be such a thing? If so, he never heard of it. Was Erickson putting him on? Was this some kind of joke?

"Boojum tree?" Erickson said, "It's a real tree. It's spelled b-o-g . . . no, it's b-o-j. . . . No, it's b-u. . . . Just wait a minute. I think it's b-u-j . . . no b-o-j . . . g . . . b-o-o-g. No, I've got it. It's b-o-o-j-u-m. That's it! Boojum tree. It's a real tree."

Lankton knew that Erickson was a major trickster, but he couldn't figure out if he was pretending to misspell it or not. In any case, he was still skeptical that such a thing really existed. Lankton had a bit of interest in botany, and the only recollection he had of such a tree was from Lewis Carroll, the guy who wrote about someone vanishing into the rabbit hole. This was not a good sign.

"Okay." Lankton said, still perplexed but wanting to play along. He'd come a long way to study with this man and knew that Erickson could be very strange at times, there was almost always a reason for what he did.

Lankton thought he might be finished with the instructions, but then Erickson leaned closer and said, "When you do find the boojum tree, your conscious mind will say, 'That's a tree' and your unconscious will say, 'I don't believe it. I don't believe it. I don't believe it.' So I want you to go into trance the way I showed you to do and look at the tree from within the trance. And when you see it in trance your unconscious mind will *knooooow* it's a tree" (Erickson drew out the word dramatically). "And then, when your conscious mind will say, 'I don't believe it. I don't believe it. I *just* don't believe it,' then I want you to look around for the creeping devils. They'll be there."

Then Erickson dismissed him and turned his wheelchair back to the group.

Lankton got the message loud and clear that if he wanted to stay in the training, he'd have to go into the desert north of Squaw Peak in the Phoenix Mountains and hunt for something. He wasn't sure what. He realized that he was expected to leave right away on this mission. So he picked himself up out of the chair feeling very much like he was being sent into exile.

Lankton went back to his hotel and changed into clothes that were more suitable for a trek in the desert. He drove out to Squaw Peak and walked around pretty aimlessly, not really taking the whole thing very seriously. He half expected Alice in Wonderland to magically appear and show him the way, but there was nothing around but cacti and sand as far as he could see. And all the while he considered what this assignment was really about. What the heck was going on when Erickson was misspelling *boojum*? Lankton knew that he was very precise about the use of language. Erickson had read the entire unabridged dictionary before he was finished with third grade. He was the editor of the *American Journal of Clinical Hypnosis*.

"I knew Milton was very good with words, and I was pretty sure he misspelled it because he was trying to give me a message. There had to be several meanings contained in that set of letters that I should somehow contemplate. So I was spelling and respelling the word *boojum* over and over as I was tramping around out there. It sounds kind of like *bum*, which is what I'll be if I don't go to college, according to some in my family. It could be *jumbo* or *boo*, which is scary. Maybe he's trying to frighten me. Or this is about all the things I do to scare myself. That must be it! There really is no tree, but it's just a way to get me to think about being a big bum who is afraid of doing certain things I wanted or needed to do throughout my life."

There Will Always Be Creeping Devils

A lot of memories were triggered for Lankton as he wandered around the desert like Moses on the way to the Promised Land. He remembered a class in behavior modification that he had once taken where the professor kept shouting at students who asked questions, "I'm not going to answer that because it's in the book." He wished he had stood up to that guy. He reviewed regrets about girls he wished he had asked out. He thought about what had prevented him from enrolling in medical school as he had originally intended. He considered many other incidents that had, at first, seemed frightening but later turned out to be not so bad after all.

"Then, all of a sudden, in the midst of this reverie, I see this gigantic upside-down carrot growing out of the desert floor. It was clearly some kind of succulent, but not a typical cactus, at least not like any normal cactus I'd ever seen. It had these tiny branches reaching up, covered in green fuzz. The thing was huge, about 30 feet high. And I said, 'Wow. That's a tree. I don't believe it.' As soon as the words were out of my mouth, I remembered Erickson telling me that's what I would say when I found the boojum tree. This was kind of perplexing but also sort of funny. Then I remembered that I was supposed to go into a trance, and so I proceeded with the ritual as reverentially as possible. I was expecting some kind of light show, or Alice to show up from Wonderland, something that would illuminate things and show me the way. But all I was thinking was that this was a boojum tree and that I couldn't believe it. I wondered if there should be something more evident to me, some deeper meaning in this elaborate assignment. What was I supposed to learn from all this? If this was indeed a boojum tree, then it wasn't a practical joke. If it was a trick, then there wouldn't have been a tree. But I just kept saying over and over, 'I don't believe it's really a tree and not a learning. I just don't believe he could have known I would think about all those times I scared myself out of action. I don't actually believe he could have known I would think that. I just don't know what to believe. . . . I don't believe it!' "

Since this part of the prediction had come true, Lankton next recalled that he should be looking around for the creeping devils. As he walked around the boojum tree he tripped on this vinelike cactus plant that was growing along the base of the tree.

Photo of creeping devils of the Sonoran Desert

"As soon as I became aware of the creeping devil, I again thought, 'I don't believe it.' The whole thing was just so bizarre that I couldn't help but laugh. Well, there it is, for sure. I was trying to figure out what this whole thing was about. It was all so paradoxical and I couldn't quite get what had happened or why, but I figured my mission was complete, so at least I earned the right to come back from exile."

Lankton returned to Erickson's office and sat in his same chair, which had been empty since he'd been gone. Erickson immediately stopped what he'd been doing, turned his wheelchair toward Lankton and looked him up and down from his shoes to his face. He looked at Lankton's shoes and saw the dirt. He studied Lankton's hands, then looked into his face with a huge grin.

"So, you've seen the boojum tree," Erickson said.

"Well, yeah," Lankton replied hesitantly. He wasn't sure what he'd seen. "Maybe. I think so."

Erickson learned in still closer, and he whispered conspiratorially, as if they shared a special secret. "Did you see the creeping devils?"

Lankton wasn't sure how to answer. He thought he might have seen the boojum tree, but he wasn't sure what a creeping devil referred to, exactly, much less whether he had tripped over one. Maybe Erickson wasn't asking about the plants at all but was talking about Lankton's scary memories. The disturbing reverie about his regrets and failures had been, after all, kind of like creeping devils.

"Well," Lankton answered finally, "I guess so."

Erickson broke out into a huge grin, leaning forward still further, and said, "Remember that!"

Lankton nodded, not sure what he was supposed to remember, exactly. "I thought he might be referring to the things I'd been thinking about in the desert. I know he was watching me carefully as I was thinking about this, watching all the little ideomotor responses in my behavior. As carefully and sensitively as he could observe things, he probably noticed a lot in my face, as I was going back in time.

After an uncomfortably long pause, Erickson nodded thoughtfully and said, "Remember that there'll always be creeping devils."

There was another long pause while Erickson waited for Lankton to digest that. Then he said, "Now I want to teach you something else."

Creating Meaning

Reflecting on this powerful experience so many years later, having thought about it a hundred, maybe a thousand times, Lankton has analyzed every nuance of what happened. He has since found mention of the boojum tree in Lewis Carroll's poem, *The Hunting of the Snark.* He has looked up the boojum tree in botanical references and discovered that indeed he had located one of these rare ocotillos of the Sonoran Desert, just as the netlike vine he had tripped over was also a creeping devil plant. He mused over the prediction Erickson had made about what Lankton would say once he spied the tree (and how on earth did Erickson know he'd find it, anyway?).

Maybe Erickson anticipated that Lankton would generate memories during the odyssey and make some sense of them. Perhaps presenting him with a conundrum that was ambiguous enough gave Lankton the opportunity to *create the meaning* in the experience.

"I still don't know what Erickson intended by the whole event. If I'd asked him, I'm sure he'd never have told me, even if he knew himself. He didn't know what I'd actually do, and it didn't matter. Perhaps he just wanted to get me out of my head. He was an innocent player in this whole scenario, simply trying to help me create a sensory experience in the desert. He could have easily told me to find a purple rock in the driveway, but he chose the boojum tree because it's an interesting thing for which he felt some affinity. He may have figured that I'd make something personal out of it; that was my job. But who knows?"

Because the experience was so mysterious and ambiguous, Lankton was left to make his own sense of it—a challenging task in the absence of many cues along the way. "So, what *was* the point of this exercise? And what were the creeping devils? Was it the self-doubt I was creating? Or was it the vines that I stumble upon in the waning light? It's all kind of the same thing, isn't it?"

The element of ambiguity was certainly present in Lankton's therapeutic journey. So, too, was the relevance factor in that he was able to make connections between the task and his own life experience. Over the years, each time he considered the episode, Lankton found a different meaning. Finally, he settled on the interpretation of how limiting self-doubt can become, because that was the meaning that held the greatest relevance and usefulness to him. It doesn't really matter what Erickson originally intended, especially considering that the work has continued for decades afterward—and continues to this day.

Playing with Spoons: An Ambiguous Function Assignment

With so many creative practitioners like Lankton, especially those of Ericksonian persuasion, we often wonder about the source of their inspiration. Where do these ideas come from, especially those that appear at first to be so wacky (going out into the desert on a boojum tree quest)? And how to do they get their clients to comply with these instructions? It's hard enough to get families to set aside a few minutes each week to talk to one another in a meaningful way, much less to convince them to devote their energy toward some task that may appear pretty unusual, if not downright crazy.

One of the remarkable qualities of Lankton is not only his improvisational skill to create extraordinary metaphors and creative interventions in his work, but also to explain the source of their power. Writers have been trying to explain and unravel the properties of Milton Erickson's work for decades, but Lankton has been singularly clearheaded in demystifying the process.

Lankton was first quick to point out that he, like Erickson, isn't just trying things with clients, crossing his fingers, and hoping for the best. There are years of professional savvy involved in figuring out what's most relevant to a given client, depending on his or her situation and context. Continual adjustments are made based on how clients respond to the first overtures, some of them deliberate and strategic, others unconscious and intuitive.

Lankton pointed out that if you asked Erickson how he could possibly know that sending someone out into the desert would have such transformative properties, he would say only that he spoke the client's experiential language. This isn't much help.

Lankton's explanation is far more illuminating. "I'm not sure that he had anything particular in mind when he tried something. Maybe he thought I was being too intellectual, so let's send him out into the desert to get some fresh air and see what he comes up with when he gets back. But I came up with something far more personal than he may have expected. On the other hand, maybe he did have some idea of what might happen. I call this an 'ambiguous function assignment,' a term he coined in 1983 to describe that the function of this assignment is ambiguous while the actual activity itself is quite specific. I have to point out that the task is not just ambiguous to the client, it's ambiguous to the therapist as well."

For those of us who were indoctrinated into the role of know-it-all experts who are supposed to have a clearly defined rationale for any intervention, which follows empirically prescribed procedures that are grounded in data, measured in behavioral terms, and clearly described outcomes, the very idea of the therapist embracing a position of "not knowing" is more than a little disorienting.

"I try to think of something that's *not* relevant to a client's problem and tell him or her to go do that; and, when the person comes back, the outcome is often far more profound than I ever imagined."

This point reminded Lankton of another case of a lawyer who came to see him from out of state. Lankton was somewhat leery about seeing the guy because he seemed more than a little strange, and possibly psychotic. When Lankton asked the lawyer, Greg, on the phone what his problem might be, Greg's reply was: "Problem? You asked what the problem is? The problem is just seven letters. You ought to be able to spell seven letters."

Greg showed up for a pretherapy appointment and Lankton agreed to meet him for one session to see whether they might work together. Before they were very far into the conversation, Lankton already had an idea. The elements in this intervention happened to utilize the main features that were available. He knew Greg was staying at the Holiday Inn on Pensacola beach and had some idea of the layout of the place and what was there. Even before he knew anything about Greg's problem, Lankton told him to go back to the motel and up to the restaurant on the top floor where there was a private area off to the side. Greg was to take two spoons off a table and hold them, scoop-to-scoop backward so they would almost be touching one another, but not quite making contact. "Got that?"

Greg wasn't sure if Lankton was putting him on or not, but he nodded nevertheless.

"Good. Now I want you to hold on to the bottom of the spoon's handle and look through the crack of space between the two spoons and watch the sun go down. I happen to know that sunset is going to be at 6:36 tonight so I want you up there, ready to go, by 6:15."

Lankton explained at this point that when instructions are so precise and specific like this, the client is less likely to question them and more likely to follow through. Such specificity implies that the therapist really knows what he or she is doing.

"You can either do this on the top floor of the restaurant, by the big picture window where you find the spoons, or if you prefer, you can go down to the beach itself and do it there."

Lankton explained it is important to give the client some choice in the matter, thus involving the person in the decision making. The choice is, of course, a bind of comparable alternatives.

"Wherever you choose to do this, on the top floor or the beach, you're going to watch the sun go down through the vertex of those two spoons. Then, tomorrow you're going to come back and tell me why I asked you to do that."

Greg came back the next day as scheduled and Lankton immediately asked him if he had done the exercise.

As soon as Greg answered that he had, he started crying. "It was perfect. It was so right. That's exactly what my problem is."

Of course, Lankton had no clue what he was talking about, because the assignment was not only ambiguous for the client, but for the therapist as well. Lankton was trying to think of some way to ask Greg to tell him what in the world he meant without revealing that he actually had no idea what the meaning was. Eventually, Greg revealed a bit more.

"They were just ordinary objects," Greg said through his sobs. "They were just spoons."

"Yes," Lankton agreed, "that's true. So, what does that mean to you?" Lankton was still stalling, trying not to compromise his image in Greg's mind as some kind of wizard who knew just what to suggest for a cure to his problem—whatever that might be.

"It's just . . . ," Greg began, then broke out in a fresh bout of crying. "It's just that the spoons were just ordinary objects, yet they revealed something so magnificent, watching the sun setting between them. It just reminded me how I get so preoccupied with everything that I worry about that I've forgotten how to find beauty in things."

"I'm with you on that, Greg. And how is that relevant for you?" Lankton was saying inside his head, "Tell me or I'll scream!"

Greg continued, "That's why I had the affair . . . because I had to look for beauty in life through someone else's eyes."

"Tah dah!" Lankton said to us with a dramatic flourish, completing the example. "And so we now know two things: One is that lawyers can actually feel guilt. Just kidding. Second, this explains why he was feeling so horrible and wanted to seek therapy and seek it out of state. As it turns out, it was because he was a big-deal lawyer in his state and he'd had an affair to make life more beautiful and meaningful."

Lankton mentioned this as an example of how an ambiguous function assignment, such as asking someone to look at a sunset through the vortex of two spoons, can have an infinite number of meanings for any client. You have to trust that the client will choose the meaning that has the most relevance and appropriateness, given the situation and context.

"Greg probably remembers the assignment to this day. And I do, too! There are many things I ask clients to do that I can't remember, but this one stands out because it came right out of the gate, before I knew anything about what was going on. And this brings us back to creativity in the sense that it's how we take ambiguity and relevance and continue to work with them until they are usable for us. Creativity is what is most novel and interesting, almost always generated out of uncertainty, ambiguity, and a position of creative indifference or not knowing."

CHAPTER 3

Bradford Keeney: Creating Nonsense through Connections of Love

Brad Keeney was an easy choice to include in this project. We have known Brad for several years and included him in several of our other books about seminal cases. It was during our first collaboration about his most unusual helping session that we were first exposed to Keeney's extraordinarily creative thinking, which was so far outside our realm of experience that we couldn't begin to make sense of what he was doing.

At the time, Keeney had all but abandoned his professional identification as a therapist and was working with indigenous groups around the world, documenting shamanic practices and developing a reputation among certain tribes as a powerful shaman in his own right. After listening to one of Keeney's stories about helping an Ojibwa medicine man learn to have visions, we were stunned by the rather unusual therapeutic approach taken, one that involved singing, chanting, and praying in a darkened room, capped off with a homework assignment in which the medicine man was instructed to collect sticks and place them under his bed. Needless to say, the intervention worked spectacularly well, and we were left pondering what had happened and why. When we asked Keeney to explain his rather unorthodox behavior, he just shrugged and said something appropriately cryptic and shamanic about preferring to enjoy watching a fire burn rather than pulling out a log to see it cool.

When we pressed him further for an explanation about how he comes up with some of his ideas, Keeney invited us to come with him to Bushmanland in Namibia to see for ourselves how he works. What we witnessed during those weeks in the Kalahari Desert was Keeney working within the most ancient healing tradition in the world, participating in ceremonies with the Bushmen, dancing and shaking throughout the night. We were so amazed by how far beyond our imaginations this therapeutic work took place that we documented the ways that shamanic practices might be incorporated within Western psychotherapy to access greater creativity (Kottler, Carlson, & Keeney, 2004).

It was with particularly eager anticipation that we settled in for Keeney's story of a creative breakthrough, knowing that it would be a whopper. In the few years that we had lost contact with him, he had moved on from his project of studying master shamans in Africa, Asia, North America, and South America and had returned to his roots as a trainer of family therapists. Keeney was now splitting his time between an academic position in California and a clinical supervision position in rural Louisiana where he had bought a home. Keeney has long felt an affinity for African American churches in Mississippi and Louisiana, where he feels some of the most authentic, heartfelt, spontaneous, and moving spiritual transformations take place, not unlike what he has studied within indigenous groups. He has been particularly impressed with the active, emotional, evocative nature of the religious services, which look nothing like the polite, restrained rituals that take place in most Western houses of worship. Parishioners sing, chant, dance, cry out, speak in tongues, and shake—they literally *move* with the spirit. This is what led Keeney to settle in this area. If he were going to live full time in the United States again, he wanted to do so in a place where he could work with people who embodied soulful and spirited expression.

Counseling in the Dark

Keeney's clinical work is located in the midst of what might very well be the most impoverished area of North America. Many of the people are so poor on the Louisiana side of the Mississippi Delta that they make Appalachia look privileged by comparison. The townships reminded Keeney of what he had seen in Southern Africa—people living in shacks, sometimes without utilities and phones. Floors are rotted out. Roofs are falling in, patched with whatever junk can be located to stuff the holes.

Many of the cases that Keeney sees involve families that have been court-ordered to seek therapy, usually because one of the children has committed a crime. One such teenager was referred to the clinic because he had been fighting in school. Zeke was the eldest of five children who all lived with their grandmother in a dwelling that can only loosely be described as a home. The wood was rotting inside and out. Collapsed floorboards in the middle of the main room were covered with a door.

"Walking into that house with my clinical supervisees," Keeney remembered, "was like entering another world. I was very conscious of wanting to step very lightly, concerned that I might fall through one of the holes in the floor. This was even more difficult because all the blinds in the house were drawn closed, no lights on, so I could barely see anything."

Keeney explained that it was common for families to turn off all the lights (if they had electricity) and draw the blinds when a therapist or social worker came to visit. They resented the intrusion into their lives and felt that the judge was punishing them by sending someone to look into their lives and make trouble. They didn't want therapy; they wanted jobs.

Although Keeney had some idea of what to expect when he visited the shanty with his staff in tow, he was unprepared for the depth of the darkness. He could hear movement, revealed by the creaking floorboards, but wasn't certain who in the family was actually present. The only person he could see clearly was the grandmother, a heavy-set woman in her late fifties, arms folded over her sizable belly.

Once they settled into chairs, and with his eyes now adjusted to the darkness, Keeney began the conversation by jumping in right away with a question: "If you could pick any of your children to become a role model for the other kids, who would you choose?"

To Keeney's surprise, the grandmother immediately picked the second youngest of the five children, Michael. "Wish he was the oldest," she said. "He ain't but nine, but he's got the most sense."

Keeney expressed his surprise at the choice, asking why Michael seemed the most responsible. Grandma admitted that the other kids resented that she favored Michael the most, but he was about the only one she could depend on consistently. She also disclosed that with this kind of vote of confidence, nine-year-old Michael acted much older than his age.

Keeney had originally been mentored by Gregory Bateson and Carl Whitaker, two of the originators of family therapy, so it was no surprise that he retains a lot of systemic thinking even with his forays into indigenous healing. He immediately recognized that Michael had become the "parentified" child within the family structure. Within five minutes of the first session, he already felt a clinical hunch come upon him. If, during that moment, one of the other staff members had pressed him about where the idea had come from, Keeney would probably have shrugged; at this point, all he knew is that he had a working hypothesis about the family that he wanted to explore further. Literally operating in the dark, he found the first glimpse of some muted light.

A Birthday Party That Doesn't Make Sense

Having been trained and functioning as a shaman for most of the past decade, Keeney isn't used to doing much talk therapy. Any self-respecting shaman would laugh at the very idea that talk can do much good. In fact, when we were in Namibia interviewing Bushmen shamans about Keeney's healing practices, one older shaman, !Cgunte, turned the tables on us, asking what we did in our own villages to help people. When we described in simple terms that basically we sit with people, listen to their stories, and eventually offer some response in the form of conversation, !Cgunte looked puzzled. "What about the dance?" he asked. "Where are the other villagers? Where is the music?"

After explaining that we don't dance or sing or chant with our clients, neither do we invite their spiritual ancestors to be present, nor do we hug them in shaking tremors or light fires, !Cgunte started laughing hysterically. When he finally caught his breath, he asked us if we'd ever helped anyone by just talking to them.

If you think about it, he has a point. Indeed, Keeney has learned long ago that if he really wants to help someone in a lasting way, he has to reach deep inside to access his heart, his spirit, his love, far more than mere intellect, in order to facilitate a creative breakthrough with dysfunctional clients. Creativity comes from a place of openness to whatever is simmering inside, often beyond conscious awareness and previous training.

Without deliberating about diagnosis or theoretical understanding, once Keeney became aware that Michael was located within an inappropriate power position in his family, he jumped on this as a place to begin.

"There's something I want you to do," he said to Grandma, "and I wonder if you would try something that might help your situation—not just with Zeke, who has been in trouble in school, not just with Michael, who seems overly serious, but with all the kids."

Grandma hesitated, not sure exactly what she was agreeing to, but there was something in this man that inspired trust. She liked his smile and the playful way he talked to her, as if he realized that they were just checking each other out. Finally she nodded.

"Good," he said. "Why don't you have a surprise birthday party for Michael?"

"A birthday party?" Grandma answered. "That don't make no sense. It ain't his birthday. He an April baby, though he wasn't supposed to come till May. He always been little."

"Well," Keeney said with a big grin. "That's what would make it a surprise."

Grandma smiled back, still not sure what this was all about.

"It might be a nice surprise for everyone in the family," Keeney continued. "Things have been tough for ya'll. Zeke got into trouble. Michael seems to be getting a rough time from his brothers. The other kids aren't doing that well, either. It just might be an interesting thing for you to do, to give Michael a surprise party when he least expects it."

Grandma nodded, still not sure where this was leading.

"And when you make a cake for Michael's party, I want you to put 15 candles on it."

"Fifteen? But I told you he's but nine. He's just a little man, my baby in the family."

"Right. He's only 9 but he acts 15—or even older. You said he acts like the man of the house even though he's still just a little boy."

Keeney wanted the family to face the contradiction and confusion surrounding this paradox that a child was being saddled with the responsibility of an adult. This was hardly the only dysfunctional aspect of the family structure, but it was a place to start. Sitting in the darkened room, it was the only thing that Keeney could find to hold onto.

Grandma seemed to understand a little better what Keeney had in mind, even if it still didn't make much sense. That's fine, Keeney reasoned. After working with shaman healers for so many years, he was well accustomed to embracing the power of mystery. To any self-respecting shaman (or Ericksonian hypnotherapist), the goal of any therapeutic ordeal or task is specifically *not* to make logical sense, but rather to shake things up.

"Michael needs to become comfortable with his actual age," Keeney explained to Grandma. "And he needs to go through all the appropriate developmental stages so he can grow in a natural and positive way."

Keeney's immediate concern was that if nine-year-old Michael was in a position in which he had to behave like an adult, then he would miss some of the experiences, skills, and education of a child his age. Grandma listened to Keeney's persuasive case, still not too sure what it all meant, but she was willing to give things a try. She literally felt there was nothing to lose, as their lives were so desperate. "Okay," she said, "tell me what I should do."

Keeney smiled and grabbed her hand in warmth. In that moment, he felt that even if he asked her to do something nonsensical she might still comply to humor him. He sensed that they shared a playfulness that connected them.

"So you're going to bake a cake with 15 candles, right?"

Grandma nodded, totally with the program now.

"I want the other kids to give Michael birthday presents, but one very special present."

"What's that?"

"Give him a pair of pants that are much too large for him to fill."

"Heck, that's easy. All them other boys is much bigger than him." Grandma giggled as she said this.

"Then what I want you to do is to have the other boys take Michael aside, Zeke in particular, and teach him what he needs to know to be successful from his current age of 9 until 15. Got that?"

Grandma did understand what Keeney was saying. She needed to help Michael start being a little boy again. As long as he was acting like the man of the house, so incongruently in his little body, there wasn't room for any of the older boys like Zeke to take more responsibility as young adults.

During the conversation that followed, Grandma admitted that Michael was a "pleaser," always doing what everyone wants but never really taking care of himself.

"Don't you think that could hurt him," Keeney asked, "becoming too much of a pleaser? Ya'll live in a tough part of town. Life is hard here, and he needs to be able to take care of himself."

Keeney explained that he was just doing traditional family therapy at this point, realigning the social hierarchy of the family. He now reframed Zeke's behavior of fighting in school as actually being helpful to his younger brother, showing him how to stand up for himself.

"That true," Grandma agreed. "That boy, Zeke, he always looking out for the boy. He scared for him."

"So, in a way, Zeke is just trying to be helpful even if he's doing it in a way that gets him in trouble." Throughout the whole conversation up to this point, not once did Keeney talk about Zeke and his expulsion from school, the so-called presenting complaint, as the main problem. He actually cast the boy in the role as a kind of hero who was trying to teach his little brother how to be a man, although Zeke was proceeding in a way that had some negative side effects.

Keeney switched back to talk about the birthday party for Michael and the cake that Grandma would bake for him. Grandma loved to cook for the children, spoiling them with the treats she would make.

"That is one way to show your love for the children," Keeney said, "but there are other ways, too."

Grandma looked quizzical, so Keeney continued: "The grandkids already know about your easy love, the way you take care of them and cook for them. Now it's time for you to show another side of love. It's called *surprising love*. It's the kind of love where you do things that they'll never expect."

This idea immediately caught Grandma's attention. She loved the idea of surprises. She had so little to offer the children. They had no parents, and they were living in the basement of the poverty level. As the first session came to an end, she was fired up to get the party rolling.

The Deer Head That Hadn't Been Named

The first thing Keeney noticed when he returned the following week was that the room was lit up. Not only were there lights on in the room, but sunlight was streaming in through the open windows. It wasn't much of a stretch to take this as a positive sign that things might have gone pretty well that week. In fact, he learned right away that the birthday party had been a huge success. Before they even settled inside, Grandma announced that she was tickled by the whole idea of surprise love and it worked just fine. She was eager to see what this crazy therapist had in mind for them next.

As Keeney scanned the surroundings for the first time, he was immediately struck by this huge deer head mounted on the wall. It was clearly the most prominent thing in the house, so, naturally, he asked about it: "How long has it been there?"

Grandma shrugged. "It's always been there. Long as I can remember."

Still working to get his bearings, digesting this little bit of information, he also noticed that as poor as the family was, they had a fairly well maintained aquarium sitting on a table. Keeney counted six goldfish swimming inside, which he thought was pretty interesting considering that there were six people in the household.

"So," Keeney began this second session, "tell me what happened."

Grandma described the birthday party they had held for Michael and how everyone seemed to enjoy the wacky surprise of it all. Maybe it was a coincidence, but everyone seemed to be doing much better. Zeke, in particular, was doing better in school. Grandma was convinced that the birthday party somehow had something to do with it.

"That's great!" Keeney responded, "How about if we introduce everyone to this surprising love."

Keeney explained what he was thinking at this point: "This was a moment where I decided to go outside what might be considered the typical boundaries of conducting family therapy, or a home visit, because I was so struck by the presence of this gigantic deer head in this tiny shanty and I couldn't get it out of my mind. It felt to me that at first we had been in the dark and now the light had come on; it felt like we were sitting on a theatrical stage. And here was this prop, this deer head, that seemed to be screaming for attention. It was almost as if my unconscious considered it must be there as part of the script, so let's go with it."

Of course, Keeney is explaining his rationale after the events transpired. At the time, all he was aware of was that this huge deer head could not be ignored.

"So," he said, "what do you think about planning another surprise birthday party?"

Grandma started a deep belly laugh, not sure if the therapist was kidding or not. "Who we celebrating next?"

"I'm not talking about a birthday for one of the children, but for *him*." As he said this, he pointed to the head mounted on the wall.

Grandma looked at him as if he were half crazy, but then the giggle started because the idea sounded so wacky. She loved the idea of baking another cake. Any excuse to treat the kids to a special event was just fine with her.

"So, how do you want to have this party?" Keeney asked.

"Well," Grandma said, "I'll get some ice cream this time to put on the cake."

"That sounds wonderful. This time, when you have the birthday party, could you make sure that only the oldest boys sit at the end of the table?" Keeney had learned that Michael was accustomed to taking the seat at the head of the table, quite incongruent with being the youngest. Again, Keeney was trying to reorder the social hierarchy within the family.

Grandma thought that was a fine idea. In the future, she would sit at one end of the table and Zeke, as the eldest, would sit at the other end. "But how we supposed to have a surprise birthday party for that . . .?" She couldn't quite finish the sentence because she wasn't sure how to speak about the deer head on the wall. That gave Keeney another idea.

Keeney told Grandma that he wanted her to set the stage for this big event by making the announcement in a dramatic moment, one that would really surprise everyone. So the next morning, she was to wake up early, at 5:30 a.m. and start singing at the top of her lungs.

"What song will I sing?" she asked.

"Any song you like."

Grandma nodded, giving that some thought.

"What do you think everyone will do when you start singing so early in the morning?"

"Don't rightly know. I ain't ever done something like that before." Nevertheless, Grandma loved the idea of continuing this pattern of surprising the children with her love. They decided that once the kids crawled out of bed to see what the racket was all about, she would then announce that they all had a new surprise coming and she wanted them to know that first thing to start their day. All she would tell them is that they would be real excited when they found out about it.

Gathered together later in the afternoon after school, Grandma told the children they would be having a special party for someone in the family. They all tried to guess whose birthday would be celebrated next, and each time, she answered no, that wasn't it. When finally they ran out of guesses, she told them they would be celebrating the deer's birthday.

"The family needs to give the deer a name. When you're all having cake, figure out what his name is. This is very important—the family needs to name the deer."

Keeney had planned with Grandma that after they decided on a name, they would next hold a special ceremony. They were all to stand underneath the deer head and Grandma would ask the question: "If the deer could speak, it would tell ya'll something that you've never heard before, some secret that he knows about our family." Then she would reveal a family secret that they didn't know anything about.

"What kind of secret?" Grandma asked Keeney.

"That's up to you. It's just got to be something they've never heard before, a surprise."

So Grandma decided to reveal to the children, while standing underneath Bill the deer head, that their great-grandfather, Grandma's own father, had been shot and killed.

"That's an interesting coincidence," Keeney observed, "since the deer had also been shot and killed. Grandma thought that was kind of funny.

Keeney instructed her not to give the children any more details; all would be revealed at Bill's party. So they ended the session with a hug, Grandma repeating her plan as it would unfold that week. Bill the deer head would finally have a name.

The Deer Head Writes a Letter

Just as she agreed, Grandma got up early in the morning—5:00 a.m., to be exact—and started singing as loud as she could. She selected "Silent Night," the only song she could remember the words to in the moment. It was a particularly suitable choice for a surprise—singing a Christmas carol in October, waking up everyone in the house.

"What's wrong, Grandma?" the kids rushed out of their bedrooms. "What's going on? Have you gone crazy? It's the middle of the night."

"I have an announcement to make," she explained to the sleepy children, "and I wanted to surprise you."

"Well, you sure did that," Zeke grumbled.

Grandma was delighted with the reaction and told the children about the new celebration plan. When they gathered for the party, Grandma had changed the seating positions, as directed, and she followed all the other instructions, as had been agreed. The younger kids were especially happy that the deer head would now get a name, and they were the ones who pressed most enthusiastically for Bill as the choice. They had always been afraid of that thing on the wall, always staring at them but never saying anything. They liked the idea that he was now a part of the family.

In telling the story to Keeney about what had transpired, Grandma related how excited the kids were, how they said this was something they'd never forget in all their lives, something to tell their own grandchildren some day, about how Bill the deer head got his name.

"I have another question for you," Keeney introduced next. "You ready for this?"

Grandma grinned her assent. She hadn't had so much fun in years.

"Okay. Which of the children would be most excited and thrilled to receive a letter from Bill the deer head?"

Without a moment's thought, Grandma said that it had to be Tania, the youngest. She was totally beguiled by Bill now that he didn't seem so scary anymore.

"Well, then, I have it on good authority that you can expect Tania will be receiving a letter from the deer in the near future. It will provide further instructions."

After leaving the house, Keeney and his therapeutic entourage went to the drugstore and purchased two cards, one to send to the family and one to send to Tania. The family card was mailed that day with an enclosed letter of instructions to Grandma. This is what the letter said:

Deer Bumbley Family:

Thank you very much for giving me a name. It helps me feel more real and more involved with each of you. Now that I have a name you can expect to hear more from me. Looking forward to all our future parties.

Love, Bill

P.S. Please pass the enclosed note to Grandma.

As promised, enclosed within the card was a letter addressed to Grandma:

Deer Grandma:

Thanks for my party and getting to meet everyone. I am proud that you were able to say things to the family that had never been said before. I think you are finding a way to have more surprises and more unexpected kinds of love with each other.

This is what I'd like you all to do. First, it's okay for you to read this to the family. Tell them how I have a special view of the family from where I sit on the wall. I see how everyone works and plays together. But I am concerned that the fish may feel left out. They, too, need a home. Please give each fish one of your names. One fish needs to be called Grandma and the others need to have the kids' names. I think you will enjoy watching yourselves in a different way as you watch them. This calls for another party. Here is some party money enclosed. Please make sure that the fish get surprised and don't forget to include me, too.

I like to be looked at, talked to, sung to, and watch you have fun together.

Love,

Bill the Deer

The day after this card and letter arrived, another mail delivery came for Tania, the nine-year-old granddaughter. It was all the more surprising and wonderful because she had never received a letter before from anyone.

Deer Tania:

I want to say something special to you because I noticed the sparkle in your eye and your special smile when you look at me. You are making me feel more real. Maybe I will see you in your dreams.

Love,

Bill Deer

The Fish Get Named, Too

Keeney arrived for their fourth meeting with the house filled with light. All the windows were open and all the lights were on. The house had been completely cleaned, and it practically gleamed. It was indeed a striking contrast with their initial visit in total darkness.

Grandma greeted Keeney with a big hug. She was dressed up in her Sunday best, looking pretty spiffy. She was so ready to talk that he didn't even have to prompt her with a question. She launched into a detailed report as soon as they were seated.

Everyone was doing great, no problems at all with any of the children. Zeke was doing better in school. Michael was acting more like a child. And Tania was talking up a storm to Bill about everything under the sun.

They had named each of the fish and were enjoying watching them swimming around, as each family member recognized a part of themselves. They seemed particularly amazed that the number of fish exactly equaled the composition of their family. As a group, they had also decided that they were so proud of Bill that they would put up a sign in their front yard saying, "Bill lives here."

Grandma handed Keeney a letter from Tania addressed to Bill. It said:

To Bill the Deer:

Bill came in our life. Hey Bill! Today is your day. What you got to say about today is your day? We put a bandana around you. What do you got to say about that?

Love,
Tania

Keeney accepted the letter with the suitable reverence that it deserved. He then said that since Halloween was coming up, it would be likely that Bill would be sending another card with more instructions. It arrived the next day.

To my deer family:

It made me very happy to watch you give the fish their names. I also like to see you enjoying these parties. I'm excited about Halloween. Aren't you? I wish I could go trick-or-treating with you. May I go? You could carry me around and let me say "trick-or-treat." I can't wait to see the sign that tells the world that I live here with you.

I would like to ask a favor. During the day when you're away at school I miss you. Could you put up your pictures next to me on the wall so I am not alone up here?

Grandma, I am planning a very big surprise that I will announce in one week. Please make sure everyone gets ready for it. One more thing: Please, please, please may I go trick-or-treating? If I can't go out, will the kids bring their friends to say hello to me? Here's money for you to buy the treats I'll give away.

Love,

Bill

The Deer Head Starts a Business

At the next session, Grandma said they had a fun and very funny Halloween. All the other kids in the neighborhood came by the house to visit Bill. He was becoming quite the celebrity, the talk of the whole town. Even relatives from far away had heard about Bill the deer. They were coming to visit for Thanksgiving and were looking forward to seeing Bill.

The next and final session was scheduled a few weeks later, after the holiday. Grandma reported that it had been a wonderful gathering. The sign proclaiming Bill's residence had been constructed. Just as Bill had requested in his letter, they had put their family portraits on the wall all around his mounted head, there to keep him company when they weren't home. The kids had also made a sign with his name on it that they put underneath his head.

Grandma had one other interesting development to report. She had so enjoyed baking cakes for the Thanksgiving holiday that she had decided to start a food catering business. She was going to bake cakes and pies.

"How do you think Bill could be part of the business?" Keeney asked her.

"I already thought of that. The company is going to be called "Bill's Pies."

A few days later, Bill wrote the family a final letter.

Deer Bumbley Family:

Thank you for making me a part of your family. I feel that I now can be called Bill Bumbley. That makes my initials

B. B. Since I sit higher than anyone in the house, looking over the family, you have made me feel like a king. Like another famous king from the Delta. I, too, am a special king who has music all around me. I would like to ask you for one more favor. Please make a special new sign to place underneath me that says: B. B. King. Your very own special B. B. King.

Love,
Bill

A follow-up visit several weeks later found that Grandma and the rest of the grandchildren had been transformed by surprises of love that entered their lives. They were all totally surprised by what had happened.

In addition to her running her catering business, Grandma had expressed concern about the run-down condition of the local school, located in a community without any money or resources. She had organized a community group to help fix it up.

"Bill must be so proud of the work you're doing," Keeney observed.

"You're right about that," she laughed.

There's nothing that B. B. King can't do in the Delta.

Creating Nonsense

In explaining the source of his creative inspirations, Keeney noted, "It is all about allowing for a space to be moved by that which is unknown. What I mean by that is there a leap into the unknown, trusting that process."

Keeney teaches creativity in a graduate program largely by helping students to access and develop their unconscious intuition. Quoting the composer Igor Stravinsky, he mentioned that the only thing that can inspire creativity is an accident, meaning an accidental encounter with the unknown.

In the case described in this chapter, Keeney admitted that he was most impacted by the presence of that huge, imposing deer head mounted on the wall. "It wasn't for any particular reason. Maybe it just looked so bizarre. But it had an impact on me. And rather than just tucking that away, I paid attention to something I did not understand in my gut and began to play with it. And that's how the dance begins."

To Keeney, creativity in clinical work begins, first, by priming the pump, getting things started. Knowing that Jeffrey Kottler is a surfer, Keeney moved into that realm as a suitable metaphor.

"Once you catch a wave, you've got to go with it and stay with it. There are two mistakes you can make once you start the ride: You can end up above it or below it. Once you're above the wave, you're gloating, telling yourself how clever you are. That's the moment you fall off. Second, you dissociate and go underneath the wave. You begin to worry. What am I going to do next? Where am I going with this? What will happen if I do this or that? Things are going pretty well right now, but what if it doesn't keep going?"

Keeney likens the process to any flow experience, such as that of a stand-up comic or a jazz player, apt analogies considering his propensity to indulge in both.

Switching gears, Keeney explained that in order to learn to become more creative it is first necessary to get outside of the box of what is familiar. Clichés and well-worn platitudes keep us inside the box, restricted to that which you think you already understand, which is often called *common sense*. "What is outside this box is called *nonsense*. There's a border between absolute nonsense and absolute sense that is the zone of creativity. If what you offer is too nonsensical, then the client will say, 'That's ridiculous,' and won't play the game. You could write all the letters you want, offer all the deer-head-naming and fish-naming instructions, and the family will just think you're nuts and dismiss you. If, on the other hand, what you offer makes too much sense, the clients see it as a cliché that doesn't feel like it holds any possibility for change, growth, healing, or transformation. You need to be in the zone between extreme sense and extreme nonsense, what I call 'meaningful nonsense.' This means that being creative involves gaining experience and expertise in the realm of nonsense so you know how to articulate meaningful nonsense. Or, to say it differently, a creative therapist is able to present and perform nonsense in a way that it becomes a source of potential meaning and transformation."

Keeney is disillusioned with the simplistic (and sometimes trivial and boring) conventionality of much of psychotherapy, along with its overreasoned assumptions and boxed-in cookie-cutter techniques. "Creativity in therapy requires getting outside the therapeutic box, going past what has been imagined by both clinical textbooks and habituated practice." The bridge out of the conventional restraints and stuck moments is often made of nonsense. Part of Keeney's goal is to teach clinicians and clients "how to move away from stuck-sense to non-sense to changed-sense." As he puts it, "Today's nonsense is tomorrow's creative sense."

"My goal is to bring students and clients into the realm of the creative process so they can act in ways they never imagined. In order for this to happen, you must have that intuition, that tug, that feeling that there's something that's calling your attention. And it typically will be the thing that doesn't apparently fit in the moment, that doesn't immediately make any sense. Pay attention to these moments, because they might awaken you to have resourceful thoughts and inspirations. This is how you find a creative mind in therapy. In this particular case, creativity announced its presence through a deer head on the wall."

CHAPTER 4

Sam Gladding: Being Unstuck without Becoming Unglued

Renfair wasn't his real name, but it was the name he had chosen as part of his goth identity. Renfair was at Sam Gladding's door because he had been kicked out of school because of his penchant for wearing all black, including long trench coats. This being a fairly conservative school in the South and during a time of school shootings by boys who looked very much like Renfair, the principal had suspended him until such time as he "reassessed" his appearance. The eyeshadow and dyed black hair probably didn't help his case, either.

"I don't want to be here," were the first words out of Renfair's mouth after he was seated in the office.

"That's okay, neither do I," Gladding answered with a kidding smile. "So, I understand you got into trouble in school."

"Look, I don't need any counseling. I just need people to leave me alone." With those words, Renfair crossed his arms, indicating that that was all he had to say on the matter.

Staring out the Window

Gladding was used to seeing reluctant kids and had been doing so for some time. He had by this time in his career begun focusing on creativity as his primary interest, especially as it relates to music, poetry, and other arts. He had developed a habit of making connections between almost any part of a conversation and the lyrics of popular songs. It was almost a kind of training exercise for him, one that encouraged him to think more creatively in his daily life.

Even though he expected a certain amount of resistance from a boy involuntarily referred by his principal, Renfair rebuffed every effort Gladding made to connect with him. After decades in the field, Gladding had within his repertoire a sizable array of therapeutic options, some especially geared for surly adolescent boys, yet Renfair would have no part of any of them. He just sat immobile in his chair with his arms crossed and a scornful look on his face. Truthfully, Gladding was a bit unnerved by the black trench coat he insisted on wearing. He could be hiding anything underneath there.

"Okay," Gladding tried one more time, "you say you don't need counseling. What is it that you need?" He'd take anything offered by the kid.

"Something you people don't seem to understand is that I've got a right to be angry."

Gladding noted that he'd been thrown in with "you people," all the rest of the adults giving him a hard time. He nodded, encouraging Renfair to continue.

"It's like this. My parents are absolute jerks. They make me go to school, where there's nothing but idiots and half-brains. The teachers are stupid. The other kids have no clue what's happening. I just hate the place. And all I did was make a visual statement by the way I dress."

"You mean wearing all black?"

"Yeah, they're violating my First Amendment rights. I'm making a statement. They just can't take a little goth. They give me a hard time just because I wear this coat." He gestured toward the trench coat.

"Well," Gladding said, "you have to admit it is a bit warm to be wearing an overcoat."

Renfair shook his head and looked at his therapist as if he was another one of the idiots.

"I agree with you," Gladding tried again. "You are certainly misunderstood by others. They look at you very differently from the way you see yourself."

"You got that right," Renfair said under his breath.

"What's that?"

"I said," Renfair screamed in a much louder voice, "that you damn well got that right."

Gladding flinched and held out his hand, palm down, indicating that Renfair should lower his voice.

"I was just saying that people definitely see me differently. They think I'm potentially violent or something just because I like to wear black. This is America, for Christ's sake! You should be able to dress any way you want, even in high school."

Gladding was feeling absolutely stuck. He was glad that his client was at least talking at this point instead of his usual silent scowl, but he wasn't sure what to do next. He thought about reflecting the young man's deep resentment and anger, but he'd already tried that, without effect. He considered confronting Renfair about the ways he was deliberately setting himself up to be a victim, but he figured that would only drive the boy further away. In fact, he had a sense that anything traditional or standard that he attempted with this case was doomed to fail. He had to try something new, something different, just like the boy, but he wasn't sure what that might be.

They had lapsed into silent mode again, so Gladding was staring out the window, looking for inspiration. It was a beautiful day, he admitted, wishing he could be outside instead of stuck in the office with this obstinate, obnoxious kid. He reminded himself that the boy was just doing the best he could. He felt lonely and misunderstood. Take a deep breath. He glanced back at Renfair and could feel his compassion and empathy returning, then looked out the window again. The mail truck was driving by, stopping at the mailbox for the daily delivery.

Mail truck. Mailbox. Being stuck. Coming unglued. All sorts of associations were going through his head, most of them song lyrics. He was drumming his fingers against his leg, wondering what the mailman had delivered today. Probably more bills. Then an idea struck him, born of desperation—and also creative inspiration.

Special Delivery in the Mailbox

"Hey Renfair," Gladding blurted out, startling the boy from his sphinxlike position. "I have an idea, something that might be fun for us to do."

Renfair shrugged like he could care less, but anything would be better than just sitting there watching this clown try so hard to get him to talk. "Sure, Doc, what you got in mind?"

"Just a little experiment. Who knows what you might discover? You game?"

Again the indifferent shrug.

"Okay, here's what we're going to do," Gladding said with the first burst of enthusiasm he'd felt since they'd been together. He could feel his excitement growing just at the very prospect of trying something different. He could feel the creative juices flowing now. "I've got this instant camera in the office. I thought we might go outside and take some pictures."

"Take some pictures?"

"Yeah, you know, with this camera." Gladding had pulled the Polaroid out of his bottom desk drawer and displayed it proudly. "We can go outside and take some photos."

"Outside?" Renfair repeated, now intrigued with getting the heck out of this office.

"Yeah. Out there," Gladding said as he pointed out the window. "Here, you take the camera."

They proceeded to traipse out of the office and headed toward the end of the walkway along the street where the mailbox stood. As they walked, Renfair studied the camera, working out its features and parts. For the first time, he seemed genuinely engaged with something other than his brooding posture.

"Okay," Gladding said as they approached the street. "Here's what I want you to do. Use the camera to take some photos of the mailbox here."

"You want me to take photos of the mailbox?" Renfair asked, as if it only confirmed that his therapist really was crazy. But he seemed to like the idea. "Hey, sure. Whatever."

Renfair snapped off a quick picture, seemingly more interested in the whirring sound the camera made as it spit out the undeveloped photo. He held it in his hand, smelled it, and began shaking it back and forth as if to speed up the resolution. He stared at the blurry image for a full minute until it came into focus. It was just a half-cocked photo of an old mailbox, the front half missing because of the hurried effort.

"Good," Gladding said. "Now try another. But this time take your time."

Renfair studied the mailbox for a moment, kneeled down, and snapped another photo of the mailbox from a different angle, this time trying to capture the whole object in the viewfinder. There was the familiar whirring sound of the camera ejecting the developing photo, which Renfair handed to Gladding.

"Excellent. Excellent," Gladding told the kid. Now I want you to keep taking photos of the mailbox but from as many different angles as possible."

Renfair looked at Gladding for clarification, but those were the only instructions that were offered. It was warm outside, even in the fading light, so the boy unsheathed himself from the black trench coat to give himself more freedom of movement. He began circling the mailbox as if studying it from every direction, then snapped photos when the position best appealed to him. For some, he took the pictures straight on; for others, he kneeled down. In one case, he lay on the ground and took the photo from a prone position. While Renfair was thus engaged, Gladding leaned up against the fence and watched him with amusement. It was fascinating to see the boy who had been so reticent earlier totally engaged in this activity. For the first time, he actually looked like a delightful boy having fun being creative instead of the moody, enraged child that he had presented earlier.

After each photo was ejected from the camera, Renfair walked over and handed it to Gladding who proceeded to put each of them out on the ground. The first ones were already clear images while the newer ones will still dark and muddy-looking.

Gladding looked up from where he was kneeling on the ground, arranging the photos sequentially, and saw Renfair intently studying his subject, positioning and repositioning the camera until he got the perfect angle he was looking for. Another photo spit out, then another and another, until all the film was used.

Gladding collected all the pictures that had dried, placing the newest ones on top so they didn't smudge. "Come on," he said, "let's go inside and see what you created."

Renfair shrugged as if he didn't care one way or the other but Gladding noticed that he was walking a bit more eagerly than he had on the way out.

Once they had resettled in the office, Gladding put the stack of photos on the table in front of them. "Now, what I want you to do is organize all these photos in any order you want on the floor and tell me about them."

"Whadya mean? They're just pictures."

"Humor me."

Again the indifferent shrug, but there was definitely some interest in his eyes. Renfair settled himself on the floor and leafed through the stack, slowly one by one, studying each of them. He spread them out in front of them, picking one up and placing it beside or below another that caught his fancy. He seemed to be categorizing them in some way, although his rationale was not yet apparent. It was evident that he was enjoying the task.

After several minutes, Renfair signaled that he was finished. He had arranged the photos in four rows of three pictures each, the edges lined up neatly, both horizontally and vertically, like the buttons on a big phone.

"So, tell me about them," Gladding prompted. "What do you have there?"

The shrug. "Well, this first one is the mailbox with the front cut off. That's the first one I took when the camera went off before I was ready." What he didn't say was that it went off before he cared about what he was doing.

"Uh-huh. What else?"

Renfair pointed to the second one. "I took this one from a long distance. It looks far away."

"It does," Gladding agreed.

"I like this one," Renfair said, pointing to the third. It was a dark silhouette against the sky. "And this one, too," he said, pointing to a close-up shot in the second row. "You can see the lettering, the way it's faded. It was supposed to say 'U.S. Postal Service' here on the bottom, but it looks like 'US Post Serv' because the dots and some of the letters on the end don't show up." He laughed as he said this, the first expression of real joy since Gladding had met him just a half hour earlier.

During the next few minutes, Renfair proceeded to talk about the pictures with greater enthusiasm and a lot more detail, requiring no further encouragement. He was proud of his work, telling a story about how the mailbox looked happy because it was full of letters and magazines and even junk mail. But once Gladding had removed the mail during the middle of the shooting session, the mailbox seemed sadder and lonely.

"So," Gladding asked, after Renfair was done with his narrative, "tell me why you think I asked you to do this?" Truthfully, when they first started the exercise, Gladding wasn't sure himself what they were doing, just that he had to get the kid out of the office. He had a vague notion of creating an experience that might prompt looking at things, any object, from different perspectives.

"You mean like I'm supposed to tell you the lesson in all this," Renfair asked, "like this is school or something?" He smiled as he said this.

"Exactly."

"Duh. It's pretty obvious that you can see the mailbox from many different angles, from the back, the front, the right side, the left side, from below, from above, from . . ."

"Okay, so what's that got to do with you?"

Renfair stood up at this point, startling Gladding, who wondered if he was going to walk out on the session. But instead he was just walking slowly around the room, giving the matter some thought. After going outside to "play," he seemed restless sitting in the office again.

"Okay," he said finally, turning around to face Gladding directly. "I guess I see what you mean."

"What do I mean?"

"Well, like at school there's all kinds of kids—geeks and jocks and brain-dead, and even a goth like me. We're all just kind of like mailboxes, but you can look at us from different angles."

Gladding nodded enthusiastically. "Go on."

"I don't know. Maybe we're not as simple as that. Teachers and kids at school see me as this goth weirdo, just because of the way I dress, but they don't really know me. They don't know anything about me."

"Kind of like you don't really know them when you put them in categories," Gladding offered gently.

"Yeah, maybe."

"Maybe?"

"So maybe I need to lighten up a little, is what you're saying."

Gladding smiled.

"These people keeping seeing me from just one angle, like the first, quick shot I took of the mailbox that didn't really show much. It was just a first impression. It just looked like a stupid old mailbox. But once you study it—I mean once I studied it—there was all this stuff I hadn't noticed. When I looked at the photos, there were lots of neat things I didn't even see when I looked at it. Not just the faded letters, but the way the color changed in different parts as it was bleached by the sun."

"Excellent," Gladding said. "So back to you—what does this all have to do with your situation?"

"Well, like, maybe I should show people more than one side of me?"

Gladding nodded, amazed at how quickly Renfair picked up on this, as if this lesson was becoming clear to him as well. It was similar to the way the photos began to reveal themselves slowly as they developed, first completely dark, then becoming grayish with indistinct outlines, then clear images emerging.

That was the one and only session that Gladding ever had with Renfair. He returned to school after his suspension, and that was the last that Gladding heard. Like so many of the clients we see, they leave, apparently satisfied with the outcome, but often we never know how the final story ends.

A few years later, Gladding received a letter from Renfair, arriving in that very same mailbox. Actually it wasn't a letter at all, but rather a drawing of a mailbox filled with thank-you letters.

Creativity as Transformative

Gladding has since given this case a lot of thought, as is often the case when something dramatic and bewildering happens in therapy.

In retrospect, we try to figure out what happened and why. What was the source of our inspiration? What really made the difference?

It seemed apparent that one simple insight, learned through an experiential activity, helped Renfair to realize the ways that he was doing to others what was being done to him—labeling and pigeonholing people with little actual data. That had become a self-protective defense for him, warding off rejection, but also real intimacy.

Just as Renfair had been able to view, and photograph, the mailbox from so many different angles, so, too, was he able to expand his vision of others—and himself. Being a goth hardly captured who he was—not even close. His new understanding helped him to abandon stereotypes and increase his own flexibility. At least, that's one explanation that seemed to make sense. Of course, many other possibilities could also have been at work.

"Creativity does open up many new possibilities," Gladding observed, "whether in therapy or in other domains of life. It gives us new outlooks. With such perceptions come new ways of not just seeing but *being* someone different. That kind of transformation can lead to a lifelong process both for our clients and for ourselves."

Creativity is an important part of the way Gladding works, not just in regard to his own actions, but evaluating those of his clients. Part of his assessment process is to look not just for symptoms and problems, but also for resources in the form of creative interests and talents. He is interested in finding out not only what people say is wrong with their lives but also the ways they express themselves creatively through writing or art or drama or music.

Gladding likes to ask clients to bring something into the session that represents their creativity. In one case, a young man was invited to bring in his guitar and play his life history rather than tell it. In other cases, clients are asked to draw, sculpt, or act out what they are feeling.

"I asked this one young woman to keep a poetic diary of her life between sessions. Another client would come in to each session and hand me a picture of what she was feeling that day. We would start out by talking about the meaning of the colors and forms and what that revealed to her."

In examining the source of the creativity that operated with Renfair, Gladding had already exhausted everything he knew how to do and that had worked before with other clients. He had tried interpretations of the symbolic meaning of the clothes. He tried to initiate goal setting to keep him out of trouble in the future. He reflected feelings and disputed thoughts, but Renfair was pretty concrete and he ignored or deflected any of the interventions. He just kept blaming everyone else for not accepting him the way he was, black trench coat and all.

This case was a breakthrough in that it not only freed Renfair to be self-expressive, but also encouraged Gladding to be more creatively experimental in his work—as a therapist and as a teacher and administrator. As president of several professional organizations and as an executive at a university, Gladding found ways to not only take care of business in efficient fashion but to do so in a way that expressed his value for group process and individual expression. Board meetings might begin with participants being asked to briefly share the most unusual, creative thing that happened for them since the last time they met. It was a way to help members reconnect in a personal way, but also to access more creative energy for the agenda items that would follow.

This case encouraged Gladding to become more spontaneous and intuitive in his work, as well. If there is one thing that stands out about him besides his self-deprecating humor (often making fun of his compact size), it is how *polished* he appears—always in a suit and tie, always in control of himself. Yet Renfair helped him to trust his instincts more—and especially to become more playful in his interactions.

"Creativity is what helps me to become unstuck—without becoming unglued," Gladding summarized with a laugh. "It is exciting and inviting for people. It gets them to try new things, and at the same time, encourages new insights. I still use all the major theories in my work because they work well in most situations—but they don't always work. That's when I have to come up with something new."

Gladding has been doing a lot of reading and writing about creativity during the past few years, trying to come to terms with the essence contained within play and fun. He is especially interested in how creativity manifests itself as people age. "Older people who are engaged in creative activities seem to do better in terms of enjoying their lives and contributing to society. There's a lot of research to support the ways that creativity sustains and improves the quality of life in every area—physically, emotionally, and spiritually."

Getting Out of a Rut

One of the most interesting questions for Gladding is asking himself: How can I be more creative in any moment when what I'm doing isn't working?

Through his research and writing on the subject, Gladding particularly likes Eberle's (1972) SCAMPER model to access a variety of tools designed to encourage greater experimentation and innovation. Although the model was originally designed to work with children, it is useful for any professionals seeking to enliven or revitalize their work, especially during those times when they feel stuck.

Each letter in SCAMPER refers to a different way of accessing creativity:

Substitute parts of the process for those that are not ordinarily associated.

Combine elements in new ways.

Adapt a method or technique in a new way.
Modify the properties (intensity, duration, size).
Put to alternative use, different from what is ordinarily expected or known.
Eliminate a factor or element that is usually present.
Rearrange the sequence or order of things, reversing or switching the order.

This popular model, originally designed as part of the brainstorming work of the 1970s, has been used in all kinds of professional innovation. It acts as a reminder of what strategic and solution-focused therapists have been advocating for many years: If you are doing something with a client that isn't working, try something else, usually the opposite of what you're already doing. This can often lead to some creative outcomes, even if the first or second efforts are not any more successful.

Gladding remembers one client who was really depressed, and not much was working in the sessions. "What's going on?" he asked her, feeling just as frustrated as she was.

"Well," she said, "every time I come to see you I'm driving by my ex-boyfriend's house and I get depressed."

"And is this the only route you could possibly take to get to my office?"

"Well, no, but it's the shortest way when the traffic . . ."

"I know. But I was just wondering, if driving by your boyfriend's house makes you feel so bad, why you just don't go another way?"

Of course this is an obvious solution, hardly creative, but it illustrates that any behavior can be reversed, switched, rearranged, adapted, or modified to produce an alternative result. This is something we all know, but don't often practice as often as we could because of the ways we become habituated in our own predictable patterns. We tell the same stories and anecdotes to clients because they are familiar and have worked before. We proceed through the same steps in our assessment and treatment planning because it is efficient and systematized. But it also can keep us in a rut.

Said another way, and lapsing into Gladding's favorite method of borrowing lyrics from a popular song, in this case Santana: "If you always do what you've always done, you always get what you've always gotten."

CHAPTER 5

STEVE MADIGAN: THERAPY AS COMMUNITY CONNECTIONS

A social worker at the psychiatric hospital phoned Steve Madigan about a new referral, another tough case that the mental health team couldn't help. Madigan was often called about such hopeless patients, those who didn't respond to medication, therapy, group work, or anything else the team members could deliver as part of their treatment protocols.

Pete, a man in his midthirties, had been married and had a three-year-old daughter. In this initial phone call, Madigan learned that the little girl had died in a tragic drowning accident, which seemed to have been the incident that pushed Pete over the edge and into a psychotic break. As so often happens in cases of traumatic family death, Pete and his wife, Caitlin, became estranged, leaving him further isolated and grief stricken.

The hospital staff had already exhausted every option they could think of to help Pete, but he appeared to sink deeper into depression, and eventually he attempted to kill himself. This led the social worker to call Madigan for help, because the staff was increasingly concerned that their hopeless patient would eventually succeed in his self-destructive effort. He was so despondent that he just didn't wish to live any longer. The final straw was that he got into a fight with one of the orderlies on the ward, which necessitated Pete's physical and chemical restraint. The hospital staff now resonated with the same sense of pessimism that Pete manifested in his behavior. The social worker said in no uncertain terms that she thought any kind of change would be impossible.

Asking Some Counterviewing Questions

Madigan was somewhat surprised that during their first session Pete was so forthcoming about his feelings, as depressing as they might be. He described himself as "bitter and angry," "haunted day and night," "unable to go on," and "barricading myself away from the world." It appeared as if Pete was retreating deeper and deeper into a black hole from which he would never escape. He blamed himself for his daughter's death, even though there didn't seem to be any connection between her accidental drowning and Pete's neglect or actions. He knew it didn't make much sense, but somehow he held himself responsible for the tragedy, just as he did for the estrangement from his wife.

"The worst thing," Pete said, then began sobbing, "the worst thing is . . . the thing . . . I can't even . . . I can't remember Maura's voice. I can't remember what she sounds like. I just loved . . . I loved her so much. But I can't remember her voice. It's like her memory won't last. I will even lose that." Then the tears began to flow again.

Employing a series of questions consistent with his style as a narrative therapist, Madigan began to explore more deeply the different facets of Pete's experience—his isolation from everyone, the lack of support he felt, the despair and the certainty that he would never, ever recover from this grief, his guilt in not having prevented Maura's death, and his regrets over his dissolved marriage. He used "curious questioning" as a way to bring out some of the dominant themes in Pete's story in order to better understand their cultural contexts and influences on the various problems. Madigan calls these "counterviewing" questions, and they are intended to highlight potential strengths and resources that might be useful in countering the negative and defeatist worldviews that Pete had adopted.

"You mentioned giving up on hope," Madigan summarized, but emphasizing "hope" as an externalized entity that had become abandoned, "as if that is a good answer to your problems, the only answer that is possible."

"What's the point?" Pete shrugged. "Nobody could understand what happened. I mean, they're good folks and all, but they just couldn't understand what I'm going through. They've got their own families and kids and problems, so what do they have in common with me?" Pete was referring to his family and friends.

Madigan used the term "community" to refer to all of the people in Pete's life whom he had left behind: "How do you think the community looks on a father like you who has lost his three-year-old daughter?"

Pete considered the question for a moment. Shrugging seemed to be his most frequent response. "I don't know. I'm sure they're heartbroken. But they probably don't want to deal with it because it scares the shit out of them to think the same thing could happen to their own kids. I don't know. Maybe they'd just tell me to get over it and get on with my life. That's what everyone says to me at the hospital."

"And this seems fair and reasonable to you, that everyone keeps telling you to get over it and move forward?"

"I just think that everyone wants things to get back to normal, to deal with it. But how is that possible? I mean, Maura is dead. How do you ever get over something like that? That's just a fact. So how can it be normal?"

"You're saying that the people you know have a timeline for you as to how long you should be grieving, how long any father should grieve for his daughter."

Pete nodded, intrigued by this comment.

"And you've gone past their limit?"

"Yeah, that's about it. It seems like to them I'm not getting over it quick enough. But shit, man, I lost my daughter." Pete started crying again, Madigan just sitting with him, waiting.

"You are feeling so much right now. What do you think the tears are saying to you?"

"This might seem kind of strange, but I haven't really let myself cry in a while."

Madigan waited. There was a long pause while they both sat there.

"I guess I wish I could be a bit more hopeful," Pete said finally, wiping the tears away with his arm. "I'm not talking about other people, but for me. I need to find a way to remember Maura. I don't know how to do that. I don't know how to get going again. I feel like . . . I just feel like such crap all the time. I just don't know how to get going. I don't know what else to do."

Making a connection between Pete's current troubles and those in the past, Madigan next asked him to consider times previously when he had felt blocked "by hopelessness and despair." Again, these were phrased as externalized forces rather than something within him.

"Well, now that there is snow on the ground again I've been wondering and hoping that I could go snowboarding again someday. I just wish that I could take Maura up on the mountain and teach her how to snowboard."

"You're smiling as you say that."

"This may sound stupid but I just like being outside, especially in the mountains and the snow. I've been cooped up in this place for crazies for a long time."

"So, there is hope on the mountain for you?"

"Well, I want to get moving again, like actually moving my body, and get off these damn drugs they give me and say, you know, that I loved my daughter and that's all that matters. That's all I have. I'd like to take a few snowboard runs and get my life back, my life that feels like it has been stolen, and like maybe there is something left for me out there."

Madigan nodded, pleased that for the first time Pete was talking about a future that had hope included in it. "I'm wondering if you also find any hope in your friends. I recall that one of your friends—Dave wasn't it?—was the one who saved your life when you tried to kill yourself." Pete had tried to asphyxiate himself by turning on the car with the garage door shut, but his neighbor, Dave, had pulled him out of there just in time.

"Yeah, I've thought of that. I'll need to speak to Dave at some point. Actually he's the guy I'd like to snowboard with." There is a long, thoughtful pause, after which Pete returned to his familiar rumination. "I guess there is something out there, but maybe I just don't deserve it. I told you that I think I caused Maura's death, you know?" Pete started crying again.

"You are still blaming yourself for Maura's death?"

"I know it doesn't make sense, even to me, but I can't seem to help it. I just feel responsible, like there's something I should have done to prevent it."

Stubborn Hope

Madigan began the next session by asking Pete for his opinion about whether he had been diagnosed accurately at the hospital as being severely depressed. Madigan offered an alternative conception of the situation, that maybe instead of "depression," Pete's problem was that of "not knowing how to go on."

"Maybe so," Pete agreed. "I just don't know how to make sense of all this. I mean one day my daughter's there and the next day they're putting her in the ground. How do you make sense of something like that? And then the people at the hospital, I don't know, sometimes it feels like they keep treating me like I've done something wrong. You know, they just fill me up with drugs."

"And why do you suppose they would give a grieving father so much medication?"

A shrug. "I suppose because I don't want to talk to them. I just want them to leave me alone and get out of my face."

Madigan reflected the ambivalence that Pete felt, that on the one hand he wanted people to just leave him alone and let him grieve, yet on the other hand he felt so isolated and alone. Madigan asked Pete directly about that, whether there was anyone he knew with whom he could share his sorrow.

"No . . . I don't know. . . . Maybe . . . I guess I'm not there yet. I mean, what do you say to someone about something like this?"

"I'm not sure about what you'd share, but I was wondering if there is someone, just one person, whom you could talk to about what you're feeling?"

"I suppose my wife Caitlin."

"What would you say to her?"

"For one thing, I'd tell her I'm sorry for what happened to us, to our family. But sometimes I think that if we talk about Maura that we'll end up taking each other down the rabbit hole and not come back. I don't want to make it worse for her, or for me."

Pete was being clear that while he was yearning for some sort of connection with his wife, his neighbor, his friends, he was still pretty terrified of opening up new doors to the depth of his feelings. Madigan wanted to respect Pete's pace, but he still wanted to encourage him to reach out beyond himself. So he asked again who Pete thought might hold out some hope for him to return to.

"Caitlin. Somehow I think she'll be okay. She remembers who I was and how much fun we used to have." There was a long silence while Pete thought about the question some more. "I guess my family, too. I have some good buddies who hold out a bit of hope that some day I'll be back."

"Good! So, if for a moment you could imagine that hope could be rediscovered in your life, what present qualities in you would give it staying power? How could you make hope stick around?"

Pete smiled. "Well, I guess you could ask anyone who knows me that I have a real hard head. I can be kind of stubborn." He laughed as he said this. "You know, I haven't thought of this before, but maybe I can be both stubborn *and* hopeful, you know, use my stubbornness for something good for a change, to become hopeful someday."

"That would be something good indeed," Madigan agreed. "Let me ask you something else."

Pete nodded his agreement.

"This love you hold for Maura, is it a stubborn love? Is it the kind that can restore hope in your life?"

"Hmm. Interesting. Maybe so. I love Maura and that's all I know. And sometimes I think that might be enough to go on, just keeping her inside me, talking with her, and showing her the world as I see it. I suppose that is a bit hopeful."

A Letter-Writing Campaign

Madigan viewed Pete's problem as being "saturated" within his life. The problem was isolating him, closing him off from his relationships with friends and family, stopping him from doing the things he enjoys most. Instead, he remains a medicated zombie on a psych ward, waiting and praying for his own death so he can hear his daughter's voice again. He doesn't realize the extent to which Maura remains alive within him, the source of hope.

If, up until this point, you have been admiring the deft and skilled ways that Madigan has been engaging his client, sensitively and empathically building a relationship, introducing some important resources, leading him to feel more hopeful, now things become a bit more creative and novel. Madigan has long since adapted narrative ideas within traditional individual therapy to a broader context that is just about as systemic as it can get—bringing the whole community to join in an intervention.

Madigan noted that although Pete's memory of his daughter's voice had dissipated, that was not the case with the image of himself as a parent, a worthy son, a friend, a husband; all his worst memories and failings felt very much alive.

"So, any memory that he had was a bad memory of himself," Madigan explained. "Any idea of a predicted future was also a bad memory or a bad forecast, a negative imagination of a foretold future. So he was left in a place of suspended animation in which he was continually being retraumatized over and over again. He was in the closed loop of a conversation that was going on inside his head that was filled with shame and guilt. No matter how much help the hospital gave him, it would never neutralize these feelings."

Madigan viewed Pete's isolation as the main problem at this point, the way he was walled off from those who were in the best position to provide support and love. He also recognized that, whereas Pete was his main client, there was a whole community out in the world that was also grieving and feeling unfinished because of Pete's withdrawal. Yet even if his friends and family had wanted to become involved or engaged with him, they had no way to get in touch as long as he was so literally locked away. Madigan also realized that even if Pete had lost some of the memories of Maura, there were others within the community who held such collective images to be shared. The key was to reconnect Pete with those who cared about him the most.

It has long been part of the narrative therapy approach, as originally developed by Michael White and David Epston, for the therapist to write letters to clients after and between sessions, using these communications to reinforce important points and to introduce alternative ways of conceptualizing their problems. Yet Madigan had taken this several steps further, experimenting with community-based interventions in which friends and family might construct letters that would be therapeutic not only for the client, but also for themselves.

Madigan constructed a list of a dozen people in Pete's world whom he felt close to—his brothers, guys he snowboarded with, a cousin, and few others (but not his wife Caitlin). Madigan then wrote a letter to all of them outlining Pete's struggles to rejoin the world and the problems he was having doing so. This is what the letter said:

> *Dear friends and family of Pete:*
>
> *My name is Stephen Madigan and I am a family therapist working alongside Pete. Since Maura's tragic death Pete has let me know that he hasn't known how to face the world. Up until recently a sense of hopelessness has pretty much taken over his life, to the point that it almost killed him. Another debilitating aspect of this profound loss is that Pete can't remember much of his life since before Maura's death. Pete also feels in an odd way responsible for his daughter's death, even though he knows somewhere in his mind that he was actually out of town the day of the accident. Pete believes that there is a strong message out there that he should just get on with his life. He says he finds this attitude troubling because each person is different and he believes that he might never get over this tragedy even though he would somehow like to learn to live with it.*
>
> *I am writing to ask you to write a letter in support of Pete describing (a) memories of your life with him, (b) what you shared together, (c) who Maura was to you, (d) how you plan to support Pete while he grieves, (e) what Pete has given to you in your life, and (f) what you think your lives will be like together once he leaves the hospital.*
>
> *Thank you for your help!*

None of these people had seen Pete for more than five months, so they were delighted to hear any news about how he was doing. As far as they were concerned, Pete had vanished off the face of the earth, leaving them to grieve for Maura without being able to talk to him. Every one of them was delighted to participate in this letter-writing campaign and responded enthusiastically to the invitation.

Madigan has evolved a number of guidelines for these letter-writing community interventions, which involve the following:

1. All letter writers are invited to the session (if this is geographically possible) and in turn are asked to read aloud the letter they have penned about the patient. In this case, it would be in front of Pete, Madigan, the other writers, and the treatment team.
2. After each writer reads aloud, the client (Pete) is asked to read the letter back to the writer, so both writer and client can attend to what is being said/written from the different positions of speaking and listening.
3. After each letter is read by the writer and discussed with the client, the community of others in the session (who are sitting and listening) offer a brief reflection of what the letter evoked in their own personal lives.
4. This process continues until all letters are read, reread, responded to, and reflected upon.
5. Each reflecting team member (usually made up of professionals) then writes and reads a short letter to the client and his community. They reflect on the counterview of the client offered up by them and their community, the hope that was shared, and aspects of the letters that moved them personally.
6. Copies are made of each letter and given to everyone in attendance.
7. Madigan then follows up with a therapeutic letter addressed to everyone who attended the session, including the client, the community, and the reflecting team. In this case, letters were also forwarded to the hospital team working with Pete.

There was a unique aspect to this particular letter-writing community in that it was dominated by male culture. All of the participants were men who had never been used to expressing deep feelings, especially in a public forum. After each letter was read, once by the author and then by Pete, the group talked about the messages expressed, reflecting on the meaning for all their lives. There were times when almost everyone was crying. Hugging, which had previously been rare in their relationships, was now commonplace. Just as important, there was a lot of laughter, teasing, and fun during the session, which lasted close to three hours.

Pete, most of all, was positively shocked by the caring and support in the room. He hadn't realized the extent that the guys were behind him. Once he started to read each of their letters, he remembered his relationships with each of them. Immediately, he felt less alone, and realized that his grief was shared by so many others who had been struggling without his support for them.

After the success of this first letter-reading session, another one was scheduled, to include the original group plus eight more people who could join the activity. There was now a hefty-sized community present, each of whom held memories of Pete and Maura. In addition to addressing the original six issues, Madigan had asked them to write a letter accounting for their relationship with Pete in the past, what it was like in the present, and what they hoped their relationship with him would be like after he let depression go. Again, notice the narrative use of language in which the problems are framed in terms of externalized objects rather than internal properties ("let depression go" versus "when he feels less depressed").

One of the effects of scheduling these two community meetings to read the letters was that Pete now had lots of visitors. The members of this support group began visiting Pete on a regular basis. In turn, Pete began leaving the hospital on day passes to visit with friends and family. He went snowboarding a few times with his friends. And then, when he felt ready, he returned to his home, where Caitlin was still residing. He brought with him a huge stack of letters, which the two of them reviewed together, and they decided to seek marital counseling to work on their issues. With the help of their friends and loved ones, hope had been restored in their lives—and in their marriage. They eventually reconciled and were able to deal together with the loss of their child.

A Community Defeats the Problem

Looking back on this case and its particular meaning for Madigan as a creative breakthrough, he noted that, so often, mental health experts speak about client problems like depression or despair or grief as if they are exclusively internal conditions that are best managed with chemicals. Yet confusion, depression, and hopelessness had such a powerful grip on Pete that doing traditional narrative therapy with him would have taken a very long time. The creative leap was to stop talking about isolation and bring the community into the session in much the same way that shamans have been doing their work for tens of thousands of years. It is only within Western counseling that interventions are so often constructed in private; most healing traditions all over the world bring the affected community to act as witnesses, to lend their support, and to offer their love. Even more powerfully, the ancestral spirits are invited to the "dance" (and it usually *is* a dance, with music and singing and shaking) to provide additional guidance.

Madigan helped to create a healing community for his client, one in which Pete could feel loved and also really hear how much he was missed as long as depression and hopelessness stole his life. He couldn't evict them on his own. The drugs couldn't do it. The hospital staff couldn't make a dent in it. But his community of support could work together to magnify their power and influence. They got through to Pete in ways that nothing and nobody else could.

"If I had just been dealing with Pete and grief, and just looking at the story he was telling, I might have ended up with a much more limited view of him and his situation. We needed to expand that view in order to see what the problem was saying about Pete. His community of friends and family could enrich the story and fill it with love and caring."

Madigan believes that the more creative ways that loved ones are involved in a client's treatment, the better the result will be. "I think that with traditional therapy we're just seeing the tip of the iceberg. We are never really seeing individuals, but rather, that person plus all the people they're populated by and all the stories they carry about themselves. We're really missing out on a rich resource of family members and community members, work members, all those who can really help form a connection with the client during a time of greatest need."

Echoing Murray Bowen and a long legacy of systems theorists, Madigan advocates that rather than merely talking about other people in therapy sessions, everyone can be brought into the experience. Therapy becomes reconstituted as community gatherings that are emotionally charged with the significant people in the person's life, all standing together to defeat the problem.

From Personal Experience, an Idea Is Born

One function of the letter writing is not only to provide support but also to help with "restorying" the problem. Pete's difficulties with depression and loss and grief resulted, in part, from his version of the story that kept him stuck and powerless. The staff in the hospital introduced their own version of the story, in which Pete was chronic and hopeless and difficult, and that surely didn't help. Pete's friends, on the other hand, introduced alternative versions of the narrative that were hopeful and encouraging.

Madigan developed this method not only from his roots as a narrative therapist, but also as a result of his work with eating disorders. When treating severe problems of anorexia, he would bring in multiple families with as many as 50 or 75 people in attendance along with another 25 members of the treatment team. Everyone is involved. Everyone offers their input and their support. Everyone collaborates on "restorying" the problems in such a way that they can be overcome by the collective energy and resources of the group. Nobody stands alone.

As we mentioned earlier, Madigan had first been introduced to letter writing when training with White and Epston, cofounders of narrative therapy, but like any inventive clinician he sought ways to imprint his own style on the work. Madigan found himself up against some very challenging, supposedly hopeless, cases that seemed immune to traditional methods of intervention. Instead of the therapist writing a single letter to a single client, he came up with the concept of involving a whole group. The origins of this idea were quite personal, as is so often the case with a creative breakthrough.

"My mom died of cancer, and she faded rather quickly and early in life. My sisters, father, and I were really devastated. We grew up on a very strong Irish Catholic family. When someone dies, people in our neighborhood start cooking and meeting. So we had this wake, and part of the tradition is to send a "mass card" to everyone who knew the deceased. Some people wrote us back, and we had all these unsolicited letters from friends and family telling us what my mother meant to them. It helped us all to feel connected and to appreciate just how remarkable our mother had been. There was a lot of comfort in that.

"I remember saying to my sisters, 'Hey, this is all well and great, but I really wish Mom was here to read these letters with us. I wish we could have had this celebration to honor her while she was still alive.' That was the inspiration for me to develop this letter-writing campaign for my clients—because I wish it is what we had done for my mother."

Madigan has a tremendous amount of faith in people, that each of us is far more interesting than anyone realizes. He is also frustrated with the limitations of individual therapy, with its emphasis on solitary reflection in ways that are separated from the community of which each person is a part.

Most client problems have been around for a long time. They are often chronic and intractable. This requires interventions to reach way outside the usual parameters of what we understand and know, to be creative and innovative in ways that we may not have considered previously. "If jazz and art and poetry and filmmaking can do this, then so can therapy," Madigan says. He wants to be part of a group of professionals who are always stretching themselves in new ways, similar to what occurred during the early days of family therapy when the likes of Bowen, Satir, and Haley were in their prime. "I'd rather become a prisoner to this hope than a captive to intractable problems."

Madigan still remains in awe of the power that letter writing can have to promote hope. He often thinks about Pete and the ways that he recovered largely because of group support. Just four weeks after the letter-writing meetings, Pete left the hospital for good, free of medication and worry. He and Caitlin eventually restored their marriage. "Hope is the most wonderful cure of all," Madigan summarized.

Creativity Is Contagious

There is always a challenge when we read cases such as this to figure out what is contained therein that might have universal appeal. Most of us don't have access to treatment teams that can collaborate and help coordinate large-scale group meetings; the logistics of organizing such sessions seem overwhelming, especially for those of us with huge caseloads, each one crying out for attention. Many of us also don't have the opportunity, resources, or facilities to tape all of our sessions and review them with colleagues.

Madigan reports that a big part of his own creative energy stems from the innovative colleagues with whom he is associated. "There's several friends who I know that I can call up and talk with, at any time, about any idea, and they're not going to think I'm crazy. Well, they might think

I'm a *little* crazy, but they won't say that to me. They'll get excited about the conversation and tell me what it is they're thinking."

Creativity *is* contagious. Madigan points out the importance of hanging out with colleagues who stimulate us, who push us to explore new areas, who challenge us to evaluate what we are doing and why, and who are the source of much innovation. There is only so much we can do on our own. That is the value of stories like those contained in this book: They present examples of work that we may not have considered before. They get us to think outside the usual boundaries of what we consider therapy. Madigan ascribes his own creative output to how closely he pays attention to what others are doing. "I pay attention to what my clients are saying. I pay attention to what my associates are doing. And I pay really close attention to what I am doing. To me, it is all a piece of art. That's what sustains me and keeps me going. Otherwise, I'd just do something else that was more interesting."

Madigan points out that creativity arises when we are most engaged and interested in what is happening—in the session, but also inside of ourselves. If a supportive community is critical to help clients rediscover hope and possibilities, then the same thing is true of therapists. And that is one area where Madigan has been a leader in creating therapeutic communities that teach clinicians to cover new ground. The whole idea of a "reflecting team" in narrative therapy is to capitalize on collective wisdom and group processing in order to promote breakthroughs.

Even if it is not possible to create a whole therapeutic community, one inspiration for creative development is to seek out and cultivate relationships with other professionals who are experimenting successfully with new work. Madigan didn't fall into his current situation because of luck or good fortune; it is something that he has made happen in his life because he so thrives on community action. On a small scale, it is possible for each one of us to become proactive, inviting colleagues to join us in conversations, if not peer supervision, to talk about ways that we could each take our work to the next level.

CHAPTER 6

Michael Yapko: You Don't Learn This Stuff in Graduate School

Michael Yapko makes his living being creative, so much so that he could scarcely decide which one of three different cases to talk about. He settled on a case about an attorney named Kyle, midforties, who had everything going well in his life yet felt depressed.

The Perfect Son

Kyle was successful in every facet of his life. He was an academic superstar in school, an accomplished lawyer with a thriving practice, secure in a happy and satisfying marriage, and filled with pride in his two lovely children. He had all the material comforts he could ever want, a loving and supportive family, and a great job. The only problem was that he was depressed and could almost never remember a time when he didn't feel down, as much as he had tried to hide these feelings. He had sought therapy in the past for his troubles, but without significant gains.

After a brief presentation of his symptoms and background, Kyle immediately put Yapko on the spot. "Give me the bottom line," he said, very much a bottom-line kind of guy, "what is this all about?"

He didn't really expect an answer, so before Yapko could answer, he admitted, "Look, I know I'm a perfectionist. Nothing is ever good enough for me. I just feel inadequate no matter what I do or how much I accomplish. I feel like an imposter, like I'm fooling everyone—but not myself."

"Then how have you managed to accomplish as much as you have?" Yapko asked.

"I'm just not nearly as good as people think I am—my clients, my partners, even my family. I fool them all."

"This isn't a new revelation for you," Yapko observed mildly, going slowly until he could figure out what was going on.

Kyle nodded. "Objectively, I know I'm good at what I do . . ."

"But . . .?"

"But if I had to guess I'd say that this all started with my dad."

"What's that about?"

"Well, my entire life I have spent an inordinate amount of time and effort trying to get my dad's approval."

"Yeah? And how's that worked out for you?"

"Not too well," Kyle admitted. "No matter what I do, no matter how hard I tried all my life, he still wouldn't acknowledge that I was doing anything worthwhile. So I'd try even harder to succeed, hoping he'd finally notice, but it was never enough." Kyle was shaking his head at the futility of it all.

"You seem to know the futility of your efforts quite well; you've recognized it for a long time, but you still seem powerless to stop yourself from still trying to get his approval."

"You got that right. The harder I try to succeed, the more critical he becomes. Perfect grades in school? Never enough. Getting a plumb job? Totally scornful. The perfect family? He could care less. It's always been that way with him."

"What son doesn't want his father's approval?" Yapko asked gently. "What man *doesn't* want to have the respect of his father?"

"You know, my mom was always pretty easy to get along with. She was easy to please. Whatever I did was just fine with her. No challenge."

"You needed the challenge?"

"It's not that. It's that . . . see, my dad is an attorney, too. He's always been hardworking, never around much, a hard-driving kind of a guy. When I was growing up, it was especially important for me to get his approval. So, when other kids were out playing, I was pretty much hanging around the house doing things and trying to get noticed by dad."

"Like what?"

"You know, just simple stuff, anything, like cleaning my room so it was perfect. Then I'd move to the more complex stuff of trying to be around to do the things he would want me to do, whether it was cutting the lawn or whatever. And then as I got older, some kids were getting into sports and other kids were getting into all kinds of after-school activities and there I was still hanging around dad waiting for him to notice me."

"But he never did."

Kyle's voice became lower, softer, and he slumped in his chair as if in resignation. "No, nothing worked. I was always a great student. I worked hard, studied hard, always got top grades, and even into high school, when most people got into this rebellious thing with their parents, I never did. I was always the good boy, the perfect son. I graduated number one in my high school class. I was the class valedictorian, but dad didn't even come to my high school graduation."

"Wow, that must have been so hard for you."

"Yeah, it tore me apart. I understood it, I guess. He was always busy with work. He was always in the middle of a big case. He was . . ."

"Excuses. You're making excuses for him."

"Right. I've always done that. I make excuses for him, but it really hurt me that he was always so critical and never there for me. What could I do? What would it take? So I figured I just had to try harder, you know?"

"And you did."

Kyle nodded. "So I went off to college and did very well and decided in my third year that I was going to be a lawyer like my dad."

"Now, that's a big surprise. Gee, who would've predicted that?"

Kyle laughed. "Point taken. So I went to law school and again was at the top of my class. I could have gotten a job anywhere, but I asked my dad if I could join his practice. I had just kind of assumed that's what I'd do after I graduated, and that's why I worked so hard to earn it. I had this idealistic image of us having a wonderful father-son law practice. Man, was I way off. I guess I shouldn't have been surprised, but he says to me, 'You want to come in? Well, I want to get out. I want to retire, and now's the time to do it. You think you're just going to come waltzing in to this business that I built and I'm going to hand it over to you? No way! I'll tell you what. I'll *sell* you the practice.'"

"What did you think about that?"

Kyle shrugged. "I don't know. I guess it made good business sense."

"That's what you thought at the time? Or is that what you've told yourself in the interim?"

"No, I was devastated at the time. My own father was going to sell me his practice and then retire because he apparently didn't want to work with me. This was the worst rejection of all."

"So then what happened?" Yapko was fascinated by the story.

"Once I was clear he and I wouldn't have that father-son law practice thing, I almost immediately agreed to buy the practice. The first thing I did in taking it over was modernize it. My father might have been a great litigator, but he hadn't updated anything in that office in 25 years! I brought in computers and a new file system and subscribed to specialized online research services. It was all pretty slick, absolutely cutting edge, and I was pretty proud of what I'd done. I'll never forget that day I had everything installed and up and running. I was thinking to myself, now my dad will be so blown away by the operation. He'll just be amazed. And finally I'll get some of the respect and recognition from him that I always deserved.

"I made a point of picking my father up at home, taking him out for breakfast, and telling him ahead of time that I'd made a few changes around the office. I wanted to pique his curiosity but also set up him for the big surprise. So he walks in the door and I'm looking at his face, waiting for his reaction, and he turns to me as soon as he sees all the new computers, terminals, screens, and other fancy stuff, and he says, 'What the hell's the matter with you? You blew all this money on a bunch of machines? I was a lawyer for 40 years and I never needed any of this crap. What are you going to do, take these computers into the courtroom with you? What kind of lawyer are you, anyway?' Then he turned around and walked out the door, telling me to take him home." As he ended this tragic tale, Kyle tried to hold back his tears, but eventually succumbed to his anger, frustration, and sadness. He had accomplished so much in his life to try to attain the one thing he could never have: his father's approval.

Don't Ask People for What They Don't Have

"It's understandable why you would feel so devastated by your father's reaction," Yapko responded after the long narrative was completed. "You were so sure he'd be proud of what you'd done."

Kyle nodded, grateful that his therapist understood what he had been saying. But Yapko had something far different in mind than empathic reflections for his intervention. This was such a nice, successful man in everyone's eyes except his own. Kyle had been in therapy before, so he well understood this insight, even if it didn't change his behavior. It was time to make a vital shift.

"After all his years in therapy," Yapko explained, "he had never learned one of the most important lessons in life. Kyle was reflexively blaming himself for his father's limitations. He had always assumed, obviously incorrectly, that his father was capable of approval if only he'd do the right thing to tap into it. It never occurred to Kyle that it was really his father who was impaired. He had an amazing son, the kind of son any parent would be thrilled to have, but he was so emotionally withholding that he simply *couldn't* offer praise, support, or approval, no matter how deserving his son might be. Kyle didn't understand that no matter what he did, no matter how hard he tried, he would never, ever get what he wanted from his father, not because he didn't deserve it, but because his father couldn't provide it. Knowing this, it was time to do something quite surprising, even shocking."

This case highlights how important it is for us to take stock of what has been tried before and has not worked, what has already been attempted without success, and not to repeat those ineffective approaches. Kyle had already been in insight-oriented therapy for some time. He had already been encouraged to look deeply into his past, to examine his approval-seeking patterns and unconscious desires, to confront his irrational thinking that he should be perfect in all he does, to explore his unresolved feelings of frustration and anger, but nothing significant changed for him. He had done enough focusing on himself. It was time to try something different, something *very* different.

Yapko considered his options as Kyle waited expectantly. Tears were still streaming down his cheeks. He reached over for a tissue.

Yapko made a show of deliberately pulling his chair closer to his client and then leaned forward, and said, for no obvious reason, "I want you to give me a million dollars." He said this in a loud voice.

"Excuse me?" Kyle said, taken aback by this surprising statement. Not even one minute ago his therapist had been so gentle and supportive, and now he suddenly seemed to have gone off the deep edge.

"I said," Yapko repeated, this time even slower and louder, "I want you to give me a million dollars. Right now!"

Kyle smiled hesitantly, thinking this had to be some kind of joke, but Yapko was looking totally serious. "I'm not sure . . . I mean . . . what you are saying . . ."

"I said I want a million dollars! Am I not being clear?"

Kyle started to become visibly agitated, knowing that there was something purposeful going on here that he was supposed to understand. They had been talking about something so deeply painful and now his therapist seemed to be baiting him for some reason he wasn't able to discern. He wondered just what the heck was going on.

Yapko was relentless, unwilling to back off. "Give me a million dollars," he repeated still louder. "Goddamn it, I said give me a million dollars! I want a million dollars. And I want it right now!"

Kyle thought about just getting up and walking out of the office right then and there. This guy was acting absolutely bizarre, demanding an outrageous sum of money. Was he serious? He can't be, he reasoned, but what was he going on about? This Yapko fellow had come highly recommended. He was very well known for his work in depression, apparently, had written books and keynoted conferences all over the world. There had to be some point he was trying to make, even if it eluded Kyle. While he was trying to sort out what it meant, Yapko was still repeating his demand for a million dollars, saying it over and over again, always with a perfectly straight face.

Kyle said, "I don't have a million dollars. Stop asking!" He looked very confused and earnest about figuring out what was going on here.

Yapko again said, "Gimme a million dollars!"

Finally, the flash of insight flew across Kyle's face.

"Wait a minute. Stop," Kyle said with a smile. "I get it."

"Get what?"

"Get what you're doing."

"What am I doing?"

"Come on. No games now. You're asking me over and over again for something that I don't have, something I would never give you even if I did have it. That's it, right?"

Yapko nodded and said, "Okay, there is something I want you to do. Are you willing to do a homework assignment, something important that you can do in order to finally overcome your depression? And, are you willing to do it even if it doesn't make immediate sense to you or other people?"

Kyle waited a moment, considering the proposal. He was a careful man, serious about the promises he made. Given how strangely Yapko had been acting the past few minutes, he seemed to be weighing whether he was prepared to make such a commitment. But Yapko had introduced a valid point. Finally he nodded his agreement with the same sort of earnestness he would give to securing a legal contract.

"Okay, good. This is what I want you to do. It is a rather simple assignment, but one that you might find a bit challenging, especially considering your history. Ready?"

Kyle nodded.

"Remember, your problem is that you keep asking your father for exactly what he can't give you—ever. You can wish for it. You can hope for it. You can strive for it, but you're still not going to get what he is unable to give you—even if he wanted to. Right?"

"Yeah, that's become pretty clear now."

"So, to drive this point home, what I want you to spend the next week doing is asking people for things that they will never give you. I want you to ask people for totally ridiculous things, outrageous things that you can never have in your wildest dreams. Ask someone who you know doesn't have one to borrow his yacht for the weekend. Call the White House and ask if you can rent the place for a party you're having. Call the Hawaiian tourist bureau and tell them you want to buy the whole state."

Kyle was laughing.

"No, I'm serious," Yapko insisted. "You've got to go out and actually do this. This isn't a game. You promised you would do what I asked, so this is what I'm asking you to do. It's going to be a focused, fun, and effective way to finally get this issue settled once and for all."

Yapko explained that he was trying to get Kyle to realize the extent to which he was internalizing the defects of his father, viewing them as his own limitations. His depression resulted from this lifelong sense of hopelessness that he would never get what he wanted most. It never occurred to him that although he was wonderfully deserving, he was asking his father for something that wasn't possible. It seemed so reasonable to him that a father would support a son, just as he was doing with his own children. He presumed that his father was holding off giving approval until such time as he actually deserved it.

Yapko wanted to get Kyle used to the idea that there are lots of times that you want something from someone, even a parent, but that doesn't mean you're ever going to get it, nor does it mean you can't be more than a little disappointed by that. Of course, the people he would approach to ask for things would tell him that he's out of his mind—of course they wouldn't buy him a new car or send him on a cruise around the world or stand on their heads naked in the middle of a park. But it was time that he got used to asking for things he wasn't going to get and that he got used to being turned down. Asking for things he really didn't want or expect would take the emotional sting out of the rejections and build an awareness in him that there are lots of reasons why people say no that have nothing to do with how nice or deserving you are. And it was time for him to understand that even though some people might be in a position to provide what he wants most, they *still* won't comply, and that is their right. As a lawyer and businessman, of course, he understood this idea in principle—he had encountered his fair share of hopeless cases and disappointments—but he had never learned to apply this to his relationship with his father.

Hypnosis to Cement the Gains

Kyle returned the next week utterly transformed. He was practically vibrating with energy; his posture, voice, his whole demeanor was different. With little preamble he announced that he had indeed completed the assignment and had fun with it, too. "But I need to tell you," he said, "I have to cut this session short by about 15 minutes, because I have a meeting with a potential partner over an issue that we need to resolve. Now I don't know if he's going to be able to do what I need him to do or not, but I'm going to ask him anyway. The worst that can happen is that he'll tell me no. It's no big deal, really, but I have to ask."

Clearly, Kyle had gotten the message and had learned his lesson well. In this second, abbreviated session, Yapko induced a brief, hypnotic experience in order to focus Kyle on a variety of other situations in which he might ask for things he would never receive in which he could use his new perspective as insulation. "I was teaching him one of the basic lessons of life that apparently his parents had never taught him, and that is to never ask anyone for anything unless, number one, they are in a position to give it, and number two, that they are capable of sharing it, and number three, you can accept no as an answer without personalizing it. Not everyone is capable of love or showing affection or approval. There are some people who are incredibly emotionally stingy, like his father. Once Kyle understood that this was his father's nature, not his lack of deserving approval, he seemed able to let his unrealistic expectations go."

In order to make this point, Yapko asked Kyle, while in hypnosis, to "name three things that your father approves of."

Kyle sat there for a minute, then another, and the time stretched on and on. Even though his eyes were closed, the concentration on his face showed he was just wracking his brain, trying to think of a way to answer the question.

In the slowed motions of someone in hypnosis, Kyle finally shrugged. He couldn't actually think of a single thing that his father had ever outwardly approved of, not only toward his son, but to *anyone.*

In reflecting on this case, Yapko admitted that he might very well have interpreted this insight, or reflected to Kyle that this father had a hard time expressing positive feelings, but that would have had about as much impact as the therapy that had preceded these few sessions. Kyle's situation required something innovative and creative, something unexpected, to get his attention in ways that nothing had before.

In a follow-up session one month later, Kyle reported that he was no longer depressed, and for the first time in as long as he could remember, he had stopped thinking about what he would do next to earn his father's approval.

Perceiving Unhabitually

This story has a very happy ending. It is indeed a creative breakthrough that is both courageous and innovative. But if you are like us, you might have some difficulty imagining yourself doing something so outrageous as yelling at your clients to give you a million dollars, or telling them to go out in the world in order to be deliberately and purposefully disappointed. Such radical interventions could be easily misinterpreted. We could easily imagine ourselves trying something like this and having a client run out of the room, threatening legal action for our rude and incompetent behavior. The point is that not everyone can be a Yapko and get away with an intervention like the one just described.

Yapko insisted that this wasn't really very risky at all. "There was something purposeful and strategic about what I was doing that was meaningful to Kyle. Even within this short period of time, he trusted me. When I'm guiding someone into the focused experience of hypnosis and telling a story about elephants in Africa, for example, the client engages in a search to make it relevant. The person accepts the premise that *there is a reason* for what you're doing, even if it eludes him or her in that moment. It is their job to make sense of this in some way, to apply it to their own lives. It's how therapy is done *with* someone rather than *to* someone. Kyle knew there was something important going on in my unexpected behavior, and he took it as an invitation to examine what it might be. And the realization therefore had much more impact than if I had just said rationally, 'Gee, you're dad sure is an emotionally withholding kind of guy.'"

Yapko acknowledges that some clients who are very literal and concrete may struggle with this task of finding relevance in their own situation. In such cases, you do the intervention differently; it may become necessary to be more direct. He mentions the example of one of Aesop's fables, the wonderful story about a fox and unobtainable grapes. The fox finally gives up and walks away, shaking his head because he couldn't reach the vines, saying to himself, "They were probably sour anyway." Aesop realized that children (and some adults) are literal thinkers, so he ended the narrative with an explanation of the meaning of the story, declaring, "The moral of this story is . . ."

Yapko acknowledges that the therapeutic alliance is also a critical part of the outcome. It is important, even necessary, that the client knows that we have their best interests at heart. They must sense that what we are doing is for their good, that we know what we are doing is meaningful even if we aren't sure exactly where things will end up. This is, to some extent, about trusting the process.

"There's a quote from William James that I absolutely love. He says, 'Genius means little more than the faculty of perceiving in an unhabitual way.' The same holds true for creativity being able to see things from a totally different perspective that nudges people out of their usual frame of reference.

"There was nothing particularly wrong with Kyle's previous therapy except that the focus was on his feelings of rejection and abandonment by his father. Kyle just ended up feeling worse after accessing and expressing these hurt feelings. Nobody had ever said to him before that maybe this whole thing wasn't about him at all, but about his father's inadequacies. That goes totally against the grain of what most therapists learn about helping clients to own and accept responsibility for their problems. That just led to more self blame."

So, how does one learn to think "unhabitually" in order to discover new, more creative ways of functioning as a therapist—and as a human being?

While still an intern, Yapko remembers observing one of his supervisors, someone who consistently did things out of the ordinary, conducting a session with a female client. "I was sitting there in the corner of the room, out of the visual field of the client, and the woman said to him, 'My boyfriend always dumps on me and it's really hurtful to me and I don't know what to do. I tell him to quit dumping on me but he keeps doing it. I don't know why I let him get away with this, but he's not the only one who dumps on me. You know, my sister dumps on me and the people at work dump on me, too.' She was going on and on using that phrase of people 'dumping' on her. Then, to my absolute shock and horror, my supervisor reached into his desk and picked up a paperclip and flicked it at her. She was startled when it bounced off her chest and landed in her lap but she just continued with her story. I think I was more horrified than she was by this behavior.

"Then he picked up a rubber band and shot it at her. She was startled enough to stop talking for a moment but then she kept going. So next he threw a pencil at her, and this time she looked annoyed but still she kept talking as if none of this was happening. In the span of the next few minutes he took off his shoes and tossed them into her lap, then his socks, and then anything else he could find on his desk. He was just bombarding her with stuff and although she was flinching, she wasn't visibly protesting. And I'm sitting in the corner freaking out; this was the craziest thing done in the name of therapy that I'd ever seen.

"Finally, as her lap was filling up with stuff, the client started smiling, then laughing in this nervous kind of way. Finally, she'd had enough. She stood up and said to him, 'You know, ever since I walked in here you've been dumping on me just like everyone else does, and I've had enough!'

"My supervisor smiled at her and told her that she'd just done very well here in the office, then asked her what it would take for her to do this with others in her life. She fell back in her chair and became tearful—she'd gotten the point big-time. In the span of moments, she went from being everyone's victim to being in charge of herself."

Not only was this a turning point in the client's life, but in Yapko's as well. "You don't learn that sort of thing in graduate school. There's no class I'd ever taken or book I'd ever read that said a therapist should take off his shoes and throw them at a client to make a point. But that's just what she needed!"

Yapko learned early on from the strategic therapists about doing very unconventional things, which Jay Haley calls "uncommon therapy," in order to lead to breakthroughs. Even though Yapko deals with so many so-called hopeless, impossible cases, he has always taken great care to make sure nothing he does or asks people to do will harm them in any way. He states forcefully that any task, any intervention, must be safe for the client to experience. Kyle is a smart, strong, and thoughtful man who could accept the nonverbal challenge to find purpose in what superficially seemed puzzling. These were the specific cues that let Yapko know Kyle could handle some confusion while he sorted things out.

"I have people who walk in, sit down, and say to me, 'I'm going to give you 20 minutes to say something smart, and if you don't, I'm going to blow my brains out.' And they mean it. Those are the people that I don't tend to get too experimental with, but the point is that most people aren't that severe. Most people have enough of a sense of humor, and most people accept the premise that what you're saying and what you're doing is meant to be therapeutic. This is all meant to say that you can generally teach people more through experiential learning than through rational conversation."

The Primacy of Experience

Most definitions of creativity involve combining previously unrelated elements into something new. That is consistent with Yapko's idea about therapy in that the object is to get the client to abandon familiar patterns in order to react in an entirely different way. In the case of Kyle, he was repeatedly blaming himself for being undeserving, a rigid template that was set early in life. Yapko presented an alternative perception that maybe this wasn't Kyle's problem. Yet as powerful as that idea might be, it was the *experience* of it that made it transformative.

According to Yapko, therapists can come to recognize that experiential learning is generally more powerful than mere conversation. He says, "Our job is to ask ourselves where we can send them out in the world to learn the lessons that are most valuable to them. Sometimes, with clients who will cooperate with the absurdity of the tasks and tolerate their ambiguity, things can be taken to a more progressive level more quickly."

The next step is to help the client to generalize the key principle to other areas in life. It is what Yapko calls the "hidden gem hypothesis." Naively, people believe that if you dig deeply enough into someone's life, you will almost always find hidden gems of their resources. "People believe that everyone really is capable of greater love or responsibility or intimacy. That's not really true. A lot of people do not have and will never develop the abilities that they need to participate in sophisticated or effective living. Some of those skills they can learn and some skills are teachable, but when you figure out how to make a sociopath empathetic, go to Stockholm and pick up your prize."

Theory often gets in the way of creativity. If a clinician is overinvested in a particular paradigm, though it may provide much comfort, it also limits options. If the "rules" of a theory state that you *must* proceed in a certain way, follow prescribed steps, and think in specific language and prescribed concepts, then this is going to reduce other possibilities and experimentation.

Theory is a metaphor rather than a literal truth, Yapko points out. It can produce the kind of rigidity that leads to entrenched beliefs about certainty and absolute truth. Yapko remembers a conversation he once had with Paul Watzlawick, one of the founders of strategic therapy at the Mental Research Institute. They were sitting in the back of a limo being taken to the airport after a conference where they had both presented.

"I'm curious about something, Paul," Yapko posed the question. "Every year during the summer, the MRI has a training program in strategic therapy. There are some people who have been going to your program every year for 10 years and they just don't get the strategic approach."

"Right," Watzlawick said with a smile, "and yet there are others who get it in a week."

"So," Yapko continued, "what do you think distinguishes those who get it right away from those who never seem to get it?"

After a long and thoughtful pause, Watzlawick said simply, "I don't know."

Yapko has been thinking about that complicated question ever since, about what leads some practitioners to block their access to greater creativity. His answer? "I believe it's all about cognitive rigidity."

He is referring to the absolute theoretical rigidity of those who identify so strongly with one viewpoint that they can't allow themselves to consider others. It is the same with clients who become stuck doing the same things because it is the only way they see things. Yapko is always looking for that rigidity and a way to loosen it. In Kyle's case, his rigidity was keeping him depressed and self-blaming. Yapko's intervention, in its simplest form, was basically to "consider the source" of this perception. Nobody had ever offered that to Kyle before, not just as an idea, but as a behavior that must be tested in the world. From the moment a client walks in the door, Yapko is looking for ways to get him or her to experiment creatively with alternative behaviors. He makes this clear as part of his informed consent—he makes it clear to the client that this is work that involves you taking purposeful action. If you aren't prepared to do that, maybe we need to examine what that is about. But the talk stops until the action is completed.

The Lingering Effects of the Story

Soon after listening to Yapko's story, I (Jon) immediately returned to my own therapy practice. As fate would have it, my next client was a very unhappy 17-year-old boy who was miserable even though he admitted that he had anything that anyone could ever want. Randy was a product of privilege: Although his parents were divorced, they were unbelievably successful, showering their son with pocketfuls of cash, a sports car, and tech devices that filled his room. As if that weren't enough, he was also smart, popular, and very handsome.

Randy lived with his mother, who was totally devoted to him. Unfortunately, his father had a track record of broken promises. No matter what Randy did, his father didn't seem to notice. Randy would call him several times each week and attempt to engage his father in a conversation or a commitment to an activity they could share, but he was almost always rejected since Dad was too busy with his various business activities. Dad was on the boards of most of the art and theater guilds in a large Midwestern city and owned boxes at the major sporting venues. He had no trouble offering the seats to his only son but seldom did he accompany him.

As I was listening to Randy's tirade of all the ways his father disappointed and neglected him, I couldn't help but remember our last interview with Yapko and his wild intervention of demanding of his client something that he could never give. I was reliving this conversation when I heard Randy ask me a question.

"You'll never guess what my dad did this time."

"What's that?" I said, knowing what was coming next, having heard this scenario a dozen times already.

"So, I got this award for being the outstanding senior in my school."

"That's fabulous! Congratulations."

"No, that's not it. See, my dad actually came to the ceremony. Can you believe it?"

I nodded, knowing that probably wasn't the end of the story. I could tell by Randy's voice that he was far from excited about the situation.

"And then," Randy continued, "I saw him out in the audience one time, but the next time I looked he was gone. Can you believe it? His son gets this big-deal award and the best he can do is show his face for one minute and then take off. I was just standing there on stage like an idiot searching for him but he was gone."

Randy was looking at me, waiting for me to say something, but all I kept hearing in my head, over and over again, was Yapko yelling at his client to emphasize his point about how crazy it is to ask for something you can't ever have.

"Is it too much to think my dad would be there for me?" Randy said.

"Gimme a million dollars!" I just blurted out, surprising myself as much as the boy.

"Huh?"

"I said, gimme a million dollars. Right now!"

"What are you talking about?"

"Give—me—a—million—dollars." I said it slowly this time, drawing out each word.

"What are you talking about? What's with the million dollars? I don't have that kind of money. And even if I did, why would I give it to you?"

I just smiled, remembering that's what Yapko did.

Randy just stared at me, confused, trying to sort out what was going on. Then he broke into a grin. "I get it," he said, smart boy that he is.

"What?"

"You think I'm asking too much from my dad."

"Well, are you?"

Randy looked down at the floor, wiping away tears. Then he nodded.

"What's going on?" I prompted him.

Randy admitted that he never thought of it in that way before. He talked about how his father grew up without a father and had probably never learned much about parenting a son. Our session ended with Randy saying he needed to think more about that.

Two days later I received a call from Randy's mother.

"I know you can't talk with me about what you and Randy discuss, but I'm just wondering what in the world happened during your last session with him?"

"What do you mean?" I asked, more than a little nervous about my intervention that was indeed way out of the ordinary of what I might do.

"It's just that he seems like a completely different person. He has been walking around as if he is a happy person. No more sulking. No more feeling sorry for himself. He is actually smiling. I even heard him singing. Can you believe it?"

I suppose there were many other ways I could have gotten this point across to Randy that he was setting himself up for disappointment over and over again. But one of the effects for me, possibly for you as well, of hearing these stories of creative breakthroughs is that it frees me up to experiment in ways that I might never have done before.

CHAPTER 7

Scott Miller: I Have Creative Clients

For Scott Miller, the inspiration for creativity occurs when he hits a brick wall, when his usual models of understanding and explaining things are no longer working. And the most important thing in his work has always been assessing how he is doing and whether it is working for those he is helping. That is Miller's most consistent mantra with his clients: How are we doing? How is this working for you? What do we need to change?

Ever since graduate school, Miller has been driven, even obsessed, with figuring out what works in therapy. He is a rare combination of clinician and researcher, integrating empirical outcome studies with his own vast experience in the trenches. Looking back to his training days, Miller entered psychoanalysis as a client, struggling to deal with depression. Although there were some gains from the experience, his perception, even then, is that it was mostly the relationship he and his clinician developed together that was far more important than the techniques employed.

Opening the Blinds

It was while attending a workshop that he met another therapist, Lynn Johnson, who was very interested in accountability in therapy, evaluating client satisfaction with outcomes. At the time, Miller had been concentrating on dream analysis and reviewing childhood memories as part of his own analysis, so he was surprised to learn that therapy could be both short-term and very pragmatic. This led him to change therapists.

Miller sat down with his new therapist and reviewed his history of depression, his marital troubles, and his profound despair. During this recitation he couldn't help but notice that the therapist had a one-way mirror in the office, which was very unusual at this time. Miller filled the therapist in more about his dingy office, his listlessness at work, and all sorts of other things that he had explored in his previous therapy.

"I want to check something out," the therapist said and then left the room. He returned a few minutes later and said, "I have some advice for you."

"What's that?" Miller asked, still trying to come to grips with this peculiar style of doing therapy. The guy had asked nothing about his dreams, family history, or anything like that.

"When you go to your office tomorrow, I want you to open the blinds of your windows."

"That's it?"

"Yup. That's it. That'll be $90."

Miller remembers thinking that this new profession he was joining was full of crazy people. "I saw one guy who wanted me to talk incessantly about my mother and masturbatory fantasies to the point of which neither was enjoyable anymore. Then I go to this idiot who tells me to open the blinds in my office. I wrote the damn check to the guy and was furious that I was so stupid to listen to any of them. I was even more depressed because this was the work I would be doing myself."

Sure enough, the next day Miller showed up in his office at the university. It was a small cubicle that was cluttered with junk, dark and dreary. He had stuck drawings on all of the walls, at the behest of his previous therapist, to represent his dreams and fantasies. There were stacks of notebooks and books everywhere, many of them containing his dream fragments that he had been instructed to record. He was doggedly persistent in these activities, hopeful that maybe one of them would supply the clues to his misery.

The only light in the room came from a muted, 15-watt bulb, which was fine with Miller because he could mostly hide in the dark. And here this crazy therapist was telling him to open the blinds. What the hell, for 90 bucks, he'd give it a try. So he pulled on the ancient venetian blinds, dust flying everywhere as he tried to raise them and lock them in an open position.

"It turned out," Miller laughed, "that this was an amazing experience, almost religious, as light flooded into the room for the first time. I'd never had the blinds open even once, never even peeked out the window before. I looked outside, and there were all these people walking to and from class and all sorts of other stuff going on. I realized that I'd been living in this strange, insulated, dark little space. I had been overly preoccupied with myself and my analysis, ignoring everything else around me. Once the light was let in, I decided to quit analysis. My mood and career went in a completely different direction after that."

Miller just had to make sense of what he experienced and how it happened. How could something as simple as opening the blinds make such a huge difference? It didn't make sense. It just couldn't have been an impulsive, random suggestion and he wondered where it came from. How did the therapist know, after just an hour, exactly what Miller needed?

With his curiosity piqued, Miller sought out supervision from many of the most well-known strategic therapists of the time. He sat behind the mirror watching Lynn Hoffman, Insoo Kim Berg, John Weakland, Paul Slovich, and others, watching them carefully and trying to figure out the method in their apparent "madness." They were all so inventive, spontaneous, intuitive, and creative beyond what he could ever have imagined. That was his inspiration upon which he would base the career that followed.

Supershrinks

As intrigued as Miller was with the innovations that were developed by those at the Mental Research Institute, he didn't quite accept their explanations that did not necessarily jive with what clients reported was happening for them. In the effort to find simple solutions and explanations for how change occurs, much of the complexity was lost. This led to a huge crisis in confidence for Miller, one that motivated him to spend his life exploring the *experience* of therapy—from the client's point of view. Miller and several of his colleagues focused on four common factors that seemed to be present in almost all effective therapy, central among them the therapeutic alliance. While interesting and conceptually useful, it still didn't address his need to develop a system that could be taught and replicated.

Another crisis of confidence ensued, leading to the next stage in Miller's professional development, which still commands his attention—collecting, measuring, and creating meaning from client feedback about what is working for them and what is not. He believes that, ultimately, this will lead to another stage in his evolution, each one producing a new creative breakthrough.

Miller and his colleagues are now able to access huge databases from various health care institutions, allowing them to observe thousands of clinicians around the world, measuring their results and noting patterns that predict success and failure. He is especially interested in those extraordinary therapists who consistently outperform what is expected, who demonstrate a degree of flexibility and creativity unmatched by their colleagues. Miller explains this in the research language that has become his trademark.

"I'm just an average therapist, based on numbers. My outcome is just about one standard deviation above the norm. What does that mean? It simply means that my outcomes are about as good as the outcomes that are seen in randomized clinical trials. But the outcomes of these other therapists we call "supershrinks" are a half to a full standard deviation better than that. And it's been a puzzle to try to figure out why that was. You can watch their work and it didn't seem to have anything to do with what they were doing in the room with their clients. I didn't see any magical patterns or creative breakthroughs or the skillful use of some new technology or better diagnostic ability. I couldn't see it in there, and neither could the team members."

Even more perplexing, when Miller and his team members interviewed these superlative clinicians, they appeared surprised that they were identified as such. If asked to evaluate themselves, they would have said they were about the same as everyone else. That seemed to be another dead end.

Miller was flying back from another workshop he was doing somewhere in Norway. He was completely exhausted, jet-lagged, but unable to sleep. So he grabbed a magazine offered by the flight attendant and started leafing through a recent copy of *Fortune* that profiled the author of an academic tome about experts. It covered expertise in every field from computer science and medicine to education and chess.

"As I read this article, it occurred to me that our search to understand what it is about these great therapists has been very narrow in focus. I realized that we had been studying the wrong thing. We'd been studying therapists and therapy rather than studying greatness itself. Once we took that different frame of reference, well, then lots of things opened up to us about what it was that was different about these supershrinks. We had been looking at how they interact with their clients in the therapy room. This is where I spent my entire career, watching tapes and sitting behind the one-way mirrors. But what I finally realized is that what makes these professionals really amazing is what happens *outside* the therapy room. This was a huge shift in perspective."

What do great therapists do that is different outside the room? For one, they embody "deliberate practice," meaning that they spend an inordinate amount of time *between sessions* reflecting on their work. They also do more follow-up with their clients to find out what they thought was of greatest value during the sessions.

Miller takes these findings to heart because of the amount of time he spends in preparation for any therapy session or presentation. He is actually one of the most skilled keynote speakers and workshop presenters because of the ways that he appears so spontaneous, humorous, dramatic, and creative, all the while apparently improvising. In fact, what looks to an audience as very improvisational is very deliberate and strategic.

"It might look like I'm doing some kind of creative breakthrough, but it is really the result of hours and hours of deliberate practice. The audience thinks I'm being wildly innovative, but I'm actually just doing what I rehearsed over and over again."

Miller mentions that it is the same with Tiger Woods and similar athletes. Tiger Woods keeps reinventing his swing over and over again, even though his previous incarnation was perfect. He is always improving and practicing, so much so that people are always trying to record his swing, copying it as diligently as they can to duplicate the same results. Woods is both amused and surprised by this because in his opinion it is not what makes him great. What makes him so extraordinary is how long and hard he practices, hours and hours every day, to prepare for any conceivable situation he might face. In Miller's opinion, this is also what makes therapists so outstanding—not what they do in sessions but how they prepare for them.

In thinking of a case of a creative breakthrough to discuss, it is perhaps not surprising that Miller de-emphasizes what the therapist did in the session compared to what the client did. Therapists could do the most creative things ever conceived, but if they don't produce successful outcomes for the clients, then they are worthless. Second, unlike many of the stories in this book, very little of what Miller does is spontaneous and unplanned. If he wants excellent results, he works harder than most other people to achieve then.

Far End of the Curve

A prospective client phoned Miller and interviewed him for a half hour because of his skepticism regarding previous experiences in therapy. He had a long history of being in treatment previously, a *very* long history, stretching over four decades. During that time he had experienced just about every kind of therapy that had then been in vogue—Gestalt, cognitive, Rogerian, hypnosis, REBT, NLP, ECT, EMDR, and every other acronym you can think of. It all started with psychoanalysis when he was a preschooler.

When Nathan was four years old, while he was sitting at the family dinner table, his grandfather stood up to say a prayer and had a fatal stroke, falling dead onto the table, but not before projectile-vomiting onto his grandson. Nathan sat at the table, covered in his grandfather's vomit, viewing his first experience with death as a four-year-old. Needless to say, this was a traumatizing event in his life.

Perhaps Nathan would be entitled to a few problems after an early experience like that, but he developed a staggering number of fears and phobias. He was so immobilized by his symptoms of agoraphobia that he had been housebound for the previous 10 years. In addition, he had a host of psychosomatic complaints—nausea, headaches, bowel and bladder problems, and, of course, a fear of vomit.

Nathan had not been able to work for many years, but managed to support himself because of a modest inheritance. There was a time, years earlier, before he'd become housebound, when he still had some hope that a therapist might help him, but that was now long gone. That was why he kept Miller on the phone for so long during this first phone call, checking out what this new guy might do for him that would be any different than the dozen failed efforts previously.

"My first reaction," Miller recalled, "was to wonder what I could possibly do that would be any different. He had already seen some very talented and experienced practitioners of every persuasion. What could I do that hadn't already been tried? Then I thought to myself that maybe the reason nobody has ever helped him is because it really isn't about the therapist; logically, it might be about him. So I figured it was very important to find out what he wanted."

It was during their first meeting that Miller casually asked Nathan where they should begin.

"Maybe we should start with my birth trauma," he said, and then launched into this whole long, sad, tragic story of one misfortune after another. It was amazing that the guy was still breathing after everything he'd lived through.

Nathan then reviewed his impressive treatment history, describing each of his therapies and all the ways they didn't help him. He was giving a running account of each and every failure with remarkable detail when Miller interrupted him.

"I'm just curious," Miller said, "what, exactly, were you hoping for?"

"Not so much, really."

"Well," Miller tried again, "like what, exactly?"

"I was hoping for a normal life," Nathan said softly, "do you think that's too much to ask for?"

Miller shook his head no.

"See, most of the people I've known in my life have had careers. They've had families. They have friends. But I haven't had any of that. Instead I stay locked up in this apartment all day and I can't go outside. I can't even use the bathroom in my place if there are any other tenants around, because I don't want them to hear me flush the toilet."

Again Miller nodded as if he heard that kind of thing all the time.

"So," Nathan asked again, "is this too much to want?"

"It doesn't seem like too much to ask that you would just have the kind of life that everybody else has. You're not asking for outrageous things."

Nathan nodded, but seemed resigned to his fate. "It would be nice, sure would be nice . . ." There was a big *but* hanging at the end.

"You just don't think it's possible," Miller reflected back.

"Yeah, you know about the bell curve, that statistical graph that shows probabilities?"

"What about it?"

"You know how it's got the majority of the people in the middle who are average and normal? Well, I just think I'm one of those who are on the edge. Bad stuff is always happening to me. From the time I was little."

A Run of Bad Luck

It was at this point Miller remembers distinctly a very personal reaction to Nathan's story. He'd been listening to him talk for almost an hour when he made this connection to another case and another part of his own life. Miller had been doing some consultation and supervision at a clinic where a woman came in for help. Staff members were having a hard time working with her and were seriously concerned that she would do something harmful. Not unlike Nathan, she'd had a run of very unfortunate circumstances. She'd had cancer five different times. She'd had chronic drinking problems. Her whole life was a mess.

Miller had been listening to her talk when he was struck by something. "Wow, you've survived cancer five times?" he said.

"Yup," she answered, almost proudly. "And they weren't just recurrences. They was all different kinds."

"Wow," Miller exclaimed, "that's some run of bad luck."

"Yeah, it really sucks."

"This sounds like a lot of other areas in your life that you would really like things to be better. You want to stop drinking and have a better life, but bad luck always seems to strike you no matter where you are."

She nodded and then proceeded to recite a long list of other instances of chronic bad luck that had plagued her. Miller thought about this woman as he sat with Nathan, because both of them seemed to be victims of some very tough circumstances that they couldn't control. What could be worse luck then beginning your childhood by being struck by your grandfather's vomit as he collapsed dead in front of you? It was all very bad luck indeed.

"I agree," Miller said to Nathan, "you sure are on the far end of the bell curve." And that was the moment when Miller was struck by inspiration, remembering the woman at the clinic. "You know what your problem is?" he asked.

Nathan looked up expectantly. He could see that his therapist was revved up about something. He'd been with enough therapists in his life to know when they were excited about some idea or another. Not that any of these would have much value to him.

"I just think," Miller said slowly, pausing for dramatic effect, "that your problem is that you've got bad luck."

"You've got to be kidding me." He looked at Miller as if to add, "That's the best you can do?"

"No, I'm serious. Just look at everything that has happened to you. None of it was your fault. Stuff just happens to you."

Nathan was nodding thoughtfully, seeming to buy this hypothesis. He had to admit it made sense.

"The problem," Miller continued, "is that there's not much I can do for bad luck."

"You're really not making this shit up, are you?"

"No, I'm really not." Miller really believed that Nathan was indeed a victim of chronic misfortune. Disasters seemed to stalk him wherever he hid.

As the session came to an end, Miller handed him a brief questionnaire that he distributes to all his clients in order to get feedback on what occurred. This is what he has learned from research, that the best therapists are those who are continually finding out how things are going, making adjustments according to client needs at any moment. Rather than just relying on verbal feedback, such as that of his client today, Miller prefers to use his alliance measurement instrument that asks clients to write down answers to specific questions.

Item number three asks what is missing in therapy. Nathan had listed two things, so Miller asked him to mention what those might be.

"Well, the first thing is that I was hoping for some magic, but you're saying you don't have any of that; nothing that can fix bad luck."

Miller smiled, encouraging him to continue.

"The second thing is that I'm feeling that things are equal here. Usually, I always look up to my therapists, you know, put them on a pedestal. But with you it feels like I'm looking at another human being."

Hoping for Magic

Scott Miller is extremely interested in measuring outcomes, using the scales he developed to continually assess client perceptions of change as it is occurring. He was particularly concerned with tracking Nathan's progress, considering the poor results that had been achieved in prior therapy.

The outcome scores for Nathan had gone up significantly using the standardized measures, enough so to conclude that there had been reliable change that could not be attributed to chance. Miller pointed this out to his client, who shook his head in disagreement.

"Change?" Nathan said. "Are you kidding? Nothing is different. And besides, this scale you're using is unreliable."

"What do you mean unreliable?" Miller had been using and refining this instrument for years, gathering data, improving both reliability and validity over time.

"Yeah. It's unreliable. My life is just as shitty as it's always been."

In spite of this report, Miller trusted his scale, which had rarely failed him in the past, to give him clear indications of where things really stand in the relationship. "Maybe," he offered, "this is just another example of bad luck."

"Bad luck?"

"Remember I told you I couldn't do much for your bad luck? I just said I would hang out with you and hope your luck would change. Sometimes that sort of thing can happen when you spend time with someone who has better luck than you do. But . . . I could be wrong."

The session soon ended, and again Miller gave Nathan the evaluation form to fill out. After marking the scales, Nathan wrote on the bottom: "I would like to have a magical case and go bouncing out of here."

It's the Clients Who Are Creative

The third session scores demonstrated even more clearly that significant progress had been made. "Is this another example of my scale being unreliable?" Miller asked.

"No, not this time. I'm feeling better."

"You are? What happened?"

"It's because I have bad luck."

"What do you mean? I don't understand. If you have bad luck, then why did your scores go up indicating that you have made so much improvement?"

"Well, you really think I have bad luck."

"That's right," Miller agreed. "I do."

"Well, all of the things I've been doing to try to prevent bad luck aren't going to help me, are they?"

"No they're not."

"So, staying a prisoner in my house, restricting my diet, not going outside—none of this is going to prevent my bad luck?"

Again Miller agreed that this was so.

"I just figured that all the things I've tried to do to control my fate haven't resulted in anything better. Since it isn't doing any good to prevent my lousy breaks, and since all the steps I've been taking to prevent bad things from happening haven't been working at all, I might as well give up with that stuff. I've got nothing to lose to stop hiding and face everything. Bad luck can find me anywhere, so I might as well be out in the open."

Nathan started slowly venturing into the outside world. He began visiting restaurants. He went on a road trip to visit his relatives whom he hadn't seen in years.

"This was a major breakthrough for Nathan," Miller summarized, "but it was for me, too. I don't think this means that I was necessarily very creative. I was just listening carefully for an opportunity. Nathan said he had bad luck, so I just repeated that. It's not that I'm a very creative guy; I just have very creative clients. I just listen to what they have to say, repeat those things back to them, and it's amazing what sometimes happens as a result."

For Miller, it is not the creative process that matters as much as the outcome. This reminds him of a story about the Marx brothers, who were asked how it was they came up with a particular routine that ended with a word that broke everyone up. Groucho just shrugged, until the interviewer asked him again how they decided on that particular word. Groucho said that they never decided on a word, they just kept trying a bunch of them over and over until the audience laughed. They just kept saying it over and over again, always getting people to laugh, but Groucho admitted he didn't know why it was funny.

Miller loves that story because it captures for him the essence of creative therapy. It isn't important to explain it, or know why it works, but just to know that it is effective. "You know, frankly, I don't why what we do helps clients, and I'm not sure that I care. The important thing is that it does work."

Nathan continued to experience some of his fears and phobias, but he began working again, living out in the world. He learned to live with his bad luck while no longer fearing what the future held for him; nothing could be worse than the nightmare that he had already lived through.

Utilizing Client Resources

Scott Miller is the first to admit that he is not especially creative as a clinician. If others in this book, such as Jeff Zeig, Brad Keeney, Steve Lankton, and Michael Yapko, are similar to comedians like Robin Williams in that they are improvisational artists who find their creative inspiration in the moment, then Miller is more like Jerry Seinfeld. Miller, like Seinfeld, is a compulsive workhorse when it comes to preparation for a "performance." Both of them rehearse endlessly, anticipate various scenarios that might unfold, come up with scripted responses, study their own behavior and its outcomes, and refine their patterns until they get the desired results. It is a kind of creativity that is reliable and consistent, even if it is less dramatic.

Miller thinks that worshipping creativity might be way overrated. The focus always remains on how brilliant the clinician is, while ignoring that it is actually the client who does the work. Miller remembers a conversation he once had with Steve de Shazer who, like so many others such as Virginia Satir, Jay Haley, Bandler and Grinder, Steve Lankton, and Jeff Zeig, tried to make sense of Milton Erickson's work and how it did its magic. Volumes have been written about this. Journals have been devoted to it. Conferences are held each year deconstructing Erickson's amazing interventions. Stories are told endlessly of the magic he produced (some of them in this book). De Shazer decided to investigate this phenomenon systematically by using a Q-sort method to identify significant variables.

De Shazer related to Miller how he and his colleagues had taken every one of Erickson's cases and every intervention that had been recorded or documented and sorted them into piles according to their common features. They tried doing this in a number of ways, over and over again, and they kept ending up with five or six piles that they were able to name. They were part of his standard repertoire, the half dozen things that he did with most clients, his favored, familiar behaviors. But they always ended up with one more pile that included everything that didn't fit elsewhere. They didn't know what to call it because it included so many different, weird things, so they just called it "miscellaneous."

It so happens that this last pile contained cases in which Erickson did something once, and never repeated it again. De Shazer's conclusion, and the reason Miller mentioned it now, is because these cases represented those times when Erickson listened creatively to his clients and followed their lead, never duplicating the effort with anyone else. These were the absolute craziest things that he ever tried.

"Creativity," Miller summarized, "means utilizing clients' resources and abilities in a way that leads them beyond whatever's obstructing their path onto a more creative life. But the outcome is that ultimate arbiter of the creativity, not whatever happens during the process."

Postscript

It should make perfect sense that after we'd completed the interview, Miller asked us how he'd done, whether this was what we were looking for. In other words, he wanted to know if this had been a successful outcome. It didn't matter how *he* felt about the conversation; the important thing was whether we got what we wanted.

Miller wanted to know if he'd helped us, and if so, what it was that was most useful. Always learning, always refining his craft, he just can't resist assessing outcomes. This doesn't come from insecurity, but rather from the passionate, determined mission to get better and better at what he does.

After we were finished with the formal interview, Miller remembered a study of exceptional radiologists, those whose abilities far exceeded those of merely competent physicians. Most radiologists read film (X-rays, CT scans, etc.), write a report, and move on to the next case. But, in the study, those who were truly heads and shoulders above the rest would pick up the phone and make a phone call—not to the referring physician but to the *patient*. They just had to know whether they'd gotten it right. They had to compare their professional judgment with the experience of the patients. This is what permitted them to continually improve their craft.

"So guys," Miller asked us, "how'd I do?"

CHAPTER 8

Jeff Zeig: A White, Fluffy Cloud and a Dissociative Moment

"So, Jeff, can you tell us a story of a creative breakthrough?"

"What does creativity look like?" Jeff Zeig asked in return.

"Huh?"

"Well, if you threw this vessel that we'll call therapist creativity in my lap, what would it look like? How about you, Jeffrey [Kottler]?"

"You're asking me what physical form creativity takes?" Jeffrey repeated, stalling for time.

"Exactly. Throw it in my lap and I'll catch it."

"Okay, it looks to me like a white, fluffy cloud."

"Good. So now I've got my hands out, I'm holding this white, fluffy cloud that's called 'therapist creativity.' I want to move inside it to experience its components. I'm also going to close my eyes and experience the context of where I've got that white, fluffy cloud. I'm also aware that I've got that white, fluffy cloud in relationship to the two of you, Jeffrey and Jon. There are actually three aspects to consider: internal components, the context in which it is experienced, and the relational elements—how it happens among people. Components, context, and relationship define the totality of any state, be it hypnosis or creativity."

So, the Devil Was Strolling through Hell

Silence on our end. We're not sure what to say back to Jeff at this point. He's obviously taken charge of this conversation. We know enough about him and his interest in teaching creativity to therapists to have expected this sort of thing. Jeff Zeig doesn't like to talk about creativity; he prefers to demonstrate it through his actions.

Still, we are wondering where the heck this is going and whether or not we're going to end up with a story, after all.

On five previous occasions we had asked Zeig to participate in our projects, telling us a story about his worst therapy session, his best session, his most memorable client, an experience that transformed him spiritually, and a client who changed him. In each case, he declined. We were frankly surprised that he had finally agreed to tell us a story for this book, and so we were a little skittish that maybe this would end up somewhere quite unexpected. The only consolation was that, considering this is a collection of creative breakthroughs, it might be a good thing to have something altogether different.

"Now," Zeig continued, "I'm going to put myself inside that white, fluffy cloud. I'm going to try to understand some of the components that make up that white, fluffy cloud. I'm going to explore its visual and sensory properties. I'm going to try to fully experience its components. I've got this white, fluffy cloud, and I want something to happen with it. In order for this to take place, there is going to be a dissociative moment, because there is no way I can get inside the cloud by just willing myself into it. I can put myself into a state in which I am attentive, in which I feel curious, but if I'm going to be creative, there has to be some dissociation, some separation from ordinary reality. Something is going to have to 'just happen.' A component of creativity is that it has to leap out at you. It cannot be forced."

Happen, indeed. We aren't sure if Jeff is inducting himself into a hypnotic state, or whether his melodic voice is directed to one or both of us. On some level, it does feel as if we are transported inside a white, fluffy cloud for a moment, floating along with Zeig wherever this may lead next.

As it turned out, one reason why Zeig had been so reluctant to share a story for one of our earlier books is that he doesn't like to dwell on the past. He told us up front that he'd rather not talk about a case that had happened in the distant past. It would be so much more interesting, not to mention more fun, to explore something going on right now, or in a session that just occurred. For Zeig, doing psychotherapy means accessing as many creative moments as possible, to make the experience more alive for all participants.

"This reminds me of a joke," Zeig said next, abruptly moving away from the white, fluffy cloud.

"A joke?"

"So, the devil is walking down the path of hell with a compatriot, and there on the floor lies creativity. The two of them are strolling, when another poor soul runs in front of the devil and his friend, picks up creativity, and runs off with it, just like a fluffy, white cloud. The devil's friend is amazed by this incident, the guy just running by, picking up creativity, and running off with it. Even more incredible is that the devil didn't even seem to notice. He just kept walking as if nothing happened.

"Finally, the devil's companion can stand it no longer, and he says to him, 'You just let that guy get away with creativity and you didn't even do anything.'

'Hey, it's really no problem at all,' the devil said with a shrug. 'I'll just let him keep it for awhile.'

'But . . . but why? I mean the guy just took creativity right in front of you. He just . . .'

'Look,' the devil explained, 'the guy is a psychotherapist.'

'So?'

'So, he'll just take creativity and turn it into an empirically validated protocol.'"

We laughed appreciatively. This is a pet peeve of all of us, that the profession of therapy has been shanghaied by the empiricists who genuinely believe that it is possible to manualize all of psychotherapy procedures into a series of specific diagnostic entities, each with its own statistically validated, reliable, and mandated treatments that have been approved by the government, insurance companies, and review boards. Creativity has often been marginalized as unscientific and ethereal, kind of like a white, fluffy cloud.

Moments of Utilization

Jeff Zeig had spent the past 30 years organizing and presiding over conferences that have gathered together the greatest living theoreticians to discuss and demonstrate their work, as well as to interact with one another over key issues in the field. Beginning with the first Evolution of Psychotherapy Conference in 1985, in which the likes of Carl Rogers, Albert Ellis, Carl Whitaker, R. D. Laing, Virginia Satir, Murray Bowen, Rollo May, and Bruno Bettleheim came together with 20 other experts to demonstrate their theories in action, Zeig has been privileged to watch the masters work with clients. In addition, he has been spending the past six months systematically reviewing demonstration videos of master practitioners and theoreticians, watching one each day to try to identify the essence of their therapeutic work.

"What I have seen most of the time is that the white, fluffy cloud of creativity is rarely present. It is mostly just conversations that are taking place, quite ordinary moments. It is rare to see something that really jumps out at you. Psychotherapy needs to be an unusual conversation—something a bit weird. We have Freud to thank for that. He made therapy into a weird conversation. Imagine people of his era being requested to lie on a couch and talk to the ceiling, saying whatever came to their mind at the moment. But it worked: Patients improved. They lived the experience of change."

Zeig likens creativity to doing something unusual and unexpected. It is, by definition, a shift in paradigm. It is a white, fluffy cloud that is at once visible and ethereal. It doesn't have to be something ground-shaking, but it is certainly something novel.

We press for an example, a story—that is what this project is about. But Zeig insists on going at his own pace, in his own way. After all, creativity cannot be forced; it must be discovered within the moment. In order for such a creative moment to emerge, he must allow himself to let go, to dissociate. What he is striving for is a moment of utilization.

"Utilization is a foundation of an Ericksonian approach. Utilization involves taking something out of the reality situation and applying it to making the therapy work, making something therapeutic out of the client's situation, values, and personal style.

"I can't really define creativity," Zeig explained apologetically. "That's why I asked you to give it a form and substance. But I see it in three different ways. One is context-dependent, two is relationship-dependent, and three is a series of psychological elements. If I can deconstruct creativity into those three large components, then I can do my best to make this moment, *any* moment, more creative. That is much more intriguing to me than just rehashing an old case that happened long ago, as interesting as it might appear.

Hands Do the Talking

Zeig decided to talk about a client that he had just seen an hour earlier, as fresh as material can possibly get. He hadn't even had the chance to reflect on it much, much less to organize his thoughts and feelings about what happened. But it was a case that was still living vividly with him.

Carla was talking to Zeig about her difficulty in letting go of resentments and anger that she felt toward others. She was plagued by injustices of the past, so much so that she spent an extraordinary amount of time reliving the experiences and thus retraumatizing herself. She was freely able to admit that her inability to forgive people for perceived slights was a kind of defense she used.

Rather than interpreting her messages, Zeig spontaneously held out his hands into a kind of shield, a barrier between himself and Carla. As he started to talk about forgiveness, he began moving his right hand toward the side, just at the periphery of his vision, bouncing it up and down.

"Suddenly, I felt this moment in which I was holding that white cloud. Something was percolating within me that was weird, not commonplace, something I couldn't explain or grasp, but it was there. It was present."

It is worth mentioning that Carla is a creative artist, and one of her specialties is making visually appealing works of art. So it was no coincidence that Zeig was resonating with his client's own internal resources.

Zeig now has these two gestures going, his left hand rigid between them acting as a defensive barrier and his right hand bouncing up and down in the periphery to represent forgiveness. He is trying to make these ideas come alive. He doesn't want them to just become words to her, but living things that are deep within her experience.

Zeig takes his right hand, the forgiveness hand which has been bouncing up and down, and he moves it back into a defensive position so that now his face is completely obscured. If Carla seeks to peek around the barrier, Zeig just moves his hands to compensate, acting as a wall. Forgiveness is now out of the picture.

"You know, Carla, sometimes whatever is going on inside you creates a little eclipse and that gets in the way of your being able to accomplish whatever it is that's important to you."

As he says this, Zeig moves his right hand away from his face and places it over his heart. "If I take forgiveness and I bring the forgiveness into my heart, what's that going to do for me? And how will I be different?"

Carla stares at Zeig's hands, mesmerized by them. Just imperceptibly, she nods her head.

"And if I let myself remain defensive," Zeig asks, moving his right hand back into shield position, "how would that affect me and what I want in my life?" He is not requiring an answer; he is looking for an experiential realization.

Carla just watched the hands.

"Could there be some advantage to me if I learned to forgive?" Zeig asked her. "Could this have some economic benefit, not to mention interpersonal benefits?"

Zeig was well aware that Carla was having significant money troubles. She was socially isolated as well. He was trying to reach her, not with words, but with movements.

Zeig had long been frustrated with the lack of training available within the field of psychotherapy to foster creativity, so he had devoted considerable time studying acting and improvisational theater. He had been training himself to use his body and gestures as much as words to convey ideas, a way of being very consistent with his early training in Ericksonian hypnosis. Milton Erickson has long been known not for *what* he said or did, but *how* he communicated.

"I wanted there to be representations for Carla," Zeig explained, "and these representations were going to make these big words, *forgiveness* and *defensiveness*, really come alive so that she can begin to *feel* them. They're not going to just be concepts that just sit in the left hemisphere of her mind. Besides, I really do not know the experiential meaning of those words to Carla. And the words she uses are just shorthand that represents deeper inherent meaning. The symbolic gestures that I use help her to flesh out the story behind her words."

Without further prompting, Carla began to open up and talk about some of the deeper aspects of her life that had never been shared before. She grew up in an alcoholic home without a sense of security and safety. She described the abuse and neglect she suffered, all of it portrayed as utterly unforgivable. And all the while she is talking, Zeig was searching for something there, some resource that might be useful.

"There are two parts of forgiveness," Zeig said to her, shaking his right hand with an open palm facing Carla. "One part of forgiveness has to do with forgiving other people."

Carla started to object, but Zeig's open right palm signaled her to wait a moment until he was finished.

"It is true," he continued, "that some people have done things that are so wrong that they don't merit forgiveness. Yet all forgiveness is predicated on an understanding that you're never going to be hurt that way again."

Zeig waited for Carla to digest this before starting again.

"There's also another position of forgiveness." Zeig moved his right hand in an open-palm way, shaking it in such a way that it drew her attention and suggested that it could not be ignored. "This is *self*-forgiveness. Even when you can't find a way to forgive others for what they have done, you can still forgive yourself for any wrongs that you have done to yourself." As he said this, Zeig touched his heart.

Zeig was suggesting to Carla that even if she couldn't bring herself to let go of her resentment toward others, she could still do much to help herself move forward. His words were saying the essence of this, but it was actually his hands that were doing most of the talking.

The session continued with discussion of things that Carla could do to become more self-forgiving, allowing her to attain greater economic stability and social interaction. As the time drew to a close, Zeig used his hands to create another visual image in space, this time that of a closet. He used his hands to sculpt the image of a closet in the air between them.

"This closet holds all your pain and resentments, all the things that you haven't been able to forgive, both in others and yourself. They were secret and hidden in this closet. One of the things you can do is open the door to the closet." As he says this, Zeig pretends to open a door with his hands, a door that is stubborn and rusty because it has not been opened before.

"Once the door of the closet is open," Zeig repeats, gesturing with his hand, "it is no longer necessary to have a shield to protect you." Zeig's hands transform from a barrier to palm-open positions. "The things you hide in the closet can be moved out into the open. You can put them in other places, just as safe, but more accessible when you need them."

Zeig ended the session by suggesting to Carla that she start becoming more diligent, even obsessive, about listing all the ways self-forgiveness could be useful to her, all the things it would do for her. It is a kind of spring-cleaning of her closet.

Moment-to-Moment Creativity

To Zeig, the whole session with Carla was a symbolic, experiential moment. He just couldn't imagine trying to deconstruct the movements, the drama, much less the words, into an empirically validated protocol. He had never done anything quite like that before, and likely would not do so again. All the material sprang from Carla's own experiences and the interactions between the two of them.

"Blink. I felt the white, fluffy cloud. Blink. I felt the intensity of it. Blink. I allowed myself to dissociate and go into that moment of our relational field. I wasn't interested in making things explicit but rather functioning as if we were cocreating an impressionist painting. There would be these wavy lines that she would then convert into something meaningful. Like Pointillism, a form of Artistic Impressionism, one can create 'dots' that can be experienced as a whole. Rather than connecting dots, therapists can create dots and allow the patient to energize and connect the dots, thereby cocreating the art.

"For me, if there isn't a creative moment in therapy sessions, then I think I missed something. I expect it from myself that in every session I'm going to do something creative. If not, I've just become a replica of myself, or of someone else. I try to bring that white cloud into every session and try to make something happen that reflects the uniqueness of the moment and make it come alive. Most of this is neither dramatic nor spectacular, but rather, ordinary moments that can lead to something stunning."

To Zeig, the therapy room has become a context for creativity culled through associations over time. Context is an unrecognized, but essential determinant of one's state of mind. If one repeatedly associates the therapy context with slavish technique, it will become so conditioned. If one repeatedly associates the therapy context with creativity, innovation is a natural outcome.

Zeig wishes that therapists would show more of the courage of their fantasies, not just the courage of their convictions, and bring creativity into sessions in ways that could never be staged or planned. Sometimes this just involves mirroring something the client is doing. "If a client crossed her legs in the beginning of a session, then I might adopt that posture. I'm watching nonverbal behavior carefully, things that clients aren't aware of consciously, and then mirror those actions to better establish attunement and rapport. It is out of that moment of connection that impressionistic, experiential, symbolic work can take place. It is about utilizing whatever is happening, realizing that whatever I'm doing I may never do again. I might pick up something from my desk. I might use my body. I might use my hands and arms. I might utilize a chair in the room. I might lie on the floor or stand up in the corner. This is what intrigues me most about therapy, the moment-to-moment creativity that can lead to a snowballing movement forward."

Intervention Is *the Assessment*

It is interesting to hear Jeff Zeig speak about not wanting to become a replica of himself or anyone else, considering that he has been known primarily as the president of the Milton Erickson Foundation and is a leading advocate for Ericksonian therapy. Granted that Erickson was one heck of a creative guy, but it is hard finding your own way when you are so closely identified with one mentor who has been so influential.

Zeig studied with Erickson intermittently for more than six years during his most formative time as a neophyte in the field. He became one of Erickson's most devoted followers, responsible for promoting Erickson's work around the world. Even today, the psychotherapy conferences are run under the auspices of Erickson's legacy. Although Zeig agrees that Erickson has had a huge impact on who he is a person and as a therapist, he is quick to point out that he has never been a clone. "I was not going to go around wearing purple [Zeig's trademark is unusual socks] and speak in a gravelly voice."

What made Erickson and all the other masters that Zeig observed on stage and in videos so good at what they did was their ability to establish rapport with clients in such a way that they could become involved in the intricacies of their stories. Like many others, Zeig observed that the model experts use accounts for only a small fraction of whatever success they are having. Most of their power and leverage takes place at a relational level in which clients feel like they have been heard and understood.

This is not to say that "core conditions" are sufficient to promote change. One thing that stuck with Zeig after his training with Erickson entailed "unlearning" what he was taught in graduate school (i.e., doing an elaborate assessment, administering lengthy tests, taking a detailed history, and formulating a careful diagnosis before attempting treatment).

"An essential part of Erickson's art and creativity was to intervene quickly. The intervention could actually *precede* assessment, because in a social situation intervention *is* assessment. You do something and then observe how the person responds. Rather than spending a lot of time talking about things first, I can intervene in the first five minutes of a session with a new client. I just don't need to spend that much time data gathering. I want the message to be clear: Therapy is about living the experience of change, not just talking about it."

As an example of this, Zeig brings to bear the case of a new client, which unfolds in the following way.

Zeig: "What's the problem?"

Client: "The problem is depression."

Zeig: "All right. I'm going to stand up for a moment and I'm going to be a sculpture that could be static or kinetic." He gets out of his chair and stands in front of the client. In the best Virginia Satir fashion, he says, "Sculpt me to be a representation of your depression."

What Zeig finds most curious and interesting about this sort of assessment process is that the therapist is actually intervening at the same time he or she is finding out more about the nature of the complaint. There is a playful rapport that develops almost immediately. This sort of interaction signals the client right away that there is something different going on here; we're not just going to sit around and make polite conversation.

In another example of this phenomenon, we watched Zeig work with a therapist at a conference who volunteered to come on stage to do some "grief work." In the first few minutes, Zeig asked her several exploratory questions: "What does that mean, 'to do grief work' for you? How does grief come up for you? How does it feel inside you? How do you recognize it?"

All the while Zeig is questioning her, his hands are playing in accompaniment, each gesture an anchor associated with a particular word or phrase. "You start with the tears," he says to her, his right hand extended, palm up. "And you feel the tears welling up," both of his hands now extended, palms up. "Then there's pressure in your chest," he says, touching his chest with both hands, pressing inward. "And then what happens in your head," he says, touching the side of his own head with his left hand. Throughout their conversation, almost every repetitive phrase will be accompanied by a corresponding gesture, as if he is visually linking the words with more dramatic visual images that will become cemented in her memory.

Just as he promised, at exactly six minutes and two seconds into this first interview, he asks the client to stand up. Enough talk. "Let's do something a little strange," he announces. It is all the more remarkable that she complies in front of an audience of hundreds, but there is something soothing and reassuring in Zeig's voice, as though everything will be okay if she just follows his lead.

"Stand up," he invites softly, "and I want you to pretend that you are on instant replay. Just like on sports events, I want you to play back a 60-second replay of your grief, with all its components." Again he repeats what each of them are—the tears, the pressure in the chest, the thoughts in the head, each one accompanied by the hand gesture.

One thing that makes Zeig so skilled and inventive is how hard he works to study the patterns of others before and beside him. This type of assessment may be reminiscent of Satir's creativity, but it also uses ideas from Michael White's narrative therapy in that the presenting problem is externalized.

"I try to be as dramatic as I can, taking a posture of actually becoming the client's depression as if it is something outside of him or her. I become a visual representation of the depression instead of just one part of a conversation about its properties and effects. I don't want to ridicule the client in any way, but I might be a little ironic about the problem. And then I start to deconstruct the problem: What does it feel like? How does it behave? What does it think about the client? What are its ambitions and goals? Once I, as the problem, become this comical, living thing, it is hard for the client to go into this depression without revisualizing me in this role. I am trying to be a living 'virus' that destabilizes the habitual maladaptive set."

Psychotherapy exists to help make a change in habitual patterns of behavior. In Erickson's tradition, the clinician might begin a hypnotic induction within five minutes of the first session, just to see how a transformative experience might be immediately constructed. The sessions are symbolic dramas that are designed to produce experiences that are memorable.

Zeig believes that good therapy is as much dramatic enactment as it is the application of scientific principles. It is an improvisational art not unlike that of good stage performers or comedians (no matter how much they have rehearsed their performances). As we mentioned earlier, once he discovered this key, Zeig systematically trained himself in improvisational arts.

"In all the years I was with Dr. Erickson, he never once taught me the technique of how to do hypnosis. He did not teach me specific techniques of therapy. He thought I could get all that out of a book. Basically, what Erickson would do with me, what he did with others, is provide experiences in the form of metaphors, anecdotes, riddles, games, directives that would be dropped in my lap. I felt pushed to develop from the inside."

So it was with learning improvisation. Students are not first taught the rules of drama—make big gestures, do articulation, and then do modeling. Nothing about this is ever said. Instead, students are told to do things on stage and work them out. Zeig has since used these tools to promote therapist development on the most basic level. He believes that much of therapy training has lost its soul. We teach beginners how to treat social phobia, which technique to use with compulsive disorders, which method to use with every diagnosis under the sun, as if they are prescriptions that are guaranteed to work. Zeig's work on teaching creativity goes way back to Freud, before there were any techniques, when clinicians concentrated mostly what was going on in the room and responded to that.

What Is Creativity?

Returning to the question Zeig asked in the beginning of our interview, we asked him what creativity looks like to him.

"It is a little vessel, a silver vessel. It has inscribed on its side the word 'utilize.'"

"And what's inside this vessel called creativity?"

"Inside the vessel is this potpourri of experience, of everything I've learned and done. Being dramatic. Being visual. A sense of presence. Caring for people. And the vessel can be realized in a context. The context is the therapy room and the things that exist in the therapy room . . . and then the way in which the vessel interacts with the client, and the way that we can pass this vessel back and forth so the clients are giving me their creative vessel and I could be taking theirs. And the creativity is something that's going to happen in the interpersonal context."

Zeig concludes by returning to the theme that creativity must be dissociative. "You can't will yourself to be spontaneous. You can't will yourself to love. Something has to just happen. Images happen. Depth of involvement happens. Being fully present happens. And so, too, does creativity happen once you begin to dissociate, to let go of ordinary reality and utilize what is present."

CHAPTER 9

JUDY JORDAN: WHAT ABOUT LOVE?

After her initial enthusiasm for our subject, Judy Jordan struggled to settle on a single creative act in her work. There are several reasons for this. First of all, it is a daunting subject indeed. Second, she had all kinds of different ideas but was uncertain which one deserved attention. Ultimately, however, as a relational therapist she had a difficult time separating any kind of breakthrough from the relationship in which it was embedded. To Jordan, *all* therapy is a creative enterprise: "It's about change. It's about movement. It's about bringing forth new understandings and new possibilities."

Most of the changes that take place in therapy are gradual, subtle, and often beyond initial awareness, yet they can often lead to surprising shifts. In fact, the paradox of doing therapy is that we may often wonder if anything much is happening at all. We feel stuck, mired in the same inertia and hopelessness that the clients bring to their lives.

Relational Creativity

Jordan presents a view of creativity that is quite different from others discussed in this book, especially those that feature singular heroic actions on the part of a therapist. Before beginning her story, she wants to be clear that she doesn't buy into the notion that breakthroughs occur as a result of some brilliant clinical insight. Second, Jordan is troubled by the ways that clients are often objectified in the ways they are discussed: "I think it's a sign of profound disrespect for the clients we work with, many of whom suffer from isolation and objectification in their lives. Many clients actually objectify themselves; they feel dehumanized, vulnerable, and alone."

Traditional diagnostic assessments, the use of treatment manuals, and differential coding all contribute to the ways that human beings are turned into "its." They are talked about as "cases," put into boxes, and materially defined. Jordan believes this is especially destructive for people who have already been victimized and feel vulnerable. "These people are already hurt, and yet they are retraumatized by our diagnoses."

Jordan warns us that in talking about a particular client relationship that may have included some creative features, she intends to move out of what might seem familiar and comfortable. "What I want to talk about is a bit dangerous: I want to speak about love."

It's All about Relationships

Throughout her career, Jordan has been most haunted by one question: What most consistently leads to change, not only in therapy, but in the world? She recalls being a supervisor of interns and asking of them about their favored theories of change. Every one of them would mention something about relationships.

"Okay," Jordan would agree, "but *what* about relationships makes a difference?"

There were a lot of different reasons supplied, many of which are familiar to us—empathic listening, making sense of experiences, finding meaning, support, openness, and so on. But one word seemed to capture the essence of the answers, and it boiled down to caring.

Jordan's mentor, Irene Stiver, one of the founders of relational-cultural therapy, was dying of lung cancer and knew she had a very short time to live. Stiver was concerned about so abruptly ending her therapy with a number of clients under her care and so asked for Jordan's help to construct a farewell letter.

Jordan was overwhelmed with the honor, and yet the incredible responsibility, of such a task. Stiver had given her very vague directions about what to do, so Judy carefully and respectfully wrote down what she thought her mentor might wish to say to people she had been helping. She made certain to mention elements of caring, respect, and regret in the message before showing Stiver the draft of what she had created.

When Stiver reviewed the note, she just shook her head and handed the paper back. "Judy, you've missed the whole point."

"I have?" Jordan answered with disappointment, feeling that she had let down her cherished friend.

"Yes, indeed," Stiver said. "What about love?"

"Love?"

"You know, Judy, love is what it's all about."

Jordan was stunned. This was her former supervisor, her mentor, her colleague of 30 years, and yet in all their time together Jordan had been so careful about the use of the word *love* in her work. She had been taught that speaking about love was not appropriate in a professional context since it is open to so much misunderstanding. Jordan could only sit there, frozen in wonderment. Here was one of her oldest and dearest friends, one of the most influential people in her life, on her deathbed, telling her something that was utterly groundbreaking: She was talking about love as the essence of therapy.

Stiver asked Jordan to write down what she was about to say. "This is what I want to say to my clients."

It has become even clearer to me that love is what it's all about, not only at this time but throughout our relationship. I have felt your love and deep caring for me. In turn, I hope that you feel my love for you. My hope is that you will hold on to this love and build on it in your life. Thank you for the privilege of being part of your life.

Sincerely,
Irene Stiver

Betrayal by Diagnosis

It was about the same time this letter was written that Jordan was working with a client who often challenged her with respect to appearing so emotionally controlled in their sessions. The client, Donna, was fairly persistent in bringing up this issue in spite of Jordan's attempts to redirect the focus to the presenting problems.

"I have a question for you," Donna said one day.

"Yes?" Jordan prompted her to continue.

"Do you love me?"

"Excuse me?" Jordan said, not sure if she heard right, but also buying some time to figure out how to best respond.

"I asked if you love me."

"Well, of course I care a great deal for you."

"That's not what I asked," Donna pressed. "I asked if you *love* me."

"Donna, there are so many different kinds of love. There's sisterly love, maternal love, romantic love. There's courtly love and agape, which is a kind of selfless, altruistic love. There's infatuation. So when you ask that question, I'm not sure exactly what you mean." Again Jordan was stalling, very uncomfortable with the situation she now found herself in.

"Okay, okay," Donna interrupted, deciding to let her therapist off the hook. "So you care about me. I'll take that."

After the interaction was over, Jordan could have kicked herself for not asking Donna what love meant to her. She could have asked why the question was so important to her. She could have reflected the fear of rejection that she sensed underlying the question. There were so many things she could have said and done, but she had chosen to go off on an intellectual discussion, disconnecting from both herself and Donna and thereby confirming Donna's assessment of her as emotionally restricted. Of course, a number of experts might very well have commented that this was the most appropriate response in order to avoid triggering deeper transference issues. But that's not what Jordan believed.

"There were several things going through my mind during the session. My first thought was about a therapist who had recently been brought up on charges for having used the language of love in her treatment of a young man. I had been trained to be very careful about erotic transferences. I was warned that clients might not be able to make the fine distinctions between safe, therapeutic caring and sexual predation. But I also thought about the times that I heard therapists talk about how much they love certain clients—with real feeling. I've admired the ways that professionals like my mentor could be so comfortable talking about this. And I knew in my heart that this love was not only safe but the source of healing."

Although Jordan was weighing the possible advantages of being more emotionally expressive, she also realized that Donna was a very vulnerable and challenging client. She had engaged in several self-destructive patterns and was actively suicidal.

Late one night, still early in treatment, Jordan received a call from a hospital emergency room to say that Donna had been admitted for another suicide attempt, the second time in three weeks. She had cut her wrists, which were now being sutured. The nurse asked Jordan if she would mind speaking to the psychiatrist on call.

"What are you doing in therapy with this young woman?" the psychiatrist asked, implying that whatever was taking place was inadequate. The question had a shaming tone to it more than expressing curiosity about the work.

Jordan tried to explain what they had been working on, but the psychiatrist interrupted impatiently, "Yes, but here she is again."

"As you know," Jordan answered, far more defensively than she would have liked, "Donna is very troubled. We are trying to find safety in our relationship . . ."

"What's her diagnosis?" the doctor asked abruptly. It was obvious he was tired and harried.

"I'm sorry?" Jordan responded.

"What is she? Her diagnosis?"

Jordan hesitated. She and Donna had had long conversations about diagnostic labels. Donna knew that other doctors had labeled her "borderline," which for her was just about the worst name that any patient could be called. Jordan didn't much like this label, either, aware that often it was bestowed when clinicians were frustrated and angry at clients who weren't cooperating the way they preferred. Jordan was thinking about all this when the psychiatrist asked again.

"I asked her diagnosis," the doctor said, unable to keep the impatience out of his voice. "She's borderline, isn't she?"

Again Jordan hesitated. But it was late at night and she was feeling badgered. "Yes," she finally agreed.

"See?" she heard the doctor say to someone else in the room with him. "She agrees with me. You're borderline, all right."

Jordan was horrified. "More than that, I was mortified. I was sad. I was disappointed in myself. I knew this would injure her terribly. I heard Donna actually screaming in the background, but the conversation was done, the psychiatrist had gotten his diagnosis, and I was left with my regrets."

Donna was soon released from the hospital and sent home. Later that week when she showed up for her appointment, she was furious. Jordan immediately gave a heartfelt apology for the injury she knew she had inflicted with her agreement to the "borderline" diagnosis. Donna refused to leave the waiting room, saying that she didn't feel safe. She would only agree to meet with Jordan in neutral territory, a place that didn't remind her of the betrayal.

Once they were seated in the cafeteria, Donna's eyes narrowed with fury, true hate. "How could you do that? How could you betray me like that after everything we talked about? You even said you agreed that it was an awful name that had no meaning."

"Look, I'm truly sorry. I was tired. It was late at night. I was frustrated. But you're right, there's no excuse. I let you down. I did the one thing that you find most hurtful: I treated you like an object rather than a person."

Donna described in vivid detail the humiliation and abuse she had suffered in the hospital, supposedly for her own good. She had been restrained and had not even been allowed to go to the bathroom, thus forced to wet herself while tied to a gurney. And her therapist, the one person she thought she could trust, had sided with others against her.

Again Jordan apologized, but Donna would not be so easily appeased. "I am truly sorry that I hurt you," Jordan tried again. "I agree that I let you down. So, how do you think I could have handled things differently?"

"How about standing up for me? How about fighting for me against these assholes? Maybe when he asked you what I am, you could have come up with a better answer." Donna bowed her head, too exhausted to continue.

"You're right," Jordan said in a soft voice. "Maybe I could have said, 'Donna is someone I care deeply about. She deserves to be respected.'"

Donna looked up and met Jordan's eyes.

"Maybe I could have even said, 'Donna is someone I love.'"

Donna studied Jordan intently, deciding whether she believed her or not. Jordan felt very anxious, like she had taken a risk that she hoped would carry some healing potential, but also uncomfortable with the scrutiny as if she was transparent.

"You couldn't say that," Donna said, shaking her head. "You *wouldn't* say that. You're too chicken. Besides, then they'd think you're crazy, too." The beginning of a smile played on her face.

Good point, Jordan thought. She wondered if she really would have had the courage to say that out loud. She thought about all the ways that could have been misinterpreted. But then she considered that she was hardly treating this so-called borderline patient with the sort of rigid boundaries, detachment, and caution that was usually prescribed.

Mystery, Doubt, and Uncertainty

Donna never ended up in an emergency room again, nor did she ever again attempt suicide. This was all the more remarkable considering that she had more than a half dozen previous hospitalizations to her credit.

To this day, Jordan isn't totally certain what turned things around for Donna. It could have been the abandonment of diagnosis, joining the client in a more collaborative alliance. It might have been her greater realness and authenticity, taking the risk of being vulnerable with Donna, which invited her to do the same. Jordan does have some thoughts on the matter.

"I thought about Irene Stiver's letter. I thought about the whole notion of courage that we ask our clients to bring to the work. I thought about why it is that we're so scared of the healing power of love, of connection, of mutual relationship. I thought about the importance of being real as therapists and the openness that we bring in those moments of vulnerability that are so momentous.

"I don't have a formula for what was creative about our work together, but I think it had something to do with coming out into the open with Donna. Even though she doubted that I would have really told the psychiatrist that I loved her, she appreciated that I would have at least *tried* to say it. Even though I betrayed her, I also stayed present with her. I tried to move out of the same old boxes that constrain the ways we work."

Piaget's theories of assimilation and accommodation come to mind for Jordan in explaining the creative process. First, we try to put our clients in existing structures, assimilating them into what we think we know; in so doing, we objectify and distort them. When we are creative, we move into new structures that are custom-designed for each person at any moment in time. It is about, in the words of John Keats, living with uncertainty, mystery, and doubt without irritably reaching after fact and reason.

"This guides a lot of my work, particularly in those moments when I'm not sure of where I'm going. I'm not advocating utter confusion or being rudderless. I give advice. I'm active in interventions. I have people do cognitive behavioral stuff. But I think that, for me, the creativity is in staying present, with staying open to where there is hope. That's where people have an opportunity to come out of some of their old, stuck, unsatisfying patterns."

Staying Fully Present

Jordan acknowledges that there is a lot of misunderstanding around the concept of love, especially as it might apply to therapy relationships. "There is a long history of exploitation and sexual misconduct in our field, and we have a duty to protect patients from this kind of abuse. Sadly, we know that some of the ostensibly most rule-bound therapists are as likely to exploit clients as other therapists. Jordan believes that caution is in order, but that doesn't prevent the possibility of talking about love in therapy and creative transformations that it can generate.

"Irene's letter was written on her deathbed. She could say some things without others being threatened by them. People were just *moved* by what she said."

Similarly to a few other therapists in this book, Jordan doesn't think in terms of creativity as "belonging" to the therapist. "Therapists sometimes believe they are the source of movement or creativity or change, but they're not. The movement comes from the relationship in a kind of fluid expertise; it is through the movement that you're creating something new."

In order for this process to occur, control of the movement must be surrendered. The therapist's job is to ensure safety during this journey, as well as to remain fully present. "You are not the creative genius in the room, but rather learning from what's happening between you."

CHAPTER 10

Robert Neimeyer: A Little Hug from Heaven

Angela was devastated by the death of her mother, which had occurred four years earlier, manifesting lingering and debilitating symptoms of depression. A woman in her late forties, Angela had finally negotiated a loving relationship with her mother after a childhood that had been marked by conflict. Just when they had reached some resolution of their life issues, the mother had died. Angela was not only grieving the immediate loss of her mother, but also the decades of abandonment she had felt previous to that.

Angela was the youngest of nine children, growing up on an isolated farm where she had few friends or social contacts outside of her immediate family. Her parents had been overwhelmed by caring for all the children and the responsibilities of managing the farm, so Angela had received very little attention, except from her brother who was closest to her age.

Complicating matters further, there was serious disturbance in the family, especially with respect to the brother, who had very violent tendencies. While a teenager, the brother had discovered two young people having a picnic on their property, so he captured and tortured them, after which he killed them. He was convicted of the crime and sentenced to life in prison.

Angela's mother devoted the rest of her life to staying in close communication with her imprisoned son, writing to him every day.

As the mother grew older, she developed health problems and eventually moved in with Angela, expecting her to take on many of her responsibilities, such as staying in contact with her brother.

Angela became the primary caregiver of her mother during her last years. After her marriage dissolved, Angela and her own daughter moved back to the family farm, which she described as the "sweetest years" now that she and her mother had grown so close. The sicker the mother became, the more dependency she developed on her daughter, a situation that Angela had enjoyed.

After her mother's death, Angela became so grief-stricken she felt that she could never recover. Her sadness and regret took over her life, as did pervasive loneliness. She was haunted by images and memories of her mother. She was troubled by periods of "blankness," when she would "zone out" for minutes or hours and could barely recall what she did. She isolated herself, neglecting her own parenting duties, and could barely function on a daily basis.

Over time, Angela attempted to cope with her loss by transitioning into the many roles and responsibilities that her mother had assumed. Although she was the youngest child, Angela nevertheless took it upon herself to regulate the lives of her siblings. This did not go over very well with her brothers and sisters, who resented their baby sister for trying to control them. "And so," Neimeyer summarized, "Angela was caught in a difficult place where she had lost the mother she had ultimately come to love and who had come to love her as well. That's the point at which she entered therapy with me, a disheveled and profoundly depressed woman who was both tearful and emotionally out of control."

Hello rather than Goodbye

Neimeyer's initial assessment of his client was that this would likely be a long-term case. "I figured progress would be glacial because Angela was in such a frozen state of grief."

"I wonder," Neimeyer asked Angela during the end of their first session, "whether it would be possible for you to move in a direction of somehow reclaiming your life?"

"What do you mean?" she asked, in between sobs. It was difficult for her to concentrate for very long.

"I was thinking of you writing a letter."

"A letter?"

"Yes, a letter to your mother, as a way of reopening a conversation with her that was interrupted by her death."

Angela's demeanor visibly brightened for a moment at the prospect of continuing any communication with her beloved mother. "I suppose I could try that."

"Good. Let me ask you—what did you call your mother?"

"Myrtle. Like Myrtle the Turtle."

Neimeyer smiled. "Okay, so your letter begins, 'Dear Myrtle.' Just continue with what you'd like to say to her and I'll write it down for you."

"Dear Myrtle," Angela started again, "I miss you. I miss . . ." Then she dissolved into tears again.

"What is it you miss most?" Neimeyer asked, prompting her to find some way to articulate the core of her yearning.

"Well, you know, she really listened to me." That was as far as she could get before the crying began again.

"What did she hear that others did not?"

"Everything that was in my heart. She was always encouraging me. She always told me that things would be okay."

As she spoke, Neimeyer continued to sketch out the letter, prompting Angela to shift to a direct, second-person way of talking to her mom rather than using a third-person voice to talk about her. As she shifted to this more personal way of speaking—"Mom, I'm doing what you wanted me to do. . . ."—Neimeyer wrote down the main points that Angela was making. Then he handed her the paper. "I wonder if it would be possible for you to finish what we just started together? Keep writing to your mother in a way that makes sense to you. Can you do that?"

Angela nodded, still a bit confused and overwhelmed by the renewed contact she felt with her mother by talking to her in the room.

"And at some point," Neimeyer added, "You might lend your mother a hand in writing a reply note back to you!" Angela smiled slightly, having a sense of where this might be headed.

As is already evident, Neimeyer has some unusual ideas about death and grief. Rather than seeing death as the end of relationship, he sees it as a renegotiation that leads to a different kind of conversation in the future. After all, when loved ones die, we still hear their voices in our heads and hearts; we still speak to them, consult them, visit them in our dreams and fantasies. They still remain alive in our memories and accessible any time we wish. There are some cultures, such as the Bushmen of the Kalahari, where all the ancestors of an afflicted person are invited to attend a healing session and to be present to provide support. They recognize that death does not separate us from family and friends who have moved on to another world. Whether spiritually or psychologically, Neimeyer believes the dead can be very much alive in our thoughts, deeds, and conversations.

It was Neimeyer's intention to support Angela in finding a new, and still feasible, way to relate to her mother—not to let her mother go, but rather to say hello once again. "You see," Neimeyer explained, "your relationship with your mother is no longer physically available in this life, but that doesn't mean you can't continue your relationship with her on another level. Does that make sense to you?"

After a moment Angela nodded slowly.

"What would this be like for you?" Neimeyer asked, sensing her hesitation.

"I don't know. I guess a little scary. And painful. But I'd like to try this. I mean, I'd like to do this. I think it's what I need to do."

An Interesting Shift

Writing a letter to a deceased loved one, however useful, is not especially innovative and could even be considered standard procedure. But asking a client to write a letter as a way to reestablish an ongoing relationship rather than to say goodbye is a radical twist on this theme. Added to that is the invitation for the bereaved to actually write back from the standpoint of the deceased, thus providing that which is most needed—a sense of reconnection, of renewed attachment.

The second session began with Neimeyer asking Angela to talk about what happened during the preceding week. "What were some of your thoughts and feelings since our last session?"

"I feel like I've gotten through some of the *yuck*."

"What's the 'yuck?'"

Angela described the unremitting anxiety and grief that she had been living with. She actually looked a little brighter and better groomed, even more in control. She talked about the ways that she felt her mother's presence around the house. She could see her mother in her sister's mannerisms. She could feel her mother when she stood at the sink washing dishes the way her mother would. She even admitted to noticing many ways in which she was so like her mother, as though she lived within her.

Coupled with this awareness of the ways her mother still remained accessible, Angela also noticed how she had seemed less bothered by things that had irritated her in the past—appliances breaking down, hassles with her daughter, things not going the way she preferred. None of these things seemed as annoying as they had before, and she was at a loss to explain this. However, to Neimeyer it seemed that as Angela regained some control over the chaos of her emotional life, minor disruptions in the world outside seemed to have less impact.

"And what about the letter-writing assignment?" Neimeyer asked, inquiring about the homework. "How did that go for you?"

"Well, I did it like you suggested," she said, pulling out a few pages written on fine stationery and reaching over to hand them to Neimeyer. He glanced over them, saw a series of short sentences, each hitting a separate point. He handed the paper back and said, "Why don't you read it to me in your own voice?"

Angela took a deep breath, then began reading. "Dear Myrtle," she began. "I'm doing what you wanted me to do with my life. I'm pursuing a college education. I'm working very hard. I miss you a great deal. I know you're in a better place. I'm trying to become a better person. I'm using you as a model in that. I know that you're keeping track of us from where you are in heaven." The letter continued with other personal statements about her life and her grief since her mother had died, then was signed, "Your daughter and friend, Angela." Finishing, she glanced up at Neimeyer, moisture in her eyes.

Neimeyer could feel a strong sense of gratitude and connection in her words. "What part of the letter was most moving for you to write?" he asked.

"I guess the part where I tell her how hard it's been for me, how I haven't been exactly functioning very well since she died. It was hard for me to admit that to her."

Angela also talked about how proud she felt about the relationship that she and her mother had built together, how it had matured and blossomed. She also spoke at length about how much she missed her.

Neimeyer was understandably impressed with the progress that Angela had made in so short a period of time. Rather quickly, it seemed, she had responded to the invitation to reopen a more contemporary relationship with her mother and, with it, to begin to win back her own life.

Hide-and-Seek

The third session began with Neimeyer asking Angela what had become clearer to her since their previous conversation.

"I guess I felt a kind of release," she reported with a smile.

"A release?"

"Yeah. Since writing that letter to my mom I realized all the ways I was trying to fill in for my mother, to actually *be* my mother. I wasn't really doing stuff that I wanted to do or that I needed to do. It was like an obsession for me to make others feel the same way I did, that others in the family would feel like me. I was trying to replace some of the things that mother did with others in the household. I was becoming this worrywart kind of person, and that was a very negative thing for me because people weren't really wanting it. I was trying to become a replacement for mom, and you can't do that because the age span alone makes that impossible. It's like I was playing *hide-and-seek* with myself and not facing reality."

"What an extraordinary image," Neimeyer responded, "of playing hide-and-seek with yourself. What exactly were you hiding and what were you seeking?"

"Well, I guess I was just seeking acceptance from my family but I was creating an identity that wasn't my own and it wasn't even asked for. I'm just not that person. It's like I was hiding who I really am."

"You mentioned before that you'd gone on to write another letter to your mom?"

Angela nodded.

"Would you be willing to read it to me?"

"Sure," she said and then pulled the pages out of her purse.

Dear Myrtle,

You were always the key holder to the family problems. Since you've been gone I have tried to replace you. I'm returning your legacy to you. My family didn't ask me to fill the hole of your departure but I picked up your one negative characteristic of worrying about the family and I realize now that I need to let go of this need to help others. I need to let go of my own negativity and not make people into who I need them to be.

Mom, I'm going to ask your permission to let me be me, to be okay with who I am. I need to practice my own individuality. I have all the wonderful things that you taught me and one of those is the power of prayer.

Love,
Angie

Angela talked about how, once she had finished this letter, she had felt able to recapture herself. She had thought about ways she could pursue the things she really wanted to do and had held herself back. Rather than forcing herself onto family members who really didn't want her help, she had decided she wanted to devote herself to an altruistic path with people who really did need help.

"So," Neimeyer reflected, "you gave your mother's legacy back to her so you could begin your own."

"Yes, I wasn't born to be her. I was born to be me."

"Who is this self that you were born to be, as you get a clearer view in the reflective mirror of this writing and our conversation? Who is this Angie that you're becoming?"

Angela spoke about how obsessively overinvolved she'd been with her daughter, who was now an adult. She needed to back away from being so controlling. She also repeated her interest in reaching out to those beyond her own family, to break out of her isolation.

"So," Neimeyer said, "now that you've stopped being your mom, you've been able to let your daughter stop being you. She can be her own person, and so can you."

Mother Speaks Words of Wisdom

At this point, Neimeyer was thinking about the parallel process between Angela's relationship with her mother, on the one hand, and her daughter and siblings on the other. He wondered how to move forward with that to restructure both kinds of relationships, with the living and the dead. Angela was doing so well that he wanted to take things to the next level. He decided to extend an invitation to do so.

"I wondered if we could have a conversation with your mom about the person that you're becoming. Could you just switch chairs with me so we can reorganize things and let me interview *her* about *you*?" Neimeyer finds that by inviting people to physically take a different chair from their usual one, it is easier for them to take on the role of another person.

Once they resettled themselves, with Angela now in the role of her mother, Neimeyer began to interview her.

"Myrtle, I've been having this conversation with your daughter, Angela, and I think she's a very interesting person. We're talking a lot about her relationship with you and she's been worried about how you feel about her finding her own legacy rather than following yours. What do you think about that?"

"Well," Angela answered in her mother's soft and assured voice, "I do want her to carry forward the positive traits that she has and to let go of that kind of negativity, that preoccupation that I sometimes had."

"I understand," Neimeyer said. "I wonder, though, if you had a magic pencil with lead on one end and an eraser on another, what are some of the traits that you'd write out for your daughter to keep?" Neimeyer had a pad of paper on his lap, a pen in his hand, poised to take notes.

"For one thing," Angela said in the guise of her mother, "I'd want her to really keep that trait of having a loving understanding of herself. I'd want her to have the courage to stand on her own decision, having a passion for life, to continue her great love for people, her empathy for them."

"I appreciate that. I'd like to ask you something else."

"Sure."

"What do you see in your daughter that is similar to your own qualities?"

"Well, she thinks before she speaks. She's not harsh. She's comfortable with what she has and she works hard for it. She's willing to ask for help."

Neimeyer was delighted with the way that Angela had so easily slipped into the role of her mother. What had started out haltingly was now flowing quite naturally. More and more, Angela's posture, voice, and manner were taking on the characteristics of her mother. It was no wonder that she so easily slipped into imitating her.

"Okay. If you were to use the eraser end of that pencil, and you could kind of erase some characteristics or give Angela permission to relinquish them, what would you ask her to let go of?"

"Well, I'd say being the family caregiver with all the endless cycle of worry. I wish she'd know that she's worth something. I want her to stand up for herself."

"Anything else you'd like to say to your daughter as final words of wisdom today?"

"I want Angela to find something that gives total joy to her, and everything else will be okay."

"That's great. Thank you very much."

"You're welcome."

"Would it be okay if you left now and asked Angela to return?"

Angela laughed, the first real laugh that Neimeyer had heard from her since they'd met. He asked her to switch chairs with him again. "So, what was that like for you?"

"Kind of weird." Another laugh.

"Weird how?"

"My mom was never that talkative. She never said things like that to me before."

Neimeyer noticed that Angela was speaking as if that really *had* been her mother in the room. That's how real it had been for her. Tears came into her eyes and her lips started to tremble as she talked about "overhearing" the conversation that just took place.

"Say more about what it was like for you," Neimeyer asked her again.

"Those last words—they sounded just like her. That's just what she would have really said to me about finding joy within." Angela started crying, but then said through her tears, "I know I'm crying like before, but this time it feels good."

Neimeyer signaled her to continue.

"It's encouraging to me, because when I focus on the fact that she's not here, then it just brings pain. But when I hear those words she said—I mean I said—whatever! Anyway, I realize that she is still here with me."

Neimeyer handed Angela the sheet of paper on which he'd been taking notes on what had been said when Angela's "mother" was speaking. She looked it over and nodded. "Yeah, you know, I think I'd like to type this up. These are words of wisdom very similar to what she would have said to me. So whenever I want her words I can have them."

"What a beautiful idea! When you want her words you can have them," Neimeyer repeated. "Why don't you type them up and bring them in next time?"

Experiential Intensity

Angela began their fourth session by talking about how interesting it had been for her to talk to her mother and to have her mother respond. She admitted that none of the despair and blankness she had felt previously was present now. For the first time since her mother died, she felt excited about being alive. There was still some sadness, of course, but it was the right kind of sadness, not the sort that disrupted her sleep and took over her life.

While typing up the dictated words of wisdom from her mother, Angela had been reminded of the spiritual principles that had been taught to her as a child—being loving, understanding, passionate, having the courage to stand up for her convictions, seeking positive results. She put down another kind of heading under what was special about her in mom's eyes—thinking before she spoke, not being harsh, being comfortable with what she had, being willing to ask for help, having permission to relinquish being the family caregiver. "I am doing real well at that," she said. "I haven't fallen back into that overidentification with mom."

Neimeyer went back to the "blankness" that Angela had mentioned earlier, that was almost like a kind of erasure. He wondered what that felt like.

"I'm not sure, really. It's kind of like a physical hurt, or maybe a void inside that can't ever be filled."

Neimeyer assumes that all important changes that take place in therapy occur during moments of "experiential intensity" and that everything else we do and say is mere commentary. "Commentary is sometimes useful to consolidate a change, but it is never sufficient to instigate a change. So I wanted to move this in a more experiential direction, just as I had in moving toward the concrete writing or the enactment of Mom. So here she had described a kind of void that had a physical location, and I asked where that was located."

"It's around my heart," Angela answered immediately, bringing her hand to her chest. "Actually it was so painful that I checked with my doctor, and he did this cardiac testing, but there was nothing that he could identify. He said it was just my mind playing tricks on me."

"We're talking about that void feeling and doing a scan for that medically in your body. I wondered if we could do an inward scan for that now psychologically?"

Angela shrugged, not sure what she was agreeing to, but game nevertheless.

"Okay then," Neimeyer said, consciously slowing the pace of his speaking to call up a state of relaxed concentration. "So, Angela, just allow yourself to close your eyes to find a comfortable position in your chair, allowing your attention to enter your body." Neimeyer let his own eyes close with hers, and then continued, "We're going to take a walk through your body looking for any tension or feelings that seem significant, perhaps related to the void you've been holding for your mother." He paused a few seconds to allow her to do the scan, and he reopened his eyes to be alert to her nonverbal signals. "As you allow your attention to move through your body, scanning for that sense, signal to me when you find it."

"It almost starts out of my body," Angela said after a moment of reflection. "Out here, over my head," she said holding her hands above her head, but still keeping her eyes closed. "It feels like a kind of beacon of light, like a warmth . . . almost as if a feeling of understanding will come over time."

"It's a reassuring feeling."

"Yes, it's like an *embracing* feeling. It's kind of like a radiation that envelops me."

"Does that kind of radiation have a direction of movement for you?"

"Yes, it's coming down. It's right here with me now." As she said this, Angela gestured with her hands around her shoulders, her eyes still closed. "It's like it might embrace the whole of me, but right now it's right here!" Again she moved her hands above her shoulders.

As Neimeyer was listening and watching Angela, he sensed that he could actually feel his own body becoming warm, enveloped in this energy. He didn't try to analyze or make sense of this but just assumed it was part of the deep empathy and closeness that they were both feeling. After taking his time to follow the sensations within his own body that were matching those in Angela's, he prompted her further: "If you were to allow that kind of radiation, that feeling, to move forward and continue its path of movement, where would it go?"

"It would just come down, I guess," she said, gesturing downward with her hands. "It would stop at the floor, sort of embracing all of me." Angela's smile and the moisture in her eyes made it clear that she found this very moving. "It gives me comfort," she said. "It gives me courage."

"That sounds almost like those spiritual words that you attributed to your mom."

"Yeah. It almost feels like an exhale, like I'm just releasing all of that negativity."

"I wonder if you could allow your lungs to fill up and to release with slow, rhythmic breaths." As he said this, Neimeyer was aware that he was matching his own breathing to that of his client, filling his lungs and exhaling deeply in synchronized movement. Both of them were giving physical expression to the cleansing Angela described, releasing the negativity as they exhaled.

"It's hard to explain what comes with that," Angela said. "It's like a wisdom or understanding, a faith that this process will continue and that it's okay to release my mom as long as it's not extreme, as long as I don't hurt myself."

Neimeyer nodded, mostly to himself since Angela's eyes were still closed. "As you speak of that wisdom, I feel tingles enter me and they go down my spine to my feet and legs."

Angela was nodding, seeming to agree that was her experience as well.

Neimeyer continued: "It feels like an affirmation in my body of some of what you have been experiencing."

"Yes. It's almost like a peace that has been brought to me, like a key has opened that door." Angela moved her hand to her heart. "It has opened that door, that void."

"Well, can you take that key and, in this moment of peace, allow that void to open just a little bit and note what's there. What would you see or feel in that space?" Neimeyer asked, speaking slowly.

"The first thing I feel is the physical, my mother not being around, her body, her structure, her voice, her reading, speaking, and singing voice. I loved to hear her sing." Angela paused, deep into her remembrance. "I hear her laughter. I loved the way she laughed—that's what I miss the most."

"What you're describing sounds almost sacred," Neimeyer said after a moment of silence. "It's almost as if this warmth, this energy, is radiating from her to you. That energy from her is like an embrace, isn't it?"

"Yes! That's it! It's her spirit and her power, what she called God. I'm not sure how that works, but the tenderness and sweetness that was so ingrained in her is there. So maybe it's not her spirit but something else."

"You're saying that your mother's tenderness and sweetness was not lost. It was lost as a physical *voice* but it was not lost as a physical *experience.* You can feel it around you or you can feel it in you. Can you speak to that a little more?"

Angela's eyes were closed, but her face was beaming. She was smiling, nodding her head, rocking her body a little back and forth.

"It feels like a massage," she said. "Like when kids poke and tickle each other. I can feel the needles and pins with my hands, the feeling in my abdomen like when she would tickle my tummy when I was a little girl. Do you know what I mean?"

"I do. I do," Neimeyer said. "I'm feeling them, too! You're sharing those feelings with me now." Neimeyer found himself smiling, too, closing his own eyes and allowing himself to be moved by what they were both experiencing together. It seemed like a kind of transcendent empathy that was carrying them both along for the ride.

"Weird, isn't it?" Angela said.

"It's also pretty interesting that as we move into that void what we get is not only the *grief* but also *joy* in this physical, almost childlike way. Each one is right there alongside the other."

"Well," Angela said, "not everyone had that kind of wonderful mother."

Sensing that Angela was shifting from the raw experience to a natural period of commentary as a way of making sense of it, Neimeyer asked Angela to take another deep breath and open her eyes when she felt ready.

Angela opened her eyes, wiped them with her sleeve, and looked around the room as if she had just arrived. "Wow!"

Neimeyer waited. "What was that like?" he asked.

"It was like . . . I don't know. It was like a little hug from heaven!"

"Yes," Neimeyer immediately agreed, delighted with the image. "I felt like I got a little pat on the shoulder myself."

Angela laughed. "That's just like my mother. She wouldn't want to leave anyone out!"

"She even doled out a little bit to a stranger, huh? So, what was that like for you, Angela, to accept my invitation to go right into that?"

"I went to kind of a meditation place. I could almost see an endless void of pages with words on them, like in a fog. And it was hard to make out some of the words, but as I looked into the void I could start to see them."

"I wonder if, as you move forward, you could allow yourself to meditate on this and to patiently attend to those words to see what they have to teach us. See what you might read there."

"Yes! Yes! It's good to remember in this positive way. I feel almost like I've been advised in some way by this."

Neimeyer asked Angela how they might continue their work after that. Angela suggested that she could continue the meditations on her own, metaphorically peering into the void where her mother's spirit resides.

"You know," Angela said, as their session was about to end, "this was really wonderful. You asked about mom's presence, and I didn't really feel it until I felt the tickling. But then it was like electrical static. I felt her energy because that is what my mom is now—she's pure energy. It's a spiritual thing."

"And yet it's very physical as well, isn't it?"

"Yes. I felt her warmth and it was deep."

Neimeyer and Angela met for two additional sessions, talking about her spiritual beliefs that were somewhat unorthodox and undergoing a period of transformation. Angela believed in the possibility of other dimensions of being, those that are not part of this existence.

It was during these weeks that Angela consolidated the changes she'd made, not only in her grief work, but in many other areas of her life. She quite literally altered her behavior in relation to her daughter and siblings, becoming much less intrusive and controlling, allowing them space to reach out to her. She volunteered to work for a children's charity, working with the terminally ill. She found a different job that gave her life greater meaning. She resumed her exercise and diet regimes, and she began dressing more stylishly. In short, her mother's "hug from heaven" had given her the boost she needed to move on with her life.

Relishing Uncertainty

"Every psychotherapy session," in Neimeyer's words, "is an invitation to creativity. When we decline that invitation, I think we deaden ourselves as therapists and we deaden our clients as people who consult us. In many ways, I think one of the most useful exercises that we can be taught in graduate school or that can be enforced in our places of employment is to do a comprehensive case planning and case conceptualization. Really note down all the behavioral goals and all of the interventions that we will use in order to reduce the person's symptoms. Then, after doing this comprehensive planning and analysis, shred it. Just throw it away! Because that plan will tell you exactly what you should *not* do when you move into a real session with a living client."

Not a big fan of manualized treatments, especially as they relate to accessing greater creativity, Neimeyer stresses how important it is that we avoid a prescriptive, canned approach at all costs. "Once we presume to know what people need *before* they signal their receptivity in a given therapeutic moment, we close ourselves off to the most potentially powerful and creative interventions. That can never come from any book or any supervision. It needs to come from within us, from the unique relationships that we develop with our clients."

Neimeyer believes that there are many thoughtful and useful things to be said in treatment manuals, but they should be written on a level of *principles* rather than *rules*. They need to be suggestive, philosophical, and abstract in such a way that they guide our actions but don't necessarily dictate them. "That is one of the biggest mistakes that beginning therapists make, in that they obsessively rehearse conversations they want to have with their clients or overplan what they intend to do and how they will do it, writing out scripts in their heads. And that has exactly the same stilted, deadening, and distancing effect in therapy that it would have, say, in a dating situation," Neimeyer explained. Even pressing the client to implement the agenda from the previous session, Neimeyer believes, is often a mistake. "That misses all the new, rich information that is available in the present moment of any encounter."

The worst thing we therapists can do, according to Neimeyer, is to become so enamored with our theories, our "evidence-based practice" protocols, our predictions and hypothesis testing that we miss what clients are really saying and doing in the moment. "I think I am doing my best therapy when I am least able to anticipate what my client—or I—will say next. When we are both attending to and being moved by the uncertain affordances of this moment of encounter, that is when we move beyond our own comfort zones. We'll be working on our intuitive leading edge of what is possible and useful in the session rather than formulaically playing out a script that either we or someone else wrote on the basis of another person, another case, a different problem."

According to Neimeyer, creativity means relishing uncertainty. "It means discovering patterns as they unfold. It means not only attending to the literal problem and solution talk that takes place, but also the metaphors, the images, the nonverbal communication, the bodily experiences. We have to use those to create a new order that could not be envisioned on the basis of some formulated understanding of the case that existed before the session began."

Honoring the Creative Work

As a way to honor his work with Angela, Neimeyer composed a poem that captures the kind of empathic attunement that he considers so crucial for therapists to access their creative spirit. He offers it here as encouragement for both therapists and clients to allow the husk of habit and prescription to fall away and to cultivate something new and fresh in the soil of their unique encounter.

Coming Through

Fall silent and you will hear it growing,
insistent as grass through asphalt.
You know it has always been there,
pregnant with possibility, finding form.

Now it is coming through,
seeking light,
earning a visible place
in this world you have made.

Listen.
Like a known voice in a crowded room
it will come,
follow the silver thread
of attention to reach your ear.
It only requires attunement,
a paring away of excess
to hear the pure tone.

Like sculpting hands
you must work the substance
to find its essential form.
There is something inside the mass
for which your life is the template,
awaiting the accident of discovery.
Now you must caress its naked shape,
shiver at its frailty,
know its strength.

All you have been has readied you
for this beginning.

CHAPTER 11

LAURA BROWN: WORKING IN A BOX

This chapter is quite different from our other stories. Many of the others we interviewed proudly advertise themselves as creative innovators; they thrive on circumstances that allow them to invent something altogether new. If you are like us, as much as we admire these wildly creative stories, we can't actually picture ourselves doing what is described. Laura Brown thus represents the journeywomen (and -men) who work in the trenches every day, who take care of business but don't necessarily see themselves as creative geniuses by any stretch of the imagination.

This interview was a real struggle for Brown. She very much wanted to cooperate with us on the project, but found it difficult to identify herself as a particularly creative practitioner. "What I realize is that the clients I work with evoke creative moments from me, perhaps even breakthroughs, but these interactions between us remain in the room and don't seem all that special once they are taken out of that domain."

Stuck in a Box

The case that Brown wanted to discuss involved a relationship with one of her very first clients, whom she was still seeing until about a year ago. The woman is an artist who has entered and reentered therapy every few years, usually remaining for a few years at a time.

Jordan had a long history of abuse, with accompanying shame. A specialty of Brown's practice has been helping abused women come to terms with their trauma. Even among such challenging cases, Jordan proved to be the toughest of all. Every time she would make any sustained progress, she was inclined to relapse, often in an alcoholic binge. Two or three years later she would show up again, ready and eager to begin work, but with limited momentum.

After so many years of failures and setbacks, Jordan's life had become a complete wreck. In addition to her alcohol dependence, she was having problems at work and with most of her intimate relationships, of which there were few to begin with.

After about a dozen or so of Jordan's disappearances, Brown had an "aha" experience and decided to try something completely different, something that would speak to the artist energy that was Jordan's greatest strength. "I want you to build a box," she instructed her client, "and then I want you spend time in there. You have to stay inside your box for at least five minutes at a time, no matter how difficult this might be for you or how closed in you feel. Can you do that? Will you do that?"

Jordan nodded her agreement, even though this did seem a bit bizarre. She had spent so much time with Brown over the years, she came to trust her completely. In fact, one of her continuing problems was how much she felt she was letting her therapist down. She was anxious to make amends and comply with whatever Brown asked of her.

"Good," Brown said. "There's one more thing. When you construct this box that you're going to sit in, I want you to draw on the outside pictures of all things you have not been able to change, objects that represent all the things that you have avoided or failed."

"Sure, I can do that." Jordan was in one of her moods when she would try anything. She was desperate. She was also intrigued; as an artist, she had built sets for plays and done designs for retail store windows. She could make this box, even if she had no idea why Brown wanted her to do it.

Prior to suggesting this craft project, as Jordan had been talking about the misery that was her life, Brown had this very clear and vivid image of her client sitting in a box. The image was so strong that she felt compelled to ask Jordan to make this fantasy into a reality, a physical structure that seemed to capture the essence of the experience—at least as Brown viewed it. This was not an uncommon occurrence that Brown, or any of us, would have strong representational images of our clients as they are speaking, but it was certainly unusual for her to ask her client to build it.

Jordan took her homework assignment very seriously. She went to an alley where a local department store throws away its old boxes and found one that was a perfect size for her purposes. It was a huge, cratelike, supersturdy refrigerator box made of reinforced cardboard. After transporting it home, she decorated it with designs and pictures, as she had been asked to do, and spent the requisite amount of time inside. Since Brown hadn't given her much instruction about what to do once she was inside the box, she spent the time thinking about her painful and apparently wasted life. Strangely, the box became a sanctuary for her, so much so that she asked if she could transport the monstrous thing to Brown's office for a session.

Brown was tickled by the idea. She didn't know where this was going, but she liked the way Jordan was taking charge of things. It was as if she knew what she needed. And trying a therapy session with her client inside a box would certainly be something different!

For the next several sessions, Jordan crawled inside her box and talked to her therapist from inside. She talked about how safe and secure she felt in her box where nobody could hurt her. There was only Brown's voice on the outside, and that was a kind of anchor for her.

Brown would invite Jordan to talk about how she was feeling inside the box, which she could do readily. Then one day, when Brown was staring at the box that contained her client, feeling more than a little strange to be conducting a session like this (what if someone walked in?), she asked Jordan what would it be like to break out of the box?

Without hesitation, she answered, "That should be easy—not!"

Jordan then kicked and punched and struggled to get out of the box, tipping it on its side at one point, flailing and screaming, putting dents in the durable cardboard. Finally she broke through, sobbing and crying. When she regained her composure, she talked for the first time about the trauma she suffered that launched her first drinking binge.

"This trauma turned out to have been the beginning of a narrative that had been running her life for 30 years," Brown recalled. "It had happened just months before she first started in therapy with me, but had taken all of this time for her to tell anyone. It had been running her relapses, running her "stuckness," running her self-hatred, running her whole life. She had felt stuck in a box in so many ways and she couldn't get out—until she busted out in my office for the first time. That changed everything."

Hobbit Courage

Looking back, Brown is a bit surprised at herself and the way the box idea came to fruition. She had originally been trained in Gestalt therapy, way back when, and it felt like she had rediscovered those creative roots. "I think it was a breakthrough," Brown clarified, "but it wasn't mine; it was *ours*. Jordan is the one who threw herself into this project with all the passion and gusto. I may have felt a little hesitant, but it is the first time she didn't feel any shame, even though she was doing something that was pretty unusual."

Although many of the other chapters in this book feature stories that emphasize technique or creative interventions, Brown believes the source of this breakthrough came from the depth of her relationship with the client. They enjoyed a level of mutual trust and safety that allowed Brown to experiment playfully in this way, to be more herself in the session and trust her intuition.

The other crucial part of the success is that Brown knew her client well. She knew Jordan had a sense of humor, a capacity to be playful, and also that she was an artist, a person for whom art was one of the few sources of joy in life. So the assignment of decorating the box was another thing that had appealed so strongly to Jordan. It was as if the whole project took her back to being a child, when she could more easily access material that she had previously blocked and denied. But this insight was not as important as the *experience* of literally busting out of the box.

"It had to be her rather than me," Brown confessed. "I'm just not all that playful. I take myself *way* too seriously. It was as if Jordan brought that part out of me and I could join her in the play. We did it together. Otherwise, I don't know where this would have come from."

Brown struggles to see herself as creative in her work. "Sure, I can think of other clients with whom we had creative breakthroughs, but it wasn't really me; it all took place within the relational field. Jordan, or any of my other clients, could have looked at me and thought I'd lost my mind, but they appreciated me going on a limb for them. It was based on the trust we felt toward one another."

This reminds us of something that Frank Pittman once said in another of our books (Kottler & Carlson, 2002), in which we asked him to talk about a case of his worst therapy. He said that you can't do good therapy unless you're doing bad therapy, because our finest work requires taking risks; sometimes they don't work out and sometimes they do. But Brown's point is that if we have a solid relationship with our clients, then they provide us with the freedom to make mistakes, to be creative, to experiment. They forgive us when things don't work out as planned and give us another chance, and another, until we can figure out together the best solution.

We draw comfort from Brown's admission that she doesn't see herself as particularly creative. Her honesty (and humility) in admitting that she isn't as innovative as she'd prefer, or that the source of her energy comes from her clients, also echoes Scott Miller's chapter, in which he ascribes so much of the outcome to the client's effort; the therapist is merely the vehicle upon which the client moves forward.

It's not that Brown doesn't have courage, but in the words of her partner, she has "Hobbit courage." "My great preference would be to sit in my home and keep warm and comfortable and not venture outside unless I absolutely have to. But then someone comes along and says that I must go on a quest. I'm really scared, but I believe it's my duty. I must do this even if I don't really want to. My Hobbit courage as a therapist is that I must be willing to follow the people I work with to the places they need to go."

Walking Off a Cliff

In the Waite deck of tarot cards is one that is called "The Fool." This character blithely walks off a cliff with a smile on her face, but she's going to be all right because she can't be harmed. "My clients call upon me to be the Fool, to step off the cliff with them, because they are doing these incredibly painful, difficult things. Doing trauma work is not for the faint of heart. It is like stepping off a cliff. But I don't do cliffs. Besides, it's not my cliff to begin with. I'd just as soon watch as have to jump myself, even if I know I'm going to be okay."

Morally, Brown feels an obligation to go wherever she asks her clients to go. "Remember, I take myself way too seriously. I don't have that much of a sense of humor. I'm someone who behaves in a reasonably dignified manner at all times. I get teased about this stuff all the time. Everyone knows this about me.

"But when I'm with someone who is willing to risk and play and show courage, then I have to join them. I think that's why I'm a half-decent therapist, because I'm willing to follow where clients lead, wherever they go."

Brown studies martial arts particularly because it is so difficult for her. "Every time I go, I have to take a deep breath and say to myself that it is really good for me. And I actually do have fun on the mat because it has brought out a certain playfulness in me when I finally master certain things that scared me to death."

Maybe it is not that surprising for someone who doesn't like walking off cliffs with her clients that the one thing she dreads most in her martial arts training is the forward roll. Brown was not playful as a child. She describes herself as having been very serious, even depressed much of the time, "a weirdo outsider who stayed home to read." Yet this is what led to her developing a rich fantasy life, as well as the extraordinary capacity to relate to other women who have experienced trauma.

Brown sees her weaknesses as the source of the resources she brings to therapy. She is able to tolerate lots of ambiguity and uncertainty. She has infinite patience with her clients. She knows how to sit with others' suffering and allow people to go at their own pace and to proceed in a way that is compatible with their own style. The creative exercise with the box emerged precisely because it was what Jordan would want to do.

"Oh Dear. Bad Me."

These were the words that Brown blurted out at this moment in our conversation when we asked if she would expand on some of her ideas about creativity that she had only briefly touched on. It was such an honest and authentic moment, one in which she admitted once again how she struggles with seeing herself as creative.

So much of Brown's work is guided by the client's lead: "I just go into the relationship with my heart and mind open. I believe that clients inherently have what is necessary for their own healing to take place."

Brown thinks back to her very first job as a therapist working on a psychiatric unit. There was one patient on the ward who was so well defended that he literally kept his guitar in front of him at all times. He wouldn't let anyone get close to him, and when Brown approached him, he would just hold out the guitar as a barrier and a clear message to keep away. Later that week, Brown brought in her own guitar so they could play music together. This resulted in some deep conversation that occurred during this client's subsequent weeks on the unit, in which the guitars became metaphors for the materials that he could otherwise not share directly. This may seem very creative (it does to us) but to Brown it is simply the logical result of following the boy's lead.

Very early in her career, Brown learned to mirror the client's behavior in whatever form it manifested itself, nonverbally, nonrationally, and intuitively. It is interesting that she still insists that she is noncreative ("Oh dear. Bad me."), yet she often found herself in trouble with the senior clinical staff because her "interventions" were considered so far-out and weird.

If a tree falls in the forest and there is nobody there to hear it, is there actually a sound? If someone who is creative doesn't view herself that way, did innovation actually occur? Brown is not just being modest—she genuinely struggles to identify herself as being creative outside the context of interaction with her clients. "We create together; it's not me being creative all by myself." We wondered about the gender connection, because she was the second woman we interviewed for this project who felt some reluctance to see herself as creative (the first one declined to be included in this book). Yet the male therapists had no difficulty whatsoever defining themselves as such. Brown strikes us as creative and innovative in profound ways, a major force in feminist therapy, a significant advocate on behalf of gay and lesbian rights, and yet she still insists that her creativity is not owned by her, that it happens because a spark emerges in the relational space between her and others, be they her clients, her trainees, or her friends. "I'm not Joni Mitchell's 'lonely painter.'"

The adolescent on the psych ward was willing to sit with Brown for hours and play guitar with her. He would talk about how his *guitar* was feeling, but he would not use first person. The whole therapy took place within a context of one guitar counseling and resonating with another.

Looking back, Brown casually mentioned that she grew up living next door to Miriam and Erving Polster, two of the seminal voices in Gestalt therapy—and among the most creative practitioners of the past century. They were her models of what a therapist should be. She decided at age nine that she wanted to be just like them, especially like Miriam, who had been an opera singer before she was a psychologist and could frequently be heard singing arias through the open windows.

Brown brings up modeling as a key factor in how any of us learn to become creative in our work. In this she is similar to others in this book, who talk about Milton Erickson, Carl Whitaker, Virginia Satir, Michael White, and others having inspired them to be far more experimental. Seeing such radical behavior demonstrated (or, in the case of this book, reading about such cases) expands the realm of possibilities open to us, not to mention gives us permission to try things that might seem bizarre. Legends abound about the times Whitaker fell asleep during sessions, Erickson sat on top of an obstructive child, or Fritz Perls was being his usual outrageous self.

"I remember during graduate school," Brown said, "when we were in a training group and there was one guy who was, let us say, a little narcissistic—like 12 on a 10-point scale. He wouldn't let anyone else speak, and he had to always be the center of attention, never letting anyone else have any space. The group leader interrupted the guy at one point to ask if anyone in the group had a tampon in their purse. We all thought, what the hell was going on, but he insisted on getting an answer to the question, until one woman spoke up and said she had one. The leader said good and asked her to hand it over. He then looked at the narcissistic guy and told him, 'I want you to wear this around your neck.' They guy looked flustered and indignant and asked why. The leader said, 'Because that way you'll always remember that for every sentence there is a period.'"

That's the sort of story that is over the top, usually passed on from one generation of therapists to the next, a story that, however potentially misguided (and perhaps mean-spirited), contains within it the sort of inspiration we need to try dramatic things to address intractable behavior that will not respond to ordinary interventions.

With her own case, Brown knew that Jordan would soon relapse into drinking again if she didn't try something spectacular—she would never get through in time to make a difference. "I was feeling increasingly desperate," Brown explained, "to reach her. She didn't have a lot of wiggle room left. Plus I had come to appreciate the power of her artistic creativity if we could only figure out a way to harness it constructively. We had already tried everything else."

Creativity often does stem from a certain degree of desperation. This has been true of military campaigns and scientific advances as much as the practice of therapy. Yet Brown warns that the need to demonstrate our brilliance can often get in the way, too. "Every time I deliberately try to be creative and say, 'Hey, look how cool this is,' it's really all about me rather than the client." That's one reason why Brown has struggled with the solution-focused and brief therapists who are all about their wild interventions; she believes many of them come at the expense of the client's ultimate welfare.

There are those who might have tried any number of strategic methods with Jordan, but her wounds were so deep and long-lasting that she always seemed to teeter on the edge of self-destruction. She had suffered terribly growing up, from chronic illness as well as family-inflicted abuse. Other medical and mental health professionals had tried to "fix" her, but she always kept limping back.

"Jordan would come back to me every few months, as well, and say, 'You know, I screwed up again,' and I would remind her that she was doing the best she could. She knew how much I valued her. She knew that I could handle hearing about the times when she wasn't doing so well, when she was about to go over the cliff. Every time she'd relapse I'd tell her that I was glad she called for help again. I'd tell her that it was time to try again. I wouldn't give up."

After reflecting on this case and telling us the story, Brown now feels strongly that she really did a fine piece of work as a collaborator with Jordan. Brown was never quite certain whether she had helped her all throughout the many years. It wasn't until this past year that the treatment ended, with Jordan stabilized and no relapses for quite some time. Jordan got out of her box and seems, for now, to have stayed out. Maybe Brown is figuring out that her willingness to join her clients in jumping off cliffs *is* what makes her work creative.

CHAPTER 12

Bill O'Hanlon: Falling on Your Face

This chapter is structured a bit differently than others in the book, not just in its focus, but also its narrative style. Our subject needed very little prodding to tell his own story, in his own way, so we'll mostly let O'Hanlon's voice speak for itself.

Early Years

Bill O'Hanlon grew up in a large, Irish Catholic family, which held among its cherished family beliefs that once you reached the ripe age of 18, you were expected to leave home and make your own way in the world.

"That was it. They sawed off your corner of the table, broke your plate, you weren't going to come back. You were supposed to go out and work or go to university. So I went off to school, although I wasn't very well prepared to take care of myself. I was the shy one in my family, very anxious, and perhaps somewhat inept."

This was during the neo-hippie era, and O'Hanlon fit right in. It was a time to question everything, especially authorities and the status quo. "I grew my hair long, did lots of drugs, and studied philosophy. I also lost my moorings. I had a few friends, but I spent most of my time alone. I got more and more depressed until, finally, I decided I'd had enough. I'm not meant for this life. That's it.

Forget it. I just can't do it. I'm too sensitive. I can't be around people. I don't know why people get out of bed. I can't figure it out."

Having reached that conclusion, O'Hanlon figured that the most reasonable option was to end his life. "If I was going to do myself in, I felt it was only appropriate to tell my friends so they wouldn't be in for such a rude shock. I mean, I might have been depressed, but I'm not a mean person."

O'Hanlon approached each of his friends to tell them goodbye, essentially saying that the pain was too much to bear, so sayonara. He was surprised at the response he got from his first two friends, each of them admitting that they admired his courage. They said that if they weren't so afraid of dying, maybe they'd consider the same option. O'Hanlon gravely shook hands with each friend, saying as his last words he hoped would be remembered: "See you in the next life. I'm sure we'll all have it better."

O'Hanlon's third friend, Marisa, was a bit more normal, in the sense that she responded in a somewhat more socially appropriate manner: "Bill, why would you kill yourself? You just can't go ahead and announce to people that you're going to commit suicide and then go ahead and do it!"

"Why the hell not?"

"You just can't do that," Marisa pleaded. "It's not right."

"Look," O'Hanlon explained, a bit flustered that now he was being challenged after his first friends had simply accepted his decision, "I'm just not meant for this world. I feel like I have no skin on when I'm around people. I hurt all the time. I'm all exposed sores. You know, I'm writing poetry and sleeping 16 hours a day. I can't even get to class. And I'm worried that as much as I hate college, in a couple years I'll actually have to go out and get a job. I can't bear that."

"It's just a stage," Marisa tried to soothe him. "You'll get over it. It's something we all go though at some time."

"Yeah, that's what I'm afraid of. I can't even get out of bed in the morning. The very thought of going to work for some corporation makes me want to puke. I just don't see the point of going on. As bad as things are now, they're only going to get worse."

Marisa was at a loss for words, not sure how to respond to this guy. She liked Bill, but she had to admit he was more than a little unstable. She had to do something. She couldn't just walk away and let him hurt himself. "Look," she said with desperation in her voice, "don't do this. My folks are from this small town in Nebraska. You've been to Nebraska, right?

"Yeah. So?"

"I have three aunts who have never married, my mom's sisters. They live on a farm near Omaha . . . well, *kind* of near there. I'm their favorite niece. They've told me when they die I'll inherit everything."

"Hey, Marisa, this is all pretty interesting," O'Hanlon interrupted, not interested at all and feeling himself losing his momentum, "but I don't think you're listening. I was saying . . ."

"Let me finish! So I was saying that they have this farm and all, and they've got this empty house on their property. Nobody lives there. So, if you want, you can go live there for free. You don't have to deal with people—with your thin skin and all. You don't have to work for a corporation. You don't even have to stay in college. You can just go there, write your poetry, grow your own food, live off the land."

O'Hanlon had to admit this sounded pretty intriguing. Of course, as a city boy he had no idea how hard it might be to grow his own food. But this still seemed like a viable option, maybe even a better one than death. "Well," he said, giving the matter some thought, "maybe that's a possibility."

"And just think about it," Marisa added, trying to close the deal, "you won't have to pay taxes or anything. Just promise you won't kill yourself and I'll promise that you can have that house when my aunts die."

"How old are your aunts?" O'Hanlon asked, calculating in his head how much longer he thought he could endure his plight.

"They're old, almost in the grave . . . like, in their fifties or something."

"This *is* pretty old," 19-year-old O'Hanlon agreed.

Reflecting on this conversation, O'Hanlon couldn't help but laugh. "Here I am, getting close to 60, and now that seems relatively young to me. But it seemed ancient at the time. So I agreed to Marisa's scheme. I figured the odds were that the aunts would die in the next few years and I'd be all set. Little did I know, those aunts in Nebraska lived till 100. I mean, there's something in the water or something, the way they lived. In fact, I'm pretty sure they're still alive."

The Call to Be Creative

Knowing that he wouldn't be forced to follow a traditional path, O'Hanlon felt a little more inspired to hang on until he could see how things developed.

"By the time I finished undergraduate school, I had actually found something I wanted to do, and I didn't need to go live on the farm after all. I wasn't suicidal anymore and have never been again. I decided I was going to live and make my way in the world. But I was still really miserable. And that's what led me to psychotherapy.

"I started to investigate philosophy first, and I couldn't find the answers in philosophy. How do people get along with themselves and other people? And then I came across psychotherapy and that was it for me. I was amazed that there was a set of processes for how people can make themselves less miserable, how they can get along better with themselves, how they can find meaning and purpose in life. I became enamored with family systems therapy, because nobody gets blamed for the problems, and I liked that. I decided that's what I wanted to do, and once I found meaning and purpose, I was less miserable. I realized I didn't have to go to work for a corporation. I can just go out and help people."

O'Hanlon had found a way to express his creative spirit. He had found work that not only felt useful to others but also helped him to sort out the lingering suffering in his own life. He became a voracious reader of every book about therapy he could get his hands on. While still an undergraduate, he snuck into workshops that were designed for professionals. And that's where he came across the work of a mentor who would become a major guiding force in his life.

"When I was an undergraduate student, I was a work-study student at the college art gallery. This guy in a wheelchair came rolling in and bought a painting. I talked to him and he seemed pretty interesting. I didn't know who he was, but one of the graduate students said he was this famous therapist and showed me an article about him. His name was Milton Erickson."

O'Hanlon not only read the article but dug up anything he could find on this maverick psychiatrist. The more he read, the more excited he became about the creative possibilities. "I just loved that Erickson was so hopeful instead of pessimistic. I was in bliss. I now knew what I wanted to do. I felt my calling."

Gardening the Nut Grass

O'Hanlon entered graduate school to study marriage and family therapy. Although he was getting the foundational background he needed to practice, he still hadn't managed to work up the courage to approach Milton Erickson for training. For one thing, he didn't have any money to pay for the supervision. Second, he was still very shy, not to mention intimidated by Erickson's reputation.

After three years of plotting and planning ways to meet Erickson again, O'Hanlon decided to write him a letter, which said in part: "You know, I've come up with all these schemes of how I could come out and study with you. I don't have any money. I worked as a gardener between undergraduate and graduate school so I could work as *your* gardener. I think someone ought to write your story for a popular magazine or write your biography. Your life story is inspiring. You recovered from polio twice and learned to walk again, and you've done all these amazing things. So after all is said and done, I really just want to come out and study with you. So, can I do that?"

O'Hanlon sent off the letter and promptly forgot about it. After going away for the weekend, he returned to find a message from his roommate telling him that some guy kept calling him. "Who called?" he asked.

"This really strange guy," the roommate said. "I kept telling him you were gone for the weekend but he kept calling back. And that's not the weirdest part."

"What do you mean?"

"Well, he kept asking me if this was the office of O'Hanlon Gardening Service."

"Yeah," O'Hanlon said, his excitement growing to a fever pitch, "I think I know who that might be."

Sure enough, first thing Monday morning, the phone rang, and the roommate rushed into O'Hanlon's room. "It's him! It's that guy again! He's asking for O'Hanlon Gardening."

O'Hanlon jumped out of bed and grabbed the phone. "This is Bill O'Hanlon."

"O'Hanlon Gardening Service?" a deep, gravelly voice said.

"Yeah. This is Bill O'Hanlon. Is this Dr. Erickson?"

"O'Hanlon Gardening Service?" the voice repeated again.

"Yeah. This *is* he. Bill O'Hanlon." Is this Dr. Erickson calling?"

"Yes, this is Dr. Erickson."

"Dr. Erickson, I am so excited that you called. I was wondering if it was possible for me to come out and see you?"

"How's Tuesday at 11:00?"

O'Hanlon hesitated for a moment, remembering he had a class then—but only for a moment. "Sure. Fine. No problem. I'll be there."

O'Hanlon resumes the narrative. "I went out there, and I was a hippie at the time, as I mentioned—or we called ourselves freaks in those days, but hippie/post-hippie kind of thing. I had really long hair, and I thought, I'm going to meet one of my mentors/heroes/models. I gotta dress up for this. And so I dressed up in what, as I look back on it now, was a ridiculous outfit. I was wearing this polyester white suit that my girlfriend had made from a McCall's pattern so that I would look like John Lennon. So I went out there in my white suit and I sat and talked with him for a little while. He asked me to help him get in the wheelchair, and then I pushed him out to the garden, and it turned out that he actually wanted me to do gardening!"

O'Hanlon was so dumbfounded, he wasn't sure what to say. Here he had assumed he'd been invited to study with the master, accepted into one of the few spots in his training program, and instead Erickson had only wanted him to do his gardening. Erickson wanted him to get right to work, and he was standing there in his white suit, too shy to ask if he could go home to change.

"See here," Erickson pointed to the garden. "I want you get the nut grass out of the rosebushes."

O'Hanlon wasn't sure if he'd heard him right. Again, he was too shy to ask Erickson to repeat what he'd said. Was this some kind of metaphor? Was it a test to see if he was worthy? As it turned out, Erickson seemed serious about wanting this young man to go to work extracting the nut grass from his garden. Apparently, this was some type of weed that has a nutlike kernel in its root system, about 12 inches under the ground.

"I had to go down there and wrestle with these weeds, all intertwined with the thorny rosebushes. I was wearing my special John Lennon white suit. I didn't have any gloves or tools and he didn't offer any. He just pointed and told me to get the stuff out of there."

O'Hanlon returned to Erickson's garden every week for over a year, hacking away at the nut grass, pruning his rosebushes, doing odd chores. "To tell you the truth, I didn't know what the hell was going on. I wondered if he was senile or sadistic. Was he trying to teach me something? Was this hypnosis? I'd read about the kind of hypnosis he does and I thought maybe this was part of it."

Finally, O'Hanlon was rescued from his thorny fate by Mrs. Erickson who took pity on him. "Milton," O'Hanlon overheard her say one day, "can't you see this boy wants to sit in on your sessions. What's he doing out here in the garden? He wants to learn something." And then she handed over the appointment book to her husband and told him to bring the boy inside.

This was toward the end of Erickson's clinical practice years, so there weren't that many sessions going on that O'Hanlon could observe. But he did get out of the garden.

"I didn't get to see too many sessions, but I also sat in with some other students—professionals from all around, sometimes graduate students like me, and it was a weird and wonderful year. I was way more confused than when I started, and this sort of goes way back beyond the story I told you earlier. I was sexually abused when I was younger . . . by my paternal grandfather. The way he'd hook me into it was through confusion. So I had a very low tolerance for any kind of confusion, which made me very anxious. And here I am sitting with Erickson, who specializes in confusion, trying to go with the flow. Needless to say, this was very challenging for me."

Blissed Out

After that year of studying with Erickson, it took O'Hanlon the next five years to try to make some sense of his experiences, first in the garden and then in the therapy sessions as an observer. This led to O'Hanlon's first book, which represented an attempt to clarify what he believed Erickson was doing. He attended Ericksonian workshops, watched all the experts doing sessions, reviewed tapes, and studied transcripts, looking for the underlying patterns.

O'Hanlon was working in his first job after graduate school at a drug and alcohol treatment center. "I was getting great clinical experience, because if there's anything that makes you a results-oriented therapist, it's working with addicts, because they either get drunk or use drugs the next day or they don't. It's pretty clear.

"I would see people, and the next day they would be drunk or using drugs, and then I would see other people and they'd be sober in a year—and stay that way. It's a really good check on your work. And what I was noticing is that we weren't helping most people who came into the treatment center. About 20 percent of the people would get sober, or stop using drugs, or get their life together, but most of them would go right back out and do it again. I was thinking that Erickson was really good at this stuff but I wasn't very good at all—at least following the standard treatment procedures employed at the clinic."

At the time, and until this day in many treatment centers, everything is about the disease model and Alcoholics Anonymous, but these weren't working too well for many people. "I had this Zen-like realization about how to get people to stop drinking and drugging forever. It's simple: You stop putting alcohol or drugs in your mouth. That's it. Everything else is commentary and theory."

O'Hanlon realized that if he said this out loud to any of his colleagues, it would be heresy; he'd be in big trouble for challenging the dominant model. "They'd likely have burned a *Big Book* on my front lawn. My colleagues believed that the only way to stop drinking was to admit you are powerless over alcohol and join AA. I thought that this was one way, but not the only way. This helped me to realize that the people in my new chosen career were very rigid. There's nothing more dangerous than someone who only has one idea. Their idea did work, and sometimes worked quite wonderfully.

But when it didn't work, they decided the clients were resistant and they would get more aggressive with them, or they would just give up on them in a certain way. They would come up with all these explanations about why their work wasn't effective, all of which had to do with the clients—that they were 'resistant' or 'chronic' or 'borderline' or they 'needed to hit bottom.'"

As disturbing as it was for O'Hanlon to realize that most practitioners in the field were not nearly as inventive, creative, or flexible as Erickson and his crew, what he found even more upsetting were the number of his colleagues who thought that some people just couldn't change. "They thought some clients were too damaged genetically, biochemically, or traumatically and that they were never going to be any different. They talked as if their clients were playing games, as if they didn't really want to get better. They said that some people enjoyed being miserable.

"I was so angry when I heard that, I could barely contain myself. I have a little bit of a sarcastic sense of humor, so I'd be really cutting and I'd say, you know, 'Maybe if you read a book every 20 years or went to a workshop you'd discover *you* are the resistant one, not them.' For some reason, they didn't much appreciate my observations. This said I wasn't being constructive."

By this time, O'Hanlon was a workshop junkie, filling himself up with the most cutting-edge stuff he could find. He learned psychodrama, hypnosis, all of the new therapies that were emerging at the time. He was so excited about the possibilities for people, and he just couldn't stand the pessimistic, negative thinking of many colleagues who believed that some behavior is too entrenched to be altered.

O'Hanlon wondered why what seemed so obvious to him was so elusive to others. He thought to himself that he should start teaching his own stuff—if only he weren't so shy. "I could never speak in front of other people—I was terrified. I was disorganized. I'm too flakey. But then I heard my second calling. It was like I could hear the voice of God telling me to do this.

"I was a terrible teacher at first. I was just bad at it. I was nervous, but also disorganized and not very skilled at it. But it didn't matter to me. I was going to persist until I got better at it. So I practiced, and I did get better to the point where I started to get more invitations to speak. After all these years, I'm still so passionate, so excited, about my speaking and my writing. I'm blissed out with this stuff that I love, and I'm still angry about people who are unwilling to change their thinking about what we do."

Leap of Faith

It is admittedly difficult to take the risks involved in reinventing oneself. We wondered about the source of O'Hanlon's creative energy.

"It takes a leap of faith. With that big step into the unknown you create the bridge to the next place you are going to go. I loved doing clinical work, but I wanted to try something else. And after learning to teach, the next leap was to write. The next time you hear a call from the depth of your soul, you have to take the leap and believe that it will work out. It's probably going to be messy along the way. There will be times when you can't pay your bills or it's really scary or you fail miserably, but ultimately it will work out. So there was some reinforcement for that kind of risk-taking creativity."

Erickson was a great model for O'Hanlon in taking risks. His motto had always been that if you try something and it doesn't work out, just try something else. He once said to O'Hanlon (as he has said to many others) that if you fall on your face, at least you're heading in the right direction. Failing is no big deal, nor is disappointment. A common theme throughout the stories in this book is that it is very difficult to be creative if you are not prepared to deal with the fallout of making mistakes and miscalculations.

O'Hanlon has recently gone through another creative stint in which he has reinvented himself once again. He was in private practice for a long time, after which he taught workshops and wrote two dozen books, and now he is excited about his next stage, which involves using technology to coach people to access greater creativity in their lives, especially as they age.

O'Hanlon has been reading research about ways to prevent senility and Alzheimer's by learning some new skills and keeping the brain stimulated. He is not especially enamored with the idea of doing crossword puzzles or even learning to play a new musical instrument, but he is highly motivated to teach himself, and others, ways to develop more leisure time and move into new areas.

O'Hanlon bristles at the criticism sometimes directed his way that he is an opportunist, riding the next wave of popularity and calling it his own. "Well, I suppose that's one way to think about it," he admits. "But I just get so excited about the latest innovations." He has jumped on the bandwagon of new approaches, always hungry to adapt the latest ideas, even if they challenge some of his most cherished assumptions. He is always looking for something that will work better with his clients, regardless of what it is called. His greatest fear is of being stuck.

"Fear is what stops us from trying new things. Fear of looking foolish. Fear of failing. Fear of not knowing. Everyone wants to appear like an expert. We coach clients all the time to move against their fears, yet we are reluctant to do the same thing. Fear is just what comes with the territory when you're a human being. Adults are so afraid of experimenting. A child will stand up and fall down and say, 'Hmmmm. Stand up, fall down,' and they're starting to learn that gravity exists and they're starting to learn that balance exists. As therapists move along in their careers, they often become more narrow and fearful of trying new things.

"I hear a lot about boredom and burnout and fatigue in our profession, and I've never felt those things in my life. I am just so excited about my work every day. And I think one reason for this is that I pay attention to my heart and my soul. I don't let my fears stop me. I just don't know any other way for people to change without trying stuff and having some of it not work out."

The key to creativity is experimentation. And it's inevitable that in trying new things you've never done before, much of the time the outcomes will be less than desirable. Yet with each attempt, hopefully you become more proficient and responsive to the client's needs, especially if you are paying close attention to what is going on moment to moment and demonstrating sufficient flexibility to make adjustments.

CHAPTER 13

CLOÉ MADANES: A TRILOGY OF COURAGE

"You mean I have to choose only one story of creativity?" Cloé Madanes began the conversation.

"Is that a problem?" we asked. "How many did you want to share?"

"Three. No, maybe four. To tell you the truth, I have so many fun interventions that I don't know how to decide."

With that beginning, we invited Cloé to tell us a trilogy of stories to cover most of the territory. Although each story is different, they all speak to a theme of having the courage to push outside the boundaries of what is usually expected. That has been Madanes's hallmark throughout her long and distinguished career.

1. Diagnosis: Artistic Temperament

Myra, in her early twenties, consulted Madanes after a long history of emotional problems. After having tried a number of medications and seen a variety of doctors and therapists, she still engaged in self-destructive behaviors, including cutting and suicide attempts. There were frequent visits to the emergency room, long conversations in the middle of the night, and great family drama. Myra was very involved with her parents, stepparents, and siblings.

Madanes invited the whole family to come in for a consultation. Mostly, they were conventional-looking people, except for Myra, who was beautiful and sported a gothic look, with long black hair, black clothes, and many silver chains. Her air was melodramatic—every gesture expressing despair and doom.

While Madanes tried to engage each member of the family during their initial meeting, she noticed that Myra could barely remain present. She refused to answer questions directed her way or spoke in a whispery voice that could barely be heard. Most of the time she sat with her head cradled in her hands as if she felt absolutely overwhelmed.

With everyone in the family present, Madanes gathered some history, especially as it related to the divorce that had taken place when Myra was a child and her older siblings were teenagers. It was revealed that Myra, the youngest, had been most affected by the family separation and felt abandoned by her father. Madanes noticed that, even though the father obviously adored her, Myra was still resentful of the breakup of the marriage and still had the sense that she had lost her father. Madanes wondered how much Myra's problems were a way of getting revenge on the father, who was constantly upset about her lifestyle and her emotional problems.

Madanes learned that Myra was living a somewhat aimless life, striving to be an artist, working at a job she hated and feeling unfulfilled. Her only true love was her gothic paintings, which she hoped one day to exhibit. About the only time she became slightly animated during the meeting was when she talked about wanting to publish her illustrations in the form of a magazine. Unfortunately, she was now somewhat destitute, in debt, and without medical insurance or regular employment.

Myra's parents and siblings were constantly on her case to get herself together, but she could never come close to measuring up to their expectations. Her father would harass Myra continuously, complaining that she should organize her time better, create a budget, work more hours, go back to school, get a proper degree, and do something productive with her life instead of sitting around listening to music and drawing.

Myra admitted that she knew those were all good ideas, but she just couldn't concentrate. Just when she tried to focus on something, terrible thoughts would enter her mind and make her do crazy, hurtful things. She felt worthless and isolated and alone. She had virtually given up. Every attempt by her father to help Myra seemed only to make matters worse.

Madanes thought about the close bond between father and daughter, with the father constantly giving guidance and Myra failing to follow his advice. She decided that had to change—Myra and her father should bond in a happier way.

"Basically what I then proposed to the family," said Madanes, "was that they should do absolutely the opposite of what they were already doing, which was clearly not working. I asked them to agree that this was the case, and they did.

"I told them that there are many ways of living, and who is to say that a person needs to be independent and self-sufficient and have a good job and have a career. Some people are just artistic and need an angel. Myra was lucky because her father could be her angel because he was quite well off. His advice, however well intended, was not helpful, so I suggested that he assist his daughter in another way: What she needed most was financial support."

This was the last thing in the world that the father expected this famous teacher of therapists to say. Madanes could tell that he was thinking: We will be enabling lazy, withdrawn behavior. Yet they had already tried everything else they could think of and nothing else had worked. Madanes became very specific, telling the father to pay off the credit cards and debt of his wayward, irresponsible daughter. Whatever happened to "tough love" or making people accept responsibility for their behavior?

"Your daughter is a true artist," Madanes said when she saw their skeptical looks. "She has that type of personality and you have been trying to change her—without much success, I might add."

The brother and sister seemed a bit stunned by this idea, but all four parents seemed to be nodding their heads as if they were intrigued with this strange idea.

A consultation with a psychiatrist was arranged with the purpose of evaluating and reducing Myra's medications. After interviewing Myra, the psychiatrist met with the biological parents and reported that his diagnosis was "artistic temperament."

Madanes saw the family only once. Two years later, there have been no more suicide threats or attempts, no cutting, no visits to the emergency room, and Myra is happy. Crucial to the success of the consultation was that Madanes was able to convince the family of three things:

1. Myra was an artist and not a mentally ill person.
2. Instead of encouraging her to be more responsible the father should encourage her to be less concerned with doing the responsible thing and give her permission to be young, carefree, fun, and happy.
3. Everyone does not have to be independent and self-reliant in order to have a good life.

Just a few weeks prior to our interview with Madanes about this case, Myra had called Madanes saying she wanted some advice about a relationship with a guy that wasn't working out. She could tell that they were on the verge of breaking up and she wasn't sure what to do.

"How old is this man?" Madanes asked.

"Twenty-five," Myra said.

"Twenty-five?" Madanes answered, "That's not a man. That's a boy. You don't need a boy. You need a 40-year-old who will invite you to Paris for the weekend and who will have a secretary that will make the arrangements. You need a rich, 40-year-old."

Myra started giggling, then roaring with laughter. "You know, Cloé, you always make me laugh. Okay, everything's okay now. I just needed to hear your voice. I'll go look for a man. A rich one."

Madanes heard her laugh as they hung up the phone.

What strikes Madanes as particularly creative about this case is that she didn't focus on Myra's problems much at all, but instead concentrated on learning more about her nature and interests. She went against so-called conventional wisdom in our dominant culture that mental health and happiness are associated with independence, self-reliance, and responsibility. Instead, she gave Myra permission to be dependent, playful, and somewhat hedonistic.

"Families typically come with very stereotyped views of how people should live," Madanes explained. "Instead of telling them they should fight the craziness or the psychosis I told them to go along with it in a way that redefines it as a lifestyle instead of a mental illness. Everything is normalized. Nobody thinks of Myra as crazy anymore.

"Myra's mother sent me an e-mail after a few months and asked me whether enough time had elapsed to make her daughter stop being lazy and tell her to go back to work. 'How long is this going to continue?' she asked me. I just told her to leave a good thing alone and let her be who she is."

Creativity often involves questioning accepted and established norms. Madanes was able to think outside what is considered normal and instead to encourage Myra to express herself without feeling tied down. Much of her so-called crazy behavior was rebellious and punitive against her father, whom she still resented and felt anger toward. Once Madanes helped Myra—and her family—to stop seeing her behavior as crazy, and instead as that of a "free spirit" with "artistic temperament," the obstructive, self-defeating behavior ceased. No more cutting. No more suicide attempts or dramatic acting.

To Madanes, her intervention seemed to be only common sense. "You have to think all the time about what is better than what. Is it better to try to make this young woman self-supporting, taking the risk that she's going to become totally schizophrenic and kill herself? Or is it better to let her be dependent and bohemian and not be crazy? So basically, it is a value judgment, and I think that saving her life was more important than making her self-sufficient."

But what if Myra didn't have a rich family, we wondered? Then what would she have done?

Madanes shrugged. "I don't know. I guess I would have had to figure out something different. But I always have other resources available."

2. *Mixing Work with Pleasure*

Madanes received an e-mail from a prospective client who desperately wanted a consultation but couldn't really say what it was about. All she would say was that it was some kind of problem with her marriage.

Josh and Natalie appeared at the office exactly on time. Natalie was in her forties, classically dressed in a Tahari wool suit, very chic, hair, makeup, everything perfect. In contrast, Josh was big and round, like an ex–football player who had gone to seed. Their manners were just as different as their appearances. Whereas Natalie was serious, almost severe, Josh was jovial and friendly, with a sweet smile.

The couple reported that they didn't have any children, were on solid financial footing, and had a good marriage. In fact, they reported that they were best friends. They enjoyed hiking together as well as just hanging out. They stressed repeatedly that they had a great relationship.

"So, what's the problem then?" Madanes asked. She remembered from Natalie's initial e-mail that it was a bit of a mystery.

"Well," Natalie started, then looked at her husband to see if he was going to say anything, but he just seemed to be studying his shirt.

"Yes?" Madanes encouraged her to keep going.

"Well, it's . . . it's hard to talk about."

"Is it something to do with sex?" Madanes guessed, knowing it wasn't that much of a stab in the dark.

"Well, kind of, " Natalie answered, looking even more uncomfortable. Josh had looked up from his shirt and was grinning.

"Kind of?" Madanes pressed.

Natalie nodded but didn't speak. Madanes looked toward Josh, hoping he might help out, but it was clear he was sitting this one out.

"Okay," Madanes tried again, "is it some kind of performance problem between you?"

"Uh, no, not exactly," Natalie answered. But she didn't say anything else.

"I see. How about problems having orgasms, something like that?"

Natalie looked on the verge of bolting out of the room she was so uncomfortable. But she shook her head and said under her breath, "No, not that, either."

"How about infidelity?" Madanes asked, running out of guesses. "Are one or both of you having affairs?"

Jackpot! Natalie began nodding her head vigorously, as if she couldn't stop. "Yes," she said, at the exact same moment that Josh said, "No!"

"Uh, I'm a bit confused here," Madanes interjected. "One of you is saying that there is infidelity and the other is saying no. What's going on?"

Josh turned to his wife, upset with what was going on. "Come on now," he said to her, "you can't say I had an affair. I never had an affair."

"No," Natalie said, her anger rising, "but you had sex."

"How can you say that? We never had intercourse."

"Well, it was sexual wasn't it?"

"Not really. I never even spoke to the woman."

Madanes was watching this back-and-forth, more confused than ever. Natalie was accusing her husband of having an affair, which he was denying. Apparently, he was with a woman, and they had sex, but they didn't have sex. None of this was making any sense.

"Hold on, hold on," Madanes interrupted them. "Josh, you were with a woman? Is that what Natalie was saying?"

Josh hesitated, then finally nodded.

"How many times would that be?"

"How many times was I with her?"

"Exactly."

"Oh, many times, I'd say."

"Okay. So you were with this woman many times. You never spoke to her. You never had intercourse. But you did have sex. Or you didn't have sex."

While things were slowly being clarified, Natalie began crying, which seemed to break the evasive spell. Finally, Josh explained that he had a preference for sadomasochistic sex and he had been seeing a dominatrix. From time to time he would seek the services of a specialist in chains and whips who dressed in black leather and high-heeled boots. He would pay her to beat him, which ended in masturbation. So, technically, he had been correct in saying that they never spoke to one another except in the form of commands his dominatrix would issue, nor did they ever touch one another.

After Natalie discovered her husband's proclivities, she tried to play the domineering role herself. But her heart wasn't in it, and Josh claimed that it didn't satisfy him the same way as his hired specialist. To add to their problems, Natalie had an important position in the community and she had just learned that Josh had done something incredibly, spectacularly stupid that might jeopardize her career. It seems that Natalie had launched an investigation to gather evidence against an employee of hers who had been engaging in unethical, if not illegal, behavior in the company. As fate would have it, at the same time Josh had decided he was tired of paying for his recreational play and so put an advertisement on a web site, including a nude photo of himself (big belly and all), looking for someone who might dominate him for the pure pleasure of it. And guess who applied for the job? The same woman whom Natalie was trying to fire!

It turned out that Josh and the woman met several times to play their sadomasochistic games, during which time the woman was gathering her own evidence to use for blackmail purposes to keep her job. She showed up at Natalie's office armed with nude photos of Josh. It was this latest crisis that had led them both to seek the consultation at this time.

Never at a loss for words or at a loss for resources, Madanes told the couple she had a plan. "I know what you need to do," she said, "and it's really up to you whether you want to do it or not, but it is really the only solution you have to get yourselves out of this mess."

The couple looked at one another, panic on both of their faces, completely at a loss about what to do. They were desperate and without other options, it was true. Finally, they both nodded that they were ready to hear the plan.

"Okay," Madanes said, waiting until she had their full attention. "The solution is *not* for your husband to give up his sexual preference." She was careful to use neutral language and to stay away from words like "perversion."

"It isn't?" Natalie blurted.

"No, that's not the answer."

When he heard that, Josh's silly grin grew even bigger.

"Well then," Natalie said, "what then? I don't want to lose my husband. I love him . . ." she looked at him, "in spite of everything. We have so many good things together."

"That's nice," Madanes agreed. "The only solution, then, is for you to join him in his sexual preference."

"But we already tried that," she pleaded, "I tried to . . ."

"Yes, yes, I know. But I have something quite different in mind."

"You do?"

"Yes. From now on, *you* are going to be the one in charge."

"In charge?"

"Yes. What Josh is doing is potentially very dangerous, with all the whips and things. He could become injured if he isn't careful. So you need to make sure that he is safe."

Natalie was nodding, although for the first time, Josh's smile was gone.

"I want you to find Josh a dominatrix who is both safe and legal. You're going to research this extensively and find the right person for him, someone he would enjoy, yet someone you trust. Make sense?"

Strangely, it *did* make sense to Natalie.

"Then," Madanes continued, "I want you to be present at all times. You are going to be the one to pay this person and you are going to remain in the room to make sure that your husband remains safe. You have to make sure that he doesn't get in trouble or do anything that you'd consider inappropriate."

It was Madanes's reasoning in this case, and in many others, that there would be two possible outcomes to this directive: It could work either straightforwardly or paradoxically. If the couple complied with the instructions, then they would share a sexual life together that, although a bit unusual, at least kept them engaged and allowed Natalie to have some control. On the other hand, if one or both of them (most likely Josh) developed a dislike for this activity, then it would work to end future indulgence. Either way, there was potentially a satisfactory solution.

A few months later, Madanes talked with the couple. Josh and Natalie were both delighted with their new arrangement. Natalie had found a club of consenting adults who all participated in their domination fantasies together, and they made many new friends who shared common interests.

There was only one little glitch, and that was related to Natalie having found a new dominatrix who was also a personal trainer on the side. It seems she had a plan to get her chubby husband to lose weight at the same time he indulged in his sexual fantasies. Under Natalie's instructions, the dominatrix was using her resources to motivate Josh's exercise program, literally pursuing him on a treadmill with the whip at his butt. It was working, too, since Josh was losing weight, even though he complained that he didn't like mixing work with pleasure.

At one point in this new arrangement, Josh injured himself during the session, a situation that had never happened previously. There were actually very strict rules and "safe signals" during domination activities to ensure that nobody would be injured. But now Josh found himself being ordered around not only by the dominatrix, but also his wife, told to run faster, lift harder, do this or that.

"Why didn't you just use your safe word and tell them to stop?" Madanes asked him.

"I tried to," Josh said with a whimper. "I told them it was too hard, but they didn't listen. The two of them—they're friends now—and they kind of ganged up on me. I just couldn't tell them to stop. I had two women ordering me around and I couldn't say no."

With iron will, Madanes managed to keep a straight face. "I see," she said, seeing all too clearly.

"So, how are you feeling now?"

"Are you kidding? I've got bruises for God's sake! That's never happened before. And I'm so sore I can barely walk. To tell you the truth, I'm not all that interested in doing this anymore."

Indeed, Josh did lose interest in sadomasochistic sex and begged his wife to agree that they would never have to visit the dominatrix again.

Madanes summarized, "So I had the wife apologize to him for not stopping, for not realizing that the boot camp experience was too much for him. After Natalie apologized profusely for having gone too far, I asked Josh to admit that he had to accept some responsibility for not telling the women he'd had enough. Then I sent them off to discover other fun things that they can do together. I'm waiting to hear from them."

That took a heck of a lot of courage to try that intervention, we suggested to Madanes after hearing the story.

"Well," she responded, "I think the major limitation is fear. Most therapists worry, 'Am I going to get into trouble? How do I protect myself in this? What could be the bad consequence?' Instead, they should be finding courage and asking themselves, 'How can I take a completely different angle?' If you think like your clients think, you cannot solve anything. You have to think completely out of the box, taking a completely different approach than what has been tried before. That requires tremendous creativity, because the natural tendency when people tell you a story is to get into the story and see things from the point of view that they are giving you. In joining with them, you start from a position of empathy, sharing their point of view. But then you have to step completely out of that perspective and take a completely different position and be credible and feel that it is the truth. That's really important to me. I never lie. I have to believe myself that it is the truth. So, when I say to the wife, "You have to become part of it," in a different way I really believe that. And I think that's really true."

3. It's All about Love

An 80-year-old father consulted Madanes about his 40-something son who was a cocaine addict. He had just paid for a whole month for his son to stay at a residential treatment center, and his son was due to get out in a few weeks. The father and the rest of the family were certain that the son would go back to his old ways once he was released, and they were desperate to prevent that. Madanes agreed to have a consultation with the entire family.

A few weeks later, the family arrived en masse, and the tension between them was something to behold. During his cocaine binges, Fred had done some pretty awful things. In addition to the expected sexual adventures, infidelities, and financial disasters, he had been arrested for walking naked on the street and had been involved in an assortment of other crazy things that he could neither remember nor explain.

Accompanying Fred to the meeting were both his parents, now divorced, his brothers and sisters, Fred's wife, Constance, and his two teenage sons. It was a big, conflicted group. Before they even began, Madanes could see evidence of tremendous contempt on the part of the boys, who resented their father and immediately made their feelings known.

"I realized I had to take a completely different approach with this family, given the tension in the room. So I said that what was most important was love, that what is important in a family is love. So rather than putting any attention on Fred, I just asked them to talk to one another about pleasant memories from the past. I wanted them to talk about their love for one another. I wanted them to share how they loved previously and how they would love one another in the future. I asked them how they could continue to support one another during these difficult times."

Everything was going pretty well until Fred said something that annoyed one of his sons. Both boys, in chorus, reacting indignantly, screamed at their father that he was a lowlife who had ruined their lives and stomped out of the room. Although the other family members were upset by this drama, Madanes calmly asked the grandfather to go retrieve his grandsons and bring them back.

Madanes had arranged the session around a conference table, as though they were all attending a business meeting, hoping this would reduce the emotional fireworks. Once the teenage boys were resettled at the table, admittedly fuming, she continued the meeting by asking the grandfather and his former wife (the grandmother) to talk to one another about the ways they still loved each other. It was clear to everyone in the room that they still held one another in high regard and affection, even with their estrangement (and remarriages) over the years. Madanes emphasized how much they loved one another even though they couldn't live together.

The others present watched the interaction with rapt attention. The boys, in particular, were amazed to hear their grandparents speaking to one another with such tenderness. Fred and his wife, as well, were obviously moved by the conversation, even inspired to join in with talk about their own mutual love. Throughout the talk, whenever any of the participants lapsed into old habits of complaint or accusation, Madanes gently led them back to talk about love.

Fred's wife, Constance, had come into the session prepared to announce that she was filing for divorce, that she'd had enough of her husband's antics and self-destructive behavior. After hearing her in-laws speak about their lingering love for one another, she felt more willing to rethink her decision. She agreed that Fred could move back into the house and would sleep in the guest room. The two sons rolled their eyes at this, but they were clearly pleased. The session ended with an agreement that they would return in a few months.

"Well," Madanes said, "they never came back and they never called. Frankly, I forgot about them. I'm so busy, I should have called to check on them, but I didn't. I just got a call yesterday, which is what reminded me of them. It's now been 19 months, and Fred was still completely clean until this week. Apparently, the wife is suspicious that Fred might be using again. I recommended that they continue regular drug testing. But I was still pretty amazed that he went 19 months without using cocaine after being an addict for so long."

So, we asked, what does she think sustained Fred during this time, making it possible for him to remain free of drugs?

"It was the talk about love that changed their relationship in a way that could contain him in the family and keep him in the home. I have no doubt that if she had expelled him, he would have gone back to drugs."

Against Conventional Wisdom

In this trilogy of cases, however different they may appear, there is a common theme in that Madanes departed from standard operating procedure, sometimes from her own preferred strategies, in order to do something quite unusual and against conventional professional wisdom. These particular cases all worked out with happy endings, but courage also means having the courage to fail—as has been highlighted in other chapters. We asked Madanes what she would say to therapists who feel inspired to go way beyond their usual comfort levels, to experiment creatively, and yet things don't work out very well.

"You can't give up! You have to keep trying things. If I try something and it doesn't work, I'll try something else. I have spent my entire career training therapists, and this is what I teach."

In each of the cases, Cloé Madanes illustrated a dimension of creativity that highlights the spontaneous, playful nature of therapy. Clients often take themselves way too seriously, as do their therapists. Creativity is often accessed by helping clients to get outside of what is most familiar, to experiment with new ways of relating to one another and to themselves. But in order for that to occur, we have to be the ones to demonstrate courage.

CHAPTER 14

Len Sperry: Accessing the Creative Self

Diane seemed like the stereotypical Southern belle in appearance as well as manner. She exuded refinement, graciousness, and reserve, all captured in a soft accent that minimized words. When asked some basic questions, she immediately apologized that she had stuttered as a child, so she was very cautious to rehearse what she wanted to say ahead of time and then to enunciate it carefully.

"And you do this all the time?" Sperry asked her, curious about the amount of self-control this would require.

Diane nodded. It appeared that whenever a simple gesture would do, she preferred that to words.

The initial interview progressed slowly, with Sperry asking basic questions about what brought her to therapy at this time and what she hoped to get from the sessions. To each of these queries, Diane gave brief, or even one-word, responses. She admitted that she would start to stutter during periods of stress and that this encounter was very stressful for her.

"I see," Sperry said, trying to put her at ease. "And I'm curious about something else."

Diane nodded.

"I wonder how long you think the therapy will take before your symptoms are relieved?"

"I'd say 10 years, at *least* 10 years."

Sperry was not at all happy to hear that response. He agreed that she had quite a lot on her emotional plate, so to speak. She had been suffering from depression most of her life, accompanied by occasional bouts of suicidal thoughts. In addition, she was inclined toward paranoid thoughts, believing that the world conspired against her. Finally, her need for control manifested itself in a long-standing bulimic eating disorder. Coupled with her own pessimistic prognosis, this was going to be a very complex and difficult case.

As Diane spoke about the past four years, during which time she had been in therapy with three previous therapists, Sperry was mesmerized by her unique style of expression, threaded with both the controlled stutter and the Southern accent. He had to concentrate to focus on what she was saying, reviewing what her previous therapists had tried with her—behavior therapy, cognitive therapy, humanistic therapy, some kind of analytic treatment, and other approaches she couldn't quite describe.

"And what was the main reason why these therapists weren't especially helpful to you?" Sperry asked.

Diane shrugged, then offered, "I'm not sure. I just couldn't connect with any of them."

"As much as I would like to work with you," Sperry explained, "I don't see people for long-term treatment."

"You don't?" Diane said, puzzled by the statement.

"No, I see people for a matter of months rather than years. I find that most of my patients can accomplish quite a lot in shorter periods of time."

Diane looked thoughtful for a moment. "Well, these other doctors didn't do a damn thing for me. But I've serious problems, I know. I need lots of therapy."

"Yes, I can appreciate that. But I'm not thinking that it necessarily has to take years for you to make significant progress. I'd like to propose that we focus on a few of your targeted concerns and make a contract with one another for a specified period of time to accomplish those goals."

"How much time are we talking about?"

"Well, about 20 sessions or so over the course of a couple of months."

Diane tilted her head, thinking about that. She didn't look particularly enthused with the idea. In fact, she seemed downright skeptical. With her characteristic melodramatic gestures, she signed deeply. "Well," she said with a shrug, "I suppose we could give it a try." She paused for a moment, then added, "But I won't hold my breath."

The Birds Flew Away

Diane had agreed to work on a short-term basis on trying to get her eating disorder under control. She had been bulimic for years, also prone to purging at times. Although that was an important goal for her, she also mentioned that she'd like to better manage her depression.

Over the next few sessions, Sperry learned a lot more about Diane's struggles. She was indeed severely depressed and also very paranoid, as she had warned. To add to their struggle in communicating during sessions, Diane was alexithymic, unable to get in touch with or express what she was feeling. She could neither identify what she was experiencing inside, name it, nor communicate clearly about the internal states.

Diane seemed most articulate only when she was talking about her paranoid fantasies. Her information processing style was actually acutely developed, especially when it came to scanning the environment and reading the worst into the most inconsequential events. She reported how she had been walking on the street, noticed a group of women whispering together, and imagined that they were gossiping about her. She would see people laughing in a room and assume they were making fun of her.

In the middle of one therapy session, Diane interrupted the conversation with a rather dramatic startle response, almost jumping out her chair. "What's that?" she yelled.

"What's what?"

"That noise."

"What noise?"

"You didn't hear it?"

"Hear what?"

"There was a noise. Out there." And then she'd pointed toward the doorway leading out into the hall.

"I'm sorry," Sperry said patiently. "I didn't hear anything. It was probably just someone walking by."

"Are you sure?" she asked. "How do you know if you didn't hear it?"

Sperry observed that external cues that would ordinarily escape most people's attention would command Diane's interest, frequently distracting her from the internal feelings she found so disturbing. Her alexithymia and troublesome information processing style had developed early in life. As a result, she had been cut off from many internal feelings, and had misinterpreted others as physical states, such that she would frequently confuse emotions and other sensations with being tired or being sick.

As a psychiatrist, Sperry found it relatively routine to manage the worst of her depression with medication. She had responded well to antidepressants in the past, but they seemed to work for only a short period of time. Unfortunately, she expected instant relief and so would complain about other symptoms of insomnia or mood changes. Sperry explained patiently that it often took as long as a month (rather than week) for the drugs to fully kick in, so he suggested they try other techniques in the meantime to deal with the depression—an exercise program, for one thing. They also talked about ways she could identify her emotional triggers and pay closer attention to what she might be feeling prior to the onset of a depressive episode.

Once they spent more time together, Sperry began to recognize features of some of her personality dysfunctions—narcissistic, histrionic, and obsessive-compulsive behaviors, as well as the paranoia. Every time they might try to make inroads into one area or another, her delusional fantasies would pop up in ways that would prevent further exploration. It was clear at this point that unless he could help her bring the paranoia under control, it would be difficult to make much progress.

"So, I was on my way here today," Diane said abruptly, changing the subject from a discussion about her eating the previous day, "and I noticed something interesting."

"What's that?" Sperry prompted, knowing what might be coming next.

"I saw these birds on the electrical wire. No, maybe they were phone lines. Anyway, they were all lined up on the wire. There were maybe 9 or 10 of them, maybe more. They were just standing there. No, I mean they were sitting there."

Sperry was becoming impatient, but he knew that once Diane was going on like this, he had to let her finish.

"So, I was looking up at the birds," Diane continued. "And as soon as I was underneath them, they flew away!" She said this with a flourish, as if this was an amazing thing that had happened.

"You walked under the birds and they flew away," Sperry repeated.

"Yes! And I know what you're going to say, that this is normal or something. But I have to tell you that I saw other people walking beneath them and the birds just stood there—or sat there—or whatever they do when they're perched on the line. It was only when I walked by that they took off." She looked at Sperry defiantly, as though she'd just proven an important point that was now irrefutable.

"I see," Sperry answered as neutrally as possible. "And what do you think that means?"

"Isn't it rather obvious? I mean, all the other people walked by and it didn't bother the birds in the least. They were just chirping away having a grand ol' time. But as soon as I walked underneath them, they flew off. So, I ask you, what have they got against *me*? I've never done anything to them."

Sperry now found himself in somewhat of a bind. He could hardly challenge or contradict Diane without her taking offense. Recognizing her hypervigiliance and the likelihood of misinterpretation and exaggeration, he said as gently as he could, "It could mean that you're just creative."

"Whatever do you mean by that?" Diane asked suspiciously, waiting for what she suspected might be a trap.

"Just that I notice ways you are becoming more aware of things, the way creative people observe things that others can't often see. Some of the most innovative people, whether composers or artists or writers or actors, are able to get in touch with their creative parts. They see things—like the ways birds behave—that escape others' notice."

Diane smiled almost immediately. She quite liked this idea. In fact, she saw herself as quite a talented actress (and indeed she was). Being so self-centered and more than a little narcissistic, she enjoyed the conception of herself as an innovator who had the gift of extraordinary sensitivity.

For the next few sessions, Sperry began the conversation by asking Diane to talk about what she had noticed during the week that represented her "creative" awareness. Initially, she continued the narcissistic fantasies that everyone and everything around her were directly related to her life. She noticed people in church were talking together after the service and remarked that they were most likely talking about her.

"And what if that is the case?" Sperry asked her. "What would that mean? How does that relate to your creativity?" By framing things in that way, he hoped to move her from a position of imagining dangerous conspiracies to potentially positive and flattering consequences. Perhaps, for example, they were considering her for a position of authority on some committee?

Diane tried thinking more positively about situations she encountered, but it was difficult after a lifetime of self-protective, paranoid habits. She presented one of her overly dramatic sighs to punctuate her doubt.

"I'd like you to try something," Sperry suggested. "We've already found that you have this creative capacity to notice things that escape others' awareness, like the birds on the line, or overhearing conversations even though they are far away. You know what a mantra is, don't you?"

"You mean like in meditation? Yeah, look, I tried meditation before and it doesn't . . ."

"I'm not finished," Sperry interrupted. "What I'm suggesting is that you use the mantra "benign" to help you keep things in perspective.

"*Benign*? Like in cancer."

"Exactly. A benign tumor is one that isn't cancerous. It can still be dangerous if it isn't removed, but most are slow-growing and not fatal."

"And you want me to repeat the mantra "benign?"

"Yes. When you find yourself thinking that people—or birds—or anything else—might be up to no good or potentially harmful to you, I want you to repeat the mantra "benign" to yourself over and over. This will help you cut off the negative thinking that leads you to feel out of control. These thoughts interfere with your ability to continue being creative. Do you think you can do that?"

"I guess I can try."

It's Not about Me

After seven weeks of treatment, Sperry finally received the medical records from Diane's previous psychiatric hospitalization four years earlier, when she had first sought mental health care. It was all very discouraging. Her MMPI scores were off the scale in "paranoia" and "schizophrenia." Besides diagnoses of bulimia, depression, and several personality disorders, she was given a very guarded prognosis upon her release. What particularly caught Sperry's attention in the discharge summary was an example of the extent of her paranoia: "Once the patient was observed eavesdropping on a conversation in the dayroom between two clinicians talking about a particularly treatment-resistant patient whom they speculated would require at least ten years of intensive therapy to make any progress. Convinced that the clinicians were talking about her, Diane left the dayroom in a huff." So *that's* where she got that idea, Sperry realized.

They weren't even talking about Diane, but she assumed that since *every* discussion was about her own case, the clinicians were discussing the hopelessness of her situation. No wonder her subsequent treatments had not gone well. Sperry thought about bringing this up in their next session but decided against it. They were already making steady progress with the depression, and now the paranoid ideation was coming more under control.

It was during the ninth session that there was a lull in the conversation. Diane seemed more reticent than usual, the discussion starting and stopping with long pauses in between. It was during one such silence that Sperry decided to take the risk of bringing up what had happened during her prior hospitalization.

"Diane," he began cautiously, "would it be all right if I spoke to your creative self?" This was a signal that he was going to broach a difficult subject and asked for her permission to do so.

Diane thought for a moment and then nodded tentatively.

"I wonder if you wouldn't mind sitting back and letting yourself go for a few minutes. Can you do that?"

She made herself more comfortable in the chair, almost steeling herself for what was to come.

"Good," he said once she was settled. "I want to talk to your creative self about something and would like you to just listen and jump in whenever you want. About five years ago, you were hospitalized, were you not?"

Diane nodded.

"I finally received the records from that period and I found something very interesting." He paused waiting for her to ask what that was, but she just continued to wait. "There is one note that a staff member composed in which she described how they had been talking about a patient, one who was extremely disturbed, and she saw you listening in. You seemed upset by what you heard, believing that they had been talking about you. Your creative self will recognize that you often think conversations are about you. We've talked about that, right?"

Again Diane nodded but didn't say anything.

"So, I'd like to ask your creative self what they were saying when they were talking about this patient?"

"Well, they were talking about someone who frustrated them, someone who wasn't getting better."

"How do you mean 'frustrated' them?"

"We were in an eating disorders' unit, so I assume they were talking about someone who was a hopeless case."

"And what might this person have been doing that was so frustrating to the staff?" Sperry asked, continuing the complicated pretense that they were talking about "another patient," even though Diane believed it was herself. In fact, she was really talking about herself from the position of her "creative self."

"I don't think this woman had been understood for a long time. People were always talking about her, saying things that weren't really true."

"Go on."

"So she was stalling, trying to go at her own pace. She was really working through her stuff, but people didn't recognize that."

"Creative self, let me ask you something: Who *was* this person that we're discussing, the one mentioned in the chart?"

"I think her name was Joanne. I didn't know her very well. But now I wish I had."

"Do you mean to say they weren't talking about you, Diane?"

"Well, initially I thought they were talking about me. But you told me to be my creative self, so now I think they were really talking about someone else, like Joanne. Not me at all."

Sperry was not at all sure where this was going, or even clear where he was going with this line of inquiry. He was intrigued that somehow they had maneuvered into a position in which Diane's creative self was guiding her to be far more rational and thoughtful than was usually the case. She was also disclosing things she'd never shared before, such as how important it was to feel understood. For someone who could never before talk about her feelings, this was quite remarkable.

Even though this was all new ground for him, Sperry decided to follow his intuition and pursue this line of discussion. "Diane," he said to her, "I'd like to ask you something, not your creative self, but your normal, regular self."

"I'm still here," she said. They both laughed.

"So, what did you think about all you've been hearing?"

"I don't know. It's pretty amazing, actually. Now that I look at the evidence, I see that they couldn't have been talking about me. They really were talking about someone else. I was a model patient. Did everything they asked. I went to all the group sessions. Never missed any of my individual appointments. I tried as hard as I could to do whatever they wanted."

"What you're saying, then, is that they couldn't have been talking about you."

"Sure, I had a meltdown or two. Everyone did at times. But they were nothing out of the ordinary. I was as cooperative as any patient could be. I realize now that they had to have been talking about someone else."

"That's pretty impressive that you now realize that," Sperry said gently.

After that breakthrough session, Diane realized that she did have the ability to challenge her paranoid thinking. Prior to this she had felt an automatic negative reaction, often suspicious, to almost anything that happened around her. Accessing her creative self, she now had an ally who could help her keep things in perspective.

Awakening Memories

Diane had originally been referred to Sperry by a friend who had also worked with him for a period of time. The friend had also been learning meditative focusing techniques to help her relax and concentrate better, which produced results that inspired her to start a support group for women with similar issues. Diane decided to join the group, which began meeting once each week to practice focusing skills. These mindfulness exercises helped her to live more in the present, without the usual critical, if not paranoid, thinking. Rather than judging behavior—her own or anyone else's—Diane began learning how to just remain focused on sensations and feelings. This represented another major breakthrough for her in terms of being able to access and express internal states.

Sperry began working with her in sessions to concentrate on what she was experiencing inside and then to make bridges to language describing these feelings. The therapy, combined with the group mindfulness practice, began to awaken memories of her childhood, in which she had been abused by her father and neglected by her mother. This was not particularly surprising to Sperry, given Diane's presenting issues.

Diane began to talk about her father's alcoholic rages, during which he would scream at her for being useless and incompetent, at times beating her into submission. Her creative self allowed her to access these memories, to bring them to therapy, and attempt to make sense of their meaning in her life. Now abandoned was the idea that improvement would take 10 years or more; Diane was now seeing rapid improvements that had occurred within the promised few months. She was also taking on the persona of her creative self far more than the previous, wounded, defensive version.

This experience not only awakened greater creativity in Diane, but in her therapist as well. Sperry points to this case as a breakthrough in trusting his own intuition more in therapeutic work. He felt inspired to trust his patients' capacity to get more in touch with their creative selves, even in cases of seriously disturbed individuals with a vast array of defenses.

This was a case in which Sperry had every reason to be as pessimistic as his patient. Diane presented a complex pattern of psychopathological symptoms that affected her personality, thinking, and behavior, that resulted in life-threatening addictions, and that even prevented her from being able to talk about her problems. She had believed herself to be a hopeless case, destined for a lifetime of continued suffering. Yet Sperry refused to subscribe to this view of things: "I expected Diane to change. It was a matter of looking for the best opportunities for growth. I kept looking for them, testing them, and trying different things until we found something that worked for her. I gave up a cookie-cutter approach and instead trusted my intuition."

It also helped that, with his medical background, Sperry could understand at a deeper level what was going on within her body as well as her mind. He was able to stabilize her on antidepressant and thyroid medications that reduced the severity of depression, allowing her to concentrate on psychological afflictions. "By talking to her creative self, I knew that I was speaking more directly to her limbic system. What people are often doing is identifying self with the emotional brain, the subcortical brain, as opposed to the thinking brain, which is the cortex. There are often disconnects between the two parts, so I often try to help people recognize these separations and get permission from one part of self to communicate with the other part, to make the connection between them. This occurred when I asked Diane to allow the one part of her to listen to the other and then reflect on that experience."

Sperry believes that therapists can become more creative by restoring their faith in their intuitive powers, as well as in the healing energy of their clients. This involves using far more than psychiatric interventions, or even psychological techniques. Spiritual traditions like Buddhism can also help people to get out of their own way. It all begins with abandoning that which is most comfortable and familiar, reaching beyond to find the creative self.

CHAPTER 15

Fred Bemak: Getting People Up Off the Floor

Maybe it's because he likes to travel or because he hungers for new experiences, but Fred Bemak has his bags packed and ready to go wherever he feels he is most needed. When there were wildfires in San Diego, Bemak was there with some of his students to deliver support and debriefing to the underserved communities of Native Americans and Latinos. The same with Hurricane Katrina and the cyclone in Burma. He has worked with homeless children in Brazil, Colombia, and India. Bemak delivers counseling in places that desperately need help and so has derived helping strategies that are optimally suited to the cultures in which he operates.

Frozen on the Floor

Bemak was asked to see a 17-year-old girl, a Vietnamese refugee who had come to the United States on her own, leaving her family behind. She had been placed with a foster family in which the couple had no longer been able to conceive, although they had two younger children. Thuy adapted reasonably well to her new home, attaching quickly to her new siblings, a boy and a girl. She began making friends, doing well in school, and generally functioning fairly well. Her foster parents described her as "an absolute delight."

Then, all of a sudden, the parents began to notice a sudden change in Thuy's behavior. Although normally fairly cheerful, she seemed progressively withdrawn, even depressed. At one point, she began spending more time in her room and was unwilling to leave, even for meals.

Understandably, the parents became increasingly concerned, wondering whether they were doing something wrong. They tried everything they could to draw Thuy out of her shell, but she seemed to retreat further from them with every overture. They consulted with the school counselor and teachers. They took her to a mental health facility. Yet Thuy remained listless, detached, and essentially mute.

The parents had heard about Bemak and his work with refugees, and so felt they had nothing to lose by bringing him in for a consultation. Since by this time, Thuy refused to leave her room, Bemak had little choice but to make the trip to another state, in the Northeast where the family lived.

Bemak was struck by the idyllic, New England setting in which the family lived—a beautiful, large suburban home, pristine lawns, and trees draped in fall colors, in a quiet, secluded neighborhood. This was about as different an environment from Thuy's home in Vietnam as could possibly be imagined.

Bemak sat in the living room of the family's home, watching Thuy nervously looking around the room, mostly at the floor. She seemed profoundly depressed, almost as if her body were present but her spirit vacated. Since she refused to speak, her parents and siblings did all they could to fill the silence with chatter. Yet as their conversation continued, Thuy retreated further into herself, at one point hugging her knees and rocking back and forth, lost in her own world.

"Hey Thuy," Bemak tried, addressing the girl directly, "what do you say if you and I go in the other room and talk a little?"

No response. In fact, he wasn't even certain if she heard him.

"Come on, let's go," he tried again, this time standing up and extending his hand.

Still looking down, Thuy rose slowly from the chair, as if she were being pulled by unseen strings connected to her like a puppet. Just the simple act of rising seemed to exhaust her. She stood still, head down, body limp, and began to shuffle toward her room, dragging her feet.

Once they settled in the room, with Thuy sitting on her bed, hands folded in her lap, Bemak began casually asking her a few questions. "So, Thuy, how is it for you to be here? How is it different from Vietnam?"

No response. No movement. She seemed so still that Bemak wasn't even sure if her eyes were blinking.

"I understand you were adjusting pretty well here, but then things started to get hard for you. Do you want to talk about that?"

As Bemak asked the question, he noticed her starting to slide off the bed onto the floor, as if pulled downward by gravity. Once her body was prone on the floor, she curled into a fetal position with her head tucked under her arms.

On the outside, Bemak was looking calm, as though he saw this sort of behavior all the time in response to a question like, "How's it going?" Inside, he was freaking out. "Oh my God, what have I done?" he was saying to himself. "What the hell is going on? What should I do now?"

Bemak was in an advanced state of panic, worried that the parents would walk in at any moment and think he had killed the poor girl. Thuy seemed like she was frozen in suspended animation. Her eyes were open, staring into space, but she wasn't moving.

"It seems like you're really upset by the question I asked you," Bemak tried gently. "I said something that really bothered you."

Still no response. Not a single movement, no acknowledgment that he was even in the room.

"It sure is nice here this time of year," Bemak said, going into safer territory. "The leaves on the trees are beautiful, aren't they? All the yellows and oranges." He was chattering now, trying to carry on both sides of the conversation, hoping, praying that the parents wouldn't find their daughter frozen on the floor. They brought him a long way to do something, to fix the girl, and so far all he'd done was make things worse—much worse.

Taste of Chocolate

"Would you like some hot chocolate?" said a voice from the other side of the door.

It was surreal. Bemak was hunched over in his chair, whispering in a soft voice to the girl curled on the floor in a fetal position, and her mother was now offering to bring in a hot drink. He could just picture the scene as she carried in the tray of steaming mugs and a plateful of cookies, probably screaming in horror when she saw her daughter on the floor. Bemak wondered idly if she would spill the drinks and whether that might get some reaction from Thuy.

Bemak was desperate, but managed to calm his voice. "Sure," he said to the mother, "hot chocolate would be fine." He then looked down at the girl and said in the quiet voice, "How does that sound, Thuy? Would you like some hot chocolate?"

Bemak didn't expect an answer, so he wasn't disappointed. He sat back in his chair for a moment, looking around the room, even outside the window, for some inspiration. The only thing that came to mind was chocolate, so he went with that. "Thuy, did you have chocolate in Vietnam?" he asked.

Thuy looked at him! He was sure of it. Her eyes flitted upward for a moment, the first reaction since she had melted onto the floor.

"I take that as a yes, you did have chocolate back home?"

Thuy's head moved, a distinct nod.

"Did your mother in Vietnam give you chocolate sometimes?" Bemak pressed a little further, gently, quietly, softly.

"And what about your brother and sister? Did they like chocolate, too?"

"Yes." It was barely audible, but the first word she'd spoken since they'd been together.

"What kind of chocolate did you have at home?"

"Candy."

"Your mother gave you chocolate candy?"

Nod, this time more distinct. Thuy was even uncurling a bit from her protective ball.

"And did you like the candy?" Bemak asked

"Oh, yes." As she said this, Thuy sat up on the floor. She didn't exactly look at Bemak, but she faced approximately in his direction.

"Did you have the chocolate very often?"

When she shook her head, Bemak held his breath, afraid that Thuy might be regressing back to muteness. "We were very poor," she said finally. "Candy was too expensive."

"I see. So you really liked chocolate, but you didn't get to have it very often."

It was at that moment there was a knock on the door, cued perfectly, and in walked Mom with the expected tray of steaming mugs of hot chocolate. The wafting vapors immediately filled the room, and Bemak could feel himself salivating. It smelled wonderful.

Mom noticed Thuy sitting on the floor, but still smiled cheerfully, making brief eye contact with Bemak, asking with her eyes how things were going. All Bemak could do was shrug and nod, indicating that it was best not to interrupt.

"Okay then, you two," Mom said, "I'll just set this down over here." She put the tray on Thuy's desk and quietly backed out of the room as if she were afraid that any little disturbance might upset the balance of whatever was going on.

Bemak grabbed one mug for himself and set the other on the floor in front of Thuy's now crossed legs. The actual presence of the steaming chocolate, its fragrance, seemed to loosen Thuy's tongue further. Through their conversation about chocolate, Bemak began to get a clearer vision of what life was like back in Vietnam. Everything was filtered through chocolate: What kind of chocolate did her friends prefer? Did they serve chocolate on the plane ride over? What was the first kind of chocolate that she had in the United States? How was it different from what she was used to back home?

It was this last question that seemed to grab Thuy most. By comparing chocolate in the two countries, she began talking about the differences between her old life and her new life. She liked many things in the United States, she said, now reaching for the cup and taking a careful sip, but she missed her home and her family and her friends.

"So," Bemak clarified, "you like the taste of chocolate in this country." As he said this, he took a deliberate drink from his own mug. "But you really miss the kind of precious chocolate you had back home?"

Thuy nodded, staring into her cup. It was then that she began talking about her past. She spoke about the pain of leaving her mother, brother, and sister behind, how she had to leave because they were so poor. She talked about the guilt she felt because she was living in such rich splendor, enjoying such wonderful chocolate, when the people back home were starving.

The conversation continued for another hour, until Thuy eventually rose from the floor and sat back on the bed. Bemak continued to gently encourage her to speak about the grief and loss she felt for her family and country, as well as her remorse in leaving people behind. Eventually, they returned to the living room where the parents were waiting anxiously.

"So," the father asked as soon as they resettled themselves, "what did you guys talk about in there?"

Bemak looked at Thuy who just shrugged and said, "You tell them."

"Well," he began, stalling until he could figure out exactly how to describe what happened. "Mostly we talked about chocolate."

Thuy giggled at that but could think of nothing else to add.

"I elaborated a bit for the parents," Bemak explained. "I told them that our discussion about chocolate was a way for us to explore her feelings about leaving her home and her family in Vietnam. It was a way to talk about her life. At first they were puzzled by that, but eventually they understood ways that they could support their daughter. It helped for them to know about her losses and regrets, which she had not felt ready to tell them; she hadn't wanted to burden them because they were already so generous. The whole family was able to connect on a different level, not just the parents with Thuy, but Thuy with the other children as well."

Bemak ended this first story by saying he never read anywhere about using chocolate as a way to engage a mute client, but the creative inspiration is to use whatever is present. It was partially in desperation, which led him to grab onto the only thing that seemed to interest Thuy.

A Cross-Cultural Exorcism

We now abruptly change locations from bucolic New England to the streets of Mumbai. Bemak spends a lot of time working with indigent and neglected people in South Asia, which included several stints in the slums of India's most poverty-stricken city. He had been consulting with a local mental health facility when he was asked to consult on a case of man who had been washing dishes in one of the restaurants when his vision suddenly went blurry.

Gajanin had been taken by his family to the hospital, where they had told him he needed a simple operation to fix his eyes, a procedure that would take only a short time. He could just walk in and walk out within a few hours.

In spite of the reassurances from his family and patient explanations by the doctor, Gajanin went back to the tin, corrugated one-room shack where he lived and proceeded to lie down on the earthen floor, refusing to move (it seems to be a theme in Bemak's cases that his clients lie on the ground). He was absolutely terrified of the hospital, the doctors, and anything they planned to do to him. Yet in this condition, with his vision compromised, he could not earn his meager wage of less than a dollar per day to feed his wife and four children. Until this point, they were living on a little rice and vegetables, but now even that would stop.

After six months lying on the floor of their shack, the family was literally wasting away. The hospital staff had given up. The people at the mental health facility had tried everything they knew to reach Gajanin, but nothing had the slightest impact: He insisted he would not move no matter what the consequences.

A few members of the clinic escorted Bemak through the slums to places where they had never seen foreigners before. They navigated through alleyways with debris everywhere—garbage, feces, prone bodies, and horrifying smells. There was no running water or electricity in this part of the city. By the time they reached Gajanin's dwelling, quite a crowd had gathered to follow this stranger in their midst.

Standing outside the open doorway of the shack, most of the neighborhood had now gathered, as many as 70 people milling about, watching to see what this stranger would do. Bemak ducked his head and entered through the doorway, followed by a dozen heads that were watching the proceedings. This was clearly a community event that had occupied everyone's attention for many months. Whether it was out of partial concern or just entertainment, this was the most interesting thing that had happened around there for a long time.

Bemak was accompanied by a Hindi interpreter from the clinic, and through him, a conversation began, starting with introductions. Bemak respectfully tented his palms under his chin and bowed to the man on the floor. "Namaste," he said, roughly translated as "My spirit greets the divine within you."

"Namaste," Gajanin responded automatically in a voice barely audible.

"I understand you have been having some troubles," Bemak said, sitting on the floor next to the man.

Gajanin nodded.

"And," Bemak continued, "you've been spending a lot of time here on the floor."

"Yes," he answered, "I'm just here. There's nowhere else to go."

"You've been here, what, six months now without leaving your home?"

Gajanin nodded again.

"I hear your eyes are not good."

"That is so."

"What's wrong with your eyes?"

"My eyes, they are hurting," Gajanin replied, covering them with his hands for emphasis.

"What is it like for you to have your eyes hurt like that?" As he asked the question, Bemak was aware that nobody had really talked to him about what he was feeling and how he experienced the pain. The doctors only scolded him. His wife complained bitterly. His children ignored him. People in the surrounding corrugated shacks treated him like a curiosity to be mocked. All throughout the previous six months he'd felt completely isolated, the only interaction consisting of his wife yelling at him and calling him names in a voice loud enough for everyone in the alley to hear.

"It must be so difficult for you lying on the hard ground," Bemak said, "It must hurt your back terribly."

"Yes, that is so. But it is also difficult watching them."

"By *them*, you mean your family?"

Gajanin nodded, rubbing his hands together, in obvious misery.

"You see them so hungry, but you can't do anything to feed them."

Another nod.

"And you cannot work because your eyes hurt?"

This time, Gajanin looked at Bemak with piercing eyes, willing him to understand.

"Yet it is more than your eyes, isn't it? It is not just something physical. There is something wrong with your spirit. Is that so?"

By this time, some of the neighbors had lost interest in the conversation, melting back into their own dwellings. It was now just Bemak, the interpreter, and Gajanin huddled together on the dirt floor. Within this closed circle, Gajanin felt more willing to talk about what he was feeling. He spoke of his fears about going to that medical place where people died. He felt sure if he went there, he would not leave again. It was better to waste away here in his own home than to go to a place where there were strangers everywhere.

Bemak listened carefully to everything Gajanin said, finally asking whether it would be all right if Gajanin's wife joined them for a few minutes. Reluctantly, he agreed. Before they continued the conversation, Gajanin spoke to the crowd outside the door in rapid Hindi. Soon afterward, a can of soda was placed in Bemak's hand, which he immediately realized cost the family a day's wages—if they had any income at all. He was stunned by their generosity and determined that some way, somehow, they would find a way through this complicated problem.

Once Gajanin's wife joined their circle, they chatted together for a few minutes, with Bemak concentrating primarily on reducing the tension, inviting them to talk about their relationship prior to the onset of the vision problems. As members of the untouchable caste, they had actually chosen one another as spouses rather than been part of an arranged marriage. They talked about the love and respect they felt for one another, how they had rarely argued until the past few months.

Bemak turned around and faced the crowd that was still gathered outside the door, faces still peeking through, straining to catch the drift of conversation. "I want you to speak directly to them," Bemak instructed the interpreter. "I want you to ask them what they think should happen here."

There was a chorus of different voices, all speaking at once, all with strong opinions about what they thought was going on. The interpreter tried to keep up with all the comments and suggestions, but at one point could only shrug helplessly.

"Tell me what they are saying," Bemak pressed him.

"There are many opinions," the interpreter answered. "Most people think he should get help, but they believe that bad spirits have done this to him. It is a curse."

At this point, Gajanin's wife and children joined in the discussion, responding to those outside the doorway, then to their husband and father. It was the first time they had talked together as a family in many months in which there was no argument. From the urgent, gentle tone of the discussion, it sounded to Bemak as if they were offering their support to their husband and father.

Bemak decided to take up the idea suggested by one among the chorus and so asked Gajanin about the presence of spirits in their home. When he agreed that they did indeed make themselves known, Bemak wondered if they were there all the time.

"Yes," Gajanin answered, "they are here all the time." He looked toward his wife for confirmation. She nodded agreement.

"What do the spirits do when they are here?" Bemak asked

"They hurt my eyes."

"Is it a big hurt or a little hurt?"

Gajanin shrugged. "Sometimes it is strong, other times not so much."

And now the critical question Bemak had been waiting to ask ever since the subject of spirits had been broached: "Why do you suppose the spirits are so upset with you that they remain in your house and will not go away, even after all these months? Don't they have better things to do?"

Once the translation was completed, everyone laughed, everyone but Gajanin, who lowered his head. "I have done bad things," he said.

Bemak nodded his understanding but didn't think it was appropriate to get details in front of Gajanin's family and neighbors. Instead he asked if it was ever possible to please the spirits so they would go away.

Gajanin thought for a minute while the crowd present began discussing this matter among themselves. Finally, Gajanin said, yes, he thought that might be possible.

"So, if you wished to be rid of these spirits, if you wished to see beyond them," Bemak pursued, "how could that happen?"

"Maybe if I do good things."

"I see," Bemak said, and he did see even if his client could not. "I think I can help you with this. I can help you make the spirits go away so you can see again.

With this promise of hope, Gajanin actually propped himself up on his elbows off the floor. For the first time, he showed genuine interest in the conversation. They began to talk about what might happen at the hospital to fix his eyes and how the doctors there could do certain things but that they could not touch the spirits.

"If you and I are going to work this out," Bemak said, "it would be a lot easier if you would sit up so we can talk to one another face-to-face." Bemak explained what he was thinking at this point.

"There was something about his having sunk into this position on the floor and refusing to move, holding very tightly to this position. He had been determined to stay there. What surprised me is that when I asked him to sit up, he actually did so. Everyone was shocked that all I did was ask him to sit up to talk to me and he did. I asked his wife how she felt about that. I asked the children and the neighbors. They all agreed that they thought the spirits were lifting. I even asked the spirits present if they were soon ready to leave this home."

They talked for some time about the spirits, sitting facing one another, when Bemak said he needed to get up to stretch a little. "After all, we have been sitting on the ground for some time. Would you like to join me?"

Gajanin was hesitant, perhaps even a little frightened, but finally he nodded. Bemak called for others to help him move Gajanin from his position on the floor to one in which he was standing up for the first time in six months. Bemak was thinking about this alteration as a metaphor for him changing in other areas of his life.

Once they were both standing, Bemak asked him what that was like for him. "How are the spirits reacting to this change, with you standing up like this?"

Gajanin indicated that he didn't think the spirits objected.

"I wonder if they would allow you to go back to work?"

They continued talking about what the spirits might wish, all with input from the community present. The important thing was that Gajanin was standing up. He was off the ground for the first time, and this was a huge improvement. The next step Bemak initiated was asking the people present how the spirits could be recruited to help put Gajanin back in action so he wouldn't lie back on the ground. His wife and children were crying because they were so happy that their father had risen, and they promised to do anything to help fortify him. Others within the crowd volunteered to help escort Gajanin to the hospital and to help ward off the spirits along the way.

So it came to be that a few days later, Gajanin, his family, and his neighbors walked to the hospital, where he had the simple procedure and regained his sight. They saw Bemak not as a therapist but rather as a spiritual healer sent from a faraway land to harness the spirits that were infecting their home. Bemak still remembers, with tears in his eyes, how when he left the home people began expressing their gratitude by kissing his feet. As awkward and uncomfortable as this was for him, it was a reminder about the importance of creativity within a context of cultural responsiveness.

What these two cases have in common, besides helping people rise from the floor, is that you have to work with what you have. As much as we might like to follow our prescribed treatment plan, sometimes creative innovation emerges when all else fails. "I do my best work," Bemak said in conclusion, "by going with what is present in the room—or the shack—rather than bringing in my own expectations. It isn't just the individual or the family that is important, but also their cultural and physical environment."

CHAPTER 16

Nancy McWilliams: The Wisdom of Not Knowing

It is more than a little interesting that some of our other women theoreticians who have been profiled have echoed a theme similar to the one that Nancy McWilliams brought up as soon as we began talking: She doesn't see herself as particularly creative, but rather sees her clients as being the inspiration. "I've done some small things that have made a big difference," she said, "but any breakthroughs that took place were very much the result of our collaboration together that resulted in mutual creativity. It's not that I am so brilliant but that some of my clients are!"

When we pointed out this gender difference in the stories, McWilliams mentioned a study that was done several years ago in which men and women were asked to solve a difficult puzzle. After 20 minutes, the subjects were interviewed about their experience. The women said they just couldn't do it while the men said it was impossible. Later, they were given a solvable task, after which the women said that it was easy and the men said, "I did it!"

Whose Side Are You On?

"I think most of my moments of creativity come through a deep emotional immersion in the somewhat alien and painfully familiar experience of the other person." With this introduction,

McWilliams remembered one turning point in her work with a severely depressed and suicidal woman who was both angry and difficult to work with in sessions. A lot of this resistance was the result of her having worked with a number of previous therapists who had labeled her as a lost cause. Nevertheless, Mary still held on to a shred of hope, although it was expressed through an attitude of "I dare you to help me."

Mary was in her midthirties, a middle child in her family who had received very little attention from her parents as a child. Most of her life, she had believed herself to be stupid, having done poorly in school, which later turned out to be the result of learning disorders. To add to her troubles, she had not been allowed to express any emotions in her family, even frustration.

"But why does any of this crap matter, anyway?" she pressed McWilliams. "I mean, who cares?"

"I can understand why you would have your doubts that I—or anyone else—could help you after everything you've been through."

Mary just glared at her with her arms crossed.

McWilliams waited, but it seemed that Mary was far more patient—and stubborn—and so the silences would continue interminably.

"It must be difficult to trust me," McWilliams tried again.

"Trust you? Why the hell would I trust you? You can't do anything for me, anyway."

After another prompt from McWilliams soliciting her family history, Mary recited a litany of tragedies that had befallen her family—a cousin who had become addicted to drugs, her sister's marriage that had fallen apart, someone else who lost a job. In each case, the family member had sought the help of a therapist without noticeable improvement.

"Plus," McWilliams added, "your own experiences with mental health professionals who haven't helped you."

"Duh," Mary said sarcastically. "I already told you that. Why do you have to repeat things I say? Aren't you listening?" Then she smirked.

McWilliams wasn't taking any of this personally. When relating her previous mental health history, Mary had remarked that her last therapist, a psychiatrist, had encouraged her to get in touch with her anger and express angry feelings more. She had eventually done that by reaching into her purse, taking out the bottle of antidepressants he had prescribed for her, and throwing them at him as an expression of anger. The psychiatrist had "fired" her as a patient on the spot and told her never to return.

"So," McWilliams proceeded carefully when she heard that story, "he'd been telling you to get angry for the 18 months you were seeing him, and then when you did what he said, he punished you for it."

Mary stared at her, but finally nodded. It was obvious that Mary was terrified of her own anger, so all her negative feelings came through indirectly.

Recognizing some borderline features to Mary's interpersonal style, McWilliams knew she had a tough road ahead with this client. In these first sessions she concentrated primarily on listening as carefully as she could, demonstrating that she took her client seriously. Cautiously, Mary agreed to return, but first asked if McWilliams would request the records from her previous psychiatrist.

"Sure," McWilliams agreed, "if you sign a release, I can get them and we can go over them together." McWilliams sensed that this was a test to see where her loyalties lay: Would she side with the psychiatrist and therefore negate Mary's feelings, or would she make an effort to really understand her?

As much as possible, McWilliams used empathic listening to communicate her willingness to hear and understand. Unfortunately, such attempts were rarely appreciated by Mary, who would typically respond sarcastically.

"That must have been so difficult for you," McWilliams would say.

"Ya think?" Mary would respond, shaking her head as if to say, "And I thought *I* was the one who was an idiot."

A More Mature Version of Empathy

It was during one such conversation that Mary finally lost her temper in the session. "You know," she said, "I bet you've never been depressed your whole life. You have this perfect little life, with your perfect office, and your perfect clothes. What the hell could you ever know about what I'm going through?"

Wow, McWilliams thought. Rather than her usual style of being passive-aggressive and indirect, Mary was expressing herself authentically and directly for the first time. "This is huge," McWilliams said to herself, realizing the significance of this breakthrough. "I've got to get this right."

McWilliams's first impulse was to counter the attack by telling Mary that her own life was far from perfect, that she'd had her own struggles, that she knew depression intimately herself. She wanted to tell her that not only had she experienced such troubles, but more important, she knew how to pull out of them. And she could teach her that. But another voice in her head countered that this was a lie, that she really had never been as seriously depressed as Mary was and that it was dishonest to say so just to make a connection.

"You know," McWilliams admitted, "you're absolutely right. I really have never gone through the kind of mental torture that I see you experiencing. I've been sad and depressed at times, but nothing like what you've been through. And I hope to God I never do, because from where I'm sitting it looks like hell on earth."

Mary later shared that this was the turning point in their relationship. She so appreciated McWilliams's authenticity and honesty that this became the beginning of trust developing between them. After that, Mary began sharing more about her life and her struggles, which had been with her as long as she could remember.

That is not to say that the going between them didn't remain pretty rough. Any time Mary didn't like the way a conversation was going or whenever she felt that McWilliams misunderstood her, she would abruptly stand up and walk out of the session, slamming the door along the way. All this seemed to be further evidence of her borderline tendencies that had been clearly documented in her previous file. Yet it was during one of these outbursts that Mary disclosed how her mind was racing with a bunch of thoughts and feelings that she couldn't hold on to.

Interesting, McWilliams thought. This description reminded her of a bipolar manic episode manifested by rage rather than high spirits. This led to questions about how Mary was sleeping and what the racing thoughts were like. It became evident that she was prone to spending binges, sexual preoccupation, and impulsive behavior. It seemed more and more apparent that she was experiencing a mood disorder, one that was soon stabilized on Tegretol. This chemical help then allowed the therapy to deepen and progress.

Mary believes that McWilliams saved her life, not just by helping to accurately diagnose her condition, but by being the first person to really take the time to understand her. "What I did," McWilliams confessed, "didn't feel like a brilliant, creative stroke of genius. Rather, it felt like Mary forced me to be more honest. She propelled me to develop a more mature version of empathy."

Mistakes of the Heart

Looking back on this case, McWilliams sees it as a breakthrough in trusting her willingness to admit what she doesn't know and understand. "In my own analysis, my therapist acknowledged a mistake, and it touched me much more than any of the brilliant interpretive things he may have said." Such an admission may be common within humanistic traditions, but it represents a fairly recent paradigm shift within psychodynamic thought. "We can now acknowledge that therapy is an experience between two flawed people. That took pressure off me, to realize that my limitations and imperfections are just another kind of experience."

When asked how other therapists might take a lesson from what she's learned about accessing greater creativity in her work,

McWilliams admitted she was speechless. "It's odd, because I've spent my whole teaching career trying to encourage therapists to find their own unique creativity and not necessarily go by the book. What I often tell beginners is that they already know enough to be good therapists if they are loving people. Most of those who are attracted to this profession have pretty big hearts, and if they're genuinely curious about other people and want to help them, ultimately that's going to be enough. They're going to make all kinds of mistakes, but that's not necessarily a bad thing; it's not like being a surgeon where, if you make a mistake, disaster ensues. There are few mistakes you make as a therapist that you can't learn something from and even recoup—that is, recover enough to turn them into something positive."

McWilliams believes that veteran therapists have learned to trust themselves a lot more, to take leaps of faith based on intuition and experience. In this era of emphasis on the need for empirical support for our interventions, it is important to note that there is considerable empirical evidence that it is the relationship that matters most. "Our clients will forgive all kinds of mistakes, except mistakes of the heart. That is when they sense we don't really care about them, that we aren't really interested in them but we're just filling the hour and protecting ourselves. Clients will forgive almost anything except disrespect."

For beginners and experienced therapists alike, McWilliams feels strongly that it is our own therapy as clients that opens the doors to innovation. "I think my own creativity came very much out of my own therapy, where I had learned to listen to parts of myself that I had closed off for various reasons. When I'm sitting with a patient, I often hear a song going through my head, and, if I listen to the lyrics of the song in the back of my mind, I'm often aware of a kind of an undercurrent theme about me and the patient that I wasn't aware of. In my training, I try to help therapists to relax and listen more to what's coming in from their own, less conscious parts."

CHAPTER 17

Nick Cummings: A Narrative History of Creativity in Action

Nick Cummings sees creativity, in its grandest sense, as far more than aesthetic expression; he sees it as an epiphany that leads to macrochange. That has been the hallmark of his own professional life, a story that begins in his childhood.

First, a Bit of History

When Cummings first showed up for kindergarten, he couldn't speak English. His family spoke Greek at home, a language that had allowed him to communicate with anyone he had cared to, at least until this point. All of a sudden, he was faced with radically different rules. This was a time during the 1920s when new immigrants were expected to adapt quickly, and here was this kid who was perceived by his teacher as just stubborn because he wouldn't fit in. He was beaten frequently for refusing (actually, he was unable) to speak English when he was asked questions. The school authorities had the boy tested by a psychologist and concluded he must be retarded.

A social worker showed up at the Cummings home with papers to sign at the behest of the school system. They had decided to send the boy to a special school for mentally retarded children and needed parental permission. Nick's father had died when he was four, so his widowed mother was left trying to make sense of the documents. Fortunately, an uncle showed up at this time and was able to figure out what they were trying to do and what a colossal mistake this would be.

It turned out that once Cummings learned English in the next few months, it was indeed agreed that he belonged in a special school, but one for the gifted. Unfortunately, his problems were hardly over.

When he was nine, Cummings was one of thousands of children who were victims of the 1933 polio epidemic. He was left paralyzed and told that he would never walk again; the doctors said that the nerve damage was permanent and irrevocable. Yet one nurse working with the family believed that regular exercise and stimulation could restore the neurological connections in the spine; at the very least, it couldn't hurt. Cummings's grandmother decided to make it her mission to teach her grandson to walk again. She made him crawl on his belly, ride a bike with support, and even walk on his unstable hips. Every time he fell, she would shame him into getting up and trying again, over and over until he was too exhausted to move. After three years of this torturous regiment, Cummings was riding his bike 50 miles.

Again, Cummings digressed from his story to mention his skepticism toward so-called authorities. Experts had labeled him retarded, then as a hopeless medical case, yet through force of his will (plus lots of family support) he proved them wrong. This has led to lifelong mistrust of established scientific conclusions, an attitude that has served him well in his own creative breakthroughs.

Psychology didn't yet exist as a profession to any degree during the time that Cummings entered the field as a World War II veteran. His teachers were the early learning theorists, such as B. F. Skinner, Clark Hull, and Kenneth Spence. Psychoanalysis was then the dominant theory in psychotherapy, so he began analytic training, which was the thing to do during the 1940s. After graduation, he moved to San Francisco and launched his own practice as a psychoanalyst.

After a year of practice, Cummings had calculated that seeing patients four times a week for an average of seven years, he'd be lucky to help 100 people in his lifetime. He found this idea appalling, but consistent with his view of the archaic ways that medicine and psychology had been practiced. Science was advancing, yet he believed that clinical professions were not applying what was learned in their practices. This led him to begin questioning the established norms of his life's work. What was so sacrosanct about the 50-minute hour? Why must patients be seen so often and for so long a period of time? Couldn't some clients be helped in 15-minute sessions, whereas for others three hours at a time might be more appropriate? And why must change take so long and require such labor-intensive services?

About the time these ideas were percolating in his head, Kaiser Permanente Health Care was searching for a chief psychologist. One condition of his employment was that the company could fire him for any reason, at any time, without disclosing a reason. Cummings took that as a personal challenge.

The Couches Are Taken Away

Cummings's patients at Kaiser were nothing like those he had treated during his brief stint as an analyst in private practice. They were bus drivers, plumbers, maids, and other working-class folks with debilitating symptoms and little interest in mining the past. At first, he was frustrated because they wouldn't lie on the analytic couches in the office; they preferred to sit, even with no back support. Even more peculiar, they insisted on facing him directly as if they were having a normal conversation.

Cummings remembers one patient who had managed to exhaust all 34 orthopedic surgeons in the system before they gave up and told him that the problems were in his head, not his back, and he needed to see a shrink.

When he arrived at the office, the patient was puzzled because there was no place for him to sit near the doctor's desk, just a couch in the middle of the room.

"Please lie down there," Cummings directed him, seeing the confusion on his face.

The patient shrugged and sat down with his feet firmly on the floor. "Hey Doc," he said, "how are you going to examine my back if I'm laying on it?"

"Well," Cumming hesitated, "I'm not going to examine your back. We're just going to talk."

"Oh yeah?" The patient then grabbed a chair on the other side of the office and pushed it into a position opposite that of Cummings's chair. He arranged it to his satisfaction, the perfect angle and distance, then settled himself comfortably.

This was a moment of epiphany for Cummings. It now seemed ridiculous that he had been seeing his patients by having them talk while lying on a couch facing away from him. Although his immediate predecessor as chief psychologist had been the notorious Timothy Leary, a maverick in his own right who experimented with LSD in therapy later in his career, nothing had prepared the staff for what their new supervisor was going to issue as his next orders: Cummings called everyone together and announced that henceforth all the couches would be given away, replaced by chairs for the patients to sit in—face-to-face with their therapists.

We Started Listening

Among the notable mentors who worked with Cummings was his training analyst, Erik Erikson, one of the great theorists of the twentieth century, who constructed the stages of psychosocial development. Cummings had been in analysis for 10 months, four days each week, when Erikson abruptly announced in a session, "Two more months and then we terminate."

"Am I flunking?" Cummings asked, a bit surprised by the premature ending.

"No," Erikson said with a smile. "Actually, you're doing quite well."

"So what's the problem?"

"No problem. I'm just concerned that if we continue together you're going to become a very prominent and successful psychoanalyst—who will be insufferable."

Cummings wasn't sure whether that was a complement or not, so he just nodded.

"But," Erikson continued, "if we quit now before we ruin you, you'll spend the rest of your life as an innovator, challenging the status quo."

"How do you know that, Mr. Erikson?" Cummings asked, still uncertain what he was hearing. He was careful to address his analyst by this preferred title, because the great man didn't have a college degree, much less a Ph.D. or an M.D. He had been a watercolorist in the South of France when Anna Freud discovered him, painting on the beach. She had been amazed by all the children standing around him, playing within his sphere, even with the enticement of the water. There was something about Erikson that she immediately recognized as extraordinary in the way children gravitated toward him. Freud invited him to come to London to train as a child analyst. Since his paintings weren't selling, he figured he had nothing to lose.

Cummings was reminded of this story that Erikson had once told him, appreciating once again that this very nontraditional analyst was so direct and honest with him. Still, he was more than a little put off by his mentor's directive that the analysis would end so quickly.

"How will I find another training analyst?" Cummings pleaded. "You can't just let me go like this. I'm not ready. Besides, people will think I flunked out or something."

"That's your privilege," Erikson responded enigmatically, "but the blood won't be on my hands."

They spent the last two months of their sessions arguing, sometimes to the point that Cummings would become so frustrated he would get up off the couch and face his mentor. Erikson thought this was hilarious and said it was further evidence that his protégé was just not cut out for this style of work.

Cummings recalled this conversation when he decided to discard all the analytic couches on the unit; he had them picked up by a charity to distribute to needy families. The result of this rather impulsive, dramatic gesture is that Cummings and his staff now began listening to their patients in ways they never before had. Furthermore, they were discovering that they could help people in a matter of months rather than years, even if they saw them just one time per week. This may not sound unusual in today's climate of brief therapy, but this was pretty radical stuff for the 1950s.

Cummings and his team began experimenting with particular therapy interventions that seemed better suited to their working-class population, who exhibited sometimes severe disturbances. They were systematic and empirically based in their approach, developing a standardized method, applying it to 100 cases, then sharpening different variables one at a time until they settled on a treatment that produced observable, measurable results within defined time parameters. Since they were operating in a hospital setting, it made sense to follow the validation process of any new medical procedure. Over the next 20 years, Cummings and his team at Kaiser developed one of the very first brief therapy regimens, which was employed in all 39 of Kaiser's medical centers and involved over 350 psychologists.

Because of his success in developing a brief treatment regimen, Cummings was recruited by Ted Kennedy to serve on the Senate health care committee during a time when it seemed as though universal health care was just over the horizon. Unfortunately, a change in administration boded that soon health care was going to be treated as just another business.

Cummings, involved in the political debates going on at the time, warned the therapy profession that the dismantling of the mental health system would lead eventually to its industrialization. In a series of national speeches and articles, he advocated a survival strategy that became the forerunner of managed care. He formed a company, American Biodyne, to implement his new vision of the future of psychotherapy—a model that was brief, empirically supported, and responsive to the needs of everyday people. Twenty years later, Cummings was the largest employer of psychologists in the country, a group treating 25 million patients.

Struggle for Survival

One of the goals Cummings advocated for his organization was to cut down on the number of psychiatric hospitalizations, as well as on the length of stay. Usually, when a mentally disturbed patient showed up at 2:00 a.m. in an emergency room, he or she would be routinely hospitalized until a psychiatrist could conduct an examination the next day. The patient would thus often end up in the psychiatric unit for the next eight hours, by which time he or she would be even more agitated by the exposure to such a crazy place with people who acted bizarrely. Before too long, that patient would be out of control as well, which could lead to a hospital stay of a month or longer.

Cummings implemented a new procedure such that whenever a patient showed up at the emergency room, regardless of the time of day, a psychologist would be dispatched to the scene, often within 15 minutes. Outpatient therapy would begin immediately, and 95 percent of the time this was sufficient to send the person home to get some rest in his or her own home and then return the next day for treatment, perhaps then followed by daily treatment for a week or longer, but usually without requiring hospitalization.

Cummings believes that therapists have been among the last professionals to recognize that we are running a business—and that until we focus more on efficiency and accountability we will remain the stepchild of the health care system. Dentists, doctors, even nurse practitioners are required to have business courses as part of their training; only therapists neglect to do so.

Cummings ended our conversation by stating that creativity in therapy will always be hampered until clinicians wake up to the realities of the health care system today. Therapists are now working longer hours for lower compensation. There are fewer referrals. He believes that until we start thinking outside of the box, we are destined to struggle and find ourselves dissatisfied and frustrated. Creativity in therapy is no longer a luxury; it is imperative for the survival of our profession.

CHAPTER 18

Alfonso Montuori: Creative Inquiry and Discovering the Unforeseen

Alfonso Montuori teaches creativity to doctoral students who are engaged in research and/or clinical work and, in addition, consults with artists and corporate executives about creativity and innovation. He envisions creativity as the center of professional and personal development around which everything else is organized. In his work as a consultant and administrator, his focus is on creating a context in which individuals can access their own creative process.

Self-Actualizing Creativity

Montuori's parents were both diplomats, his father Italian and his mother Dutch. The family lived in Beirut until Alfonso was five, after which they moved to Greece, where he attended an Italian elementary school, and then to London, where he attended high school and university. In his English private school, he was subjected to Latin, which he found intolerably boring. "I wondered why Latin had to be so dull and was told by the teacher that this was just the way it was. I had been very lucky in Greece, where my headmaster was a wizard who could turn topics that were extremely tedious into wonderful games and explorations, so I knew nothing *had* to be intrinsically boring. At that point, I realized my English teacher was not talking about Latin at all but about himself, his way of seeing Latin, the world, and his own limitations. This increased my awareness that our understanding of the world can be constructed in many different ways, whether culturally or individually, and it was therefore possible to challenge what was taken as 'given' and create more generative, fun, and caring ways of being in the world."

After living in so many different cultures and being exposed to so many different ideas at an early age, Montuori began his lifelong quest for what he calls "creative inquiry," which he defines as the exploration of creativity and the creativity of exploration. Traditional education seemed to focus on "knowing" through the acquisition of information, theoretical frameworks, skills, and practices that provided answers and solutions. Unfortunately, in the process it devalued and often killed off precisely the "not knowing," the mystery that motivates us to be creative. Once we think we *know*, we cease real inquiry. Schooling tells us to learn what is already known and feed it back in one and only one way. We risk being boxed into frameworks that may provide us with answers, but can also become foundational givens and thus shut off the creation of alternatives and other ways of being in the world. As Montuori articulates it, "Creative inquiry does not reject traditional education and the value of knowing. But it also emphasizes that if we dig a little deeper, we see the immensity of not knowing, including all the 'Big Questions,' and even the things we think we do know are merely gallant creative constructions we use to make sense of a complex, fundamentally mysterious world. Creative inquiry is a frame that sees the world as a creative process, our understanding of the world as a creative process, and invites us to explore this creativity rather than accept what is given and immediately look for a solution or fix. Problem solving is necessary, of course, but not at the expense of opportunity finding!"

In graduate school, Montuori became particularly interested in the ways in which theoretical frames determined how topics were understood and approached. He saw, for instance, that the popular discourse about creativity emphasized *individual* initiative, often ignoring group, social, and cultural influences. After spending several years as a professional musician, Montuori was perplexed that in the mainstream discourse on creativity there was hardly any research on creative groups. He didn't find a single research article on a creative band, for instance.

He was intrigued by how creativity was framed in different disciplines. Whereas psychologists focused exclusively on the individual and ignored just about everything else, sociologists took a very different approach. For them, social factors were central, and the individual was just a vehicle for ideas that were "in the air." For example, sociologists have argued that Charles Darwin and Alfred Russell Wallace developed a theory of evolution at the same time, so the idea would ultimately have emerged regardless of who proposed it. Likewise, Sigmund Freud's theories were certainly novel and innovative, but if he had not published the ideas, then someone else would have come along and done so. Here were two very different perspectives on creativity, with very different emphases, different assumptions, and working almost entirely independently of each other. And clearly, psychology dominated the popular discourse of creativity, because in the popular imagination, creativity was entirely about the individual!

But Montuori's approach to creativity has been transdisciplinary, stressing what is relevant to the issue at hand, focusing on a constant creative interplay between theoretical frameworks and actual experience rather than on any form of theoretical or disciplinary purity. It has also focused on uncovering how different frameworks—which, after all, are themselves creations and the result of creative processes—construct their subject matter and shed light on it in different ways. In other words, how do we relate our understanding of creativity, or of disciplinary or therapeutic orientations, to specific issues? And how do these frameworks in turn create both possibilities and constraints, illuminating one aspect of a subject while obscuring others?

Montuori also came to realize that the creative process is full of paradox, bringing together disparate items that are normally considered separate from one another. For instance, many people are so afraid that if they imitate their mentors, they will lose their own individual voice. "Yet," Montuori mentions, "Charlie Parker, one of the greatest innovators of jazz, learned all of Lester Young's solos by heart, and he certainly developed his own unique voice." Creativity involves imitation and novelty, tradition and innovation, rigor and imagination, head and heart, knowing and not knowing, learning and unlearning. This helped him to conceptualize graduate education and personal development as a process of *self-creation* that emerges when we see these polarities as sources of creativity rather than as mutually exclusive oppositions. "I don't think of education or therapy or coaching or consulting as separate—I see them all as a process of creative inquiry, an investigation of how we create our understanding of self and world, and how we can create alternatives."

Creative inquiry is not just about what you know. It is also about how you know what you know, who we are as inquirers, the choices we have made and can make, and who we can be. Our most fundamental choices become an opportunity for self-inquiry. Why does a person gravitate to one subject or research topic over another? Why is one road taken rather than another? Why choose this spouse or that town or this job or that philosophical or therapeutic orientation? And who is the student or clinician becoming during this process of inquiry? What and how and why are we creating?

"One of the things that always troubled me about the conventional attitude to creativity," Montuori explained, "is that there seemed to be an excessive focus on how to become more creative by using tools like lateral thinking. But I don't think of creativity as this external thing that is generated by techniques; I think it's more useful to view it as the essential nature of who we are. The role of the educator or therapist or consultant then involves assisting individuals and organizations in unblocking all the various ways in which our natural creativity is prevented from flowing. And that is itself a creative process."

Creativity is often blocked by teachers and supervisors who focus on what you are doing wrong and admonishing you to avoid taking risks. Students and therapists start out eager and passionate about their work and then are forced to conform to established norms and rules that stifle any kind of innovation and make us lose touch with our passion. We are expected to reproduce what our teachers tell us to do rather than participating actively in the creation of new knowledge and practice. In this process, we take these norms and rules as the "right" way and lose touch with the fact that they are also creations and that other creative possibilities abound.

Montuori often hears people say that they just aren't very creative (we, too, have heard that a lot from a number of theorists we contacted for this project), but when he digs deeper into their assumptions about what that means, he hears a lot of self-limiting beliefs. "Some people confuse creativity with being artistic. I know a lot of very creative people who beat themselves up because they think they're not creative. In fact, they are creative leaders, organizers, academics, or therapists. They just don't think of their areas of expertise as being ones where creativity lives, and that's partly a function of the fact that our society has a very limited and distorted view of creativity. But when we mask our own creative contribution and feel we've *discovered* a theory or an approach rather than *invented* or created it, we also run the risk of thinking 'this is it!' and, paradoxically, can become very invested in our 'right' approach (because it's 'real'), therefore become ossified and closed to alternatives.

"I always find that asking people about creativity is fascinating—there are so many revealing assumptions that emerge almost immediately. Creativity offers a remarkable entry point into personal change, because what people tell us about creativity says a lot about who they are, how they view the process of creation and self-creation, where they create limitations and boundaries, and also where there may be opportunities for transformation. The process of creative inquiry itself can be transformative, as individuals begin to explore the way in which they have created themselves and their way of being in the world and begin to find alternatives."

Montuori has enjoyed asking people over the years who they consider to be creative role models. Baby boomers frequently name "eminent creatives" such as Einstein, Picasso, and Freud, but younger people tend to name "everyday creatives" such as friends and family members. While giving a lecture to a group of undergraduate art students at a major Midwestern university, he asked this question, and not one person mentioned a sculptor or painter. One student mentioned C. M. Punk, a World Wrestling Federation champion, after which the professor's face began to turn white, as if she were going to pass out. Another student mentioned his cousin, Fred, who could do amazing things in figuring out video games. Montuori sees this change in creative role models as further evidence we are evolving into a postmodern, MySpace world. But people of every generation have unexamined assumptions about creativity that can be unpacked in very revealing ways.

Many assumptions about creativity need to be deconstructed, that is, examined in such a way as to loosen their hold and open up a greater range of possibilities and choices. Montuori sees creativity as a process in which people create themselves, where the person is the creative product. "Creativity is really another way of saying that our experience of what we call reality is not given, but a creative construction. We co-create that 'reality' construction but are largely unaware of it. We are engaged in a creative process of reality construction all the time, and so we might as well increase our range of choices and enjoy the process so as to live and act in the most aesthetic, caring, loving, funny, smart, and entertaining way possible."

Montuori likes to help students and professionals to focus on something that ordinarily they have framed as tedious and even insignificant. For researchers, this might mean reading and reviewing the existing literature to capture the essence of prior studies before developing their own project. One reason for their reluctance to undertake such a mundane task is the assumption that they are merely supposed to report what others have said. They often think of this as list making that is neither exciting nor engaging; it is just something that they are required to do in order to prove they know what others have done so they can justify what they really want to do themselves.

Montuori prefers to frame this process as the means by which you "situate yourself among your people. These are the people who, like you, care deeply about the subject you have chosen. Think of them as your ancestors. Some of them are long dead, and some may have even been killed for having an interest in or opinion about this subject. They are your colleagues, your people. One very bright student put it very nicely when she told me the literature review gave her the grounding that allowed her to explore her more unusual ideas. She felt she was freer to explore knowing she had a history and community of like-minded people she could draw on when she felt lost, anxious, or confused.

"Rather than writing a literature review as an 'outsider,' I ask my students to write it as a 'participant' in the community. And we mustn't forget that even though we may not be aware of it, we are deeply influenced by our predecessors. Situating ourselves in the literature is also a great way of uncovering our own implicit assumptions about our chosen field and how we approach it. Somebody who wants to be a therapist may never have read Freud, for instance, but you can be sure that when they talk about therapy, they're drawing on a history of thought and using language and concepts whose origins they most likely don't know. Even though they don't think they are part of a larger history, it's important they understand that they are not blank slates, but deeply influenced by their cultural context that informs their assumptions about the field. And, of course, the fact that they want to be a therapist in the first place would not be possible if there had not been men and women who created the field and profession of 'therapist.'"

Montuori immediately gets his students to really participate in their new community. "I have my doctoral students write a publishable book review and submit it to a journal. Most get published, and before you know it, the community knows who they are, because you can bet your bottom dollar academics will read reviews of their work! So, at that point, they're not just doing some exercise for their teacher. Now they have an audience, and the audience will likely include the very people they're reading and writing about. This gives them a completely different attitude toward their work. They stop being 'students' and begin to see themselves as engaged in creative inquiry."

This is but one example of the ways that Montuori likes to make even the most mundane tasks come alive and spark creative engagement. Again, he is emphasizing breakthroughs as the result of a different frame that does not see creativity as something confined to a few individual geniuses or a few fleeting moments of insight, but as the very nature of who we are. "We normally think of creativity as a gift we receive once in a while if the muses are in the mood. But I believe creativity is there all the time, waiting for us to get out of our own way."

Improvisation

Montuori believes that asking yourself what you feel most passionate about is central to creativity. "Very often, it's only after a lot of dialogue and a lot of trust building that students will confess what they *really* would like to do with their dissertation or with a particular client, but they 'know' that's not possible. And of course that's the breakthrough. It comes about because an environment has been created where the student feels it's okay to get in touch with and express her or his real (and sometimes long-forgotten) passion and challenge their assumptions about what is and is not possible and their often self-imposed limitations."

In his own life, Montuori didn't start to enjoy school until he was in graduate training. That is when he felt enough freedom to begin exploring his own interests and when he was allowed to do more than just regurgitate what he had learned before. Pluralism had always been a big theme in his life because he has lived in so many countries and attended so many different schools: It taught him to engage complexity and paradox as well as to appreciate what can emerge with patience and perseverance. Once he can get past the confusion, frustration, and fatigue, he often finds that he is able to break through to a different and unusual perspective. "Dealing with complex and ambiguous situations, there's a tendency to want premature closure, to get an answer, a solution, and get it over with. It's stressful not to know what's going on, not know what to do, and to stick with that not knowing. But you just have to stay with it, not give in to the need to be in control, allow for periods of not knowing, and navigate the turbulence for a while."

Being a professional musician earlier in life prepared Montuori for the demands of improvisation. He points out that the word *improvisation* can be traced back to the Latin *improvisus*, meaning "unforeseen," that which is not part of daily life, that which is not anticipated. Formal education prepared him only for preexisting situations, but it was improvisational jazz that helped him deal with the unexpected.

"In classical music," Montuori explained, "there's a score, and you play the notes, and it's all there—you can't deviate from what has been written. Anything unforeseen is, by definition, wrong. In jazz, however, the unforeseen is actually embraced. Jazz is therefore sometimes called 'the sound of surprise.' The idea is to create something new and aesthetically satisfying in the context of an existing song, perhaps a standard like 'Our Love Is Here to Stay.' It's a very different view of the world: not a focus on absolute order, but rather on the continuous and delightful interplay of known and unknown, order and disorder. I think so much of the fundamentalism we see today is the result of a desperate desire to have a universal score, an absolute order that we can all stick to. But as Gregory Bateson said, 'Life is not like that.' In improvisation there is an ongoing process of navigating order and disorder, tradition and innovation, the song form and the new interpretations of that song, soloing and supporting soloists, but there's not a strict formula. That would be anathema! We explore and play together, not certain where exactly it will lead. And creativity is not just about great solos; it's also about being able to create a supportive context that makes the soloist sound good. A good accompaniment can make a soloist shine, but a bad, unsupportive accompaniment makes the whole thing crash. Rather than leading to total chaos, we are able to embrace and actually produce the unforeseen and also create a generative context where we can collaborate and create together. It's a process of collective self-creation, with the music as an emergent property."

As an administrator, Montuori does not want to control everything that's going on. If we want everything to be predictable, nothing new will ever emerge. He would rather open himself (and his organization) to the possibility of each person doing a solo, while ensuring that that everyone is playing the same song. There can be dissonance, counterpoint, rhythmic tension, but ultimately there must be individual and collaborative creativity and a dynamic relationship between predictability and innovation.

Creative Attitudes

In the practice of therapy, we can so easily slip into what is familiar rather than allowing ourselves to improvise in the moment, to create a new metaphor, intervention, or explanation that may not have ever been tried before. As enlightening and inspirational as the individuals and cases in this book may be, there is a tendency (especially for beginners) to think, "This is all very well that these famous therapists can do these amazingly innovative things, but they will never be within my grasp. I can learn them. I can apply them the way they did. But I'll never be that creative myself." Actually, nothing could be further from the truth: Each of us has the capacity to be more improvisational in what we do, inventing our own riffs that are variations of other themes. Rather than imposing preexisting melodies or structures, we can allow the music we make together to emerge through dialogue and inquiry.

Montuori has heard the complaint from beginners all the time that they are not geniuses and will never be a Milton Erickson, Virginia Satir, Fritz Perls, or Carl Whitaker, much less a poet like Sylvia Plath or Emily Dickinson, a painter like Georgia O'Keefe or Auguste Renoir, a musician like John Coltrane or Miles Davis, a writer like Ernest Hemingway or Virginia Woolf, or a performer like George Carlin or Chris Rock. Reading stories about creative breakthroughs is humbling and often discouraging and can lead to the conclusion that famous people are supernatural, or at least superhuman, acting in ways that are beyond the scope of mortal beings. Clearly, some people are born with extraordinary talent in certain areas. But we can *all* tap into our natural creativity.

Montuori suggests that along with a deconstruction of our limiting assumptions about creativity's who, what, where, and when, we can also engage in what he calls a "re-cognition" of the creativity and improvisation we engage in on a daily basis. "Many people I talk with tell me that they're just not creative, and they certainly never improvise—in fact, they mostly don't even know what improvisation is. I have to remind them that the very conversation we're having is an improvisation on a theme called 'What is this thing called improvisation?' As they understand the nature and practice of improvisation, they become aware of what they're already doing and, reframing it, they begin to pay attention to pockets of freedom, open spaces they didn't see before. It's all about increasing the number of choices."

CHAPTER 19

Some Creative Themes

You have no doubt reflected on some of the cases within this book, wondering about the appropriateness (if not the sanity) of the therapist to introduce such radical interventions. Certainly, many of us who are somewhat more traditional and conventional in our work might find it difficult to do some of the things that are described (having a deer head write letters, telling a client to watch a sunset between two spoons, asking a client to build a box to climb into, etc.).

It is sometimes difficult to assess when advancement in any discipline is considered to be a creative leap or a symptom of derangement. Before the likes of Sigmund Freud, Karl Marx, Charles Darwin, Galileo, or Albert Einstein were ever hailed as geniuses they were first marginalized as charlatans. Yet others, such as Anton Mesmer, with his views of "animal magnetism," were considered breakthroughs during their lifetimes only to be discredited soon afterward.

It was Freud who first introduced the rather crazy idea that people could cure themselves of mental afflictions by lying on a couch and spilling the contents of their consciousness into thin air. Now we think of this method as not only normal, but even obsolete and way too conservative. It was the same with Carl Rogers, who constructed rather unusual conversations in which he focused only on reflecting feelings, and Fritz Perls, who instructed people to talk to an empty chair (Zeig, 2008).

Historical Legacies

Some of our field's most creative mavericks (Fritz Perls, Carl Whitaker, Salvador Minuchin, Jacques Lacan, Milton Erickson) could just as easily have been viewed as crazy or foolish. There are hundreds of stories circulating about some of the wild things they did with their clients, many of them carefully documented, others that have grown into legends:

- In response to his students' request for supervision, Erickson sent one of them (Lankton) out into the desert to find a tree and enlisted another (O'Hanlon) to become his gardener. He also asked one of his female clients to undress in front of him to overcome her modesty and poor body image.
- Minuchin asked a mother to arm-wrestle her child to show who was stronger.
- Psychoanalyst Jacques Lacan was known to abruptly dismiss clients after just a few minutes in the session if he found them boring or reticent.
- Whitaker fell asleep during a session to display his boredom (or perhaps fatigue). He also had clients sit on his lap while he "breast-fed" them milk from a baby bottle.
- When a client of Perls complained that he couldn't feel anything, Perls (allegedly) slapped him in the face, asking if he could feel *that*. In another incident, Perls wrestled a resistant group member to the ground and pinned her to demonstrate that she shouldn't defy him.
- Psychoanalyst John Rosen joined his clients in their madness in order to push them out of insanity. When an institutional-

ized schizophrenic claimed to be the Pope, Rosen called a taxi to take him to the airport since he obviously belonged in the Vatican rather than a hospital.

- William Glasser adopted a depressed, lonely client into his family, inviting the man to join them for holiday functions for many years thereafter.
- Ralph Greenson, founder of the Los Angeles Psychoanalytic Society, psychiatrist to Hollywood celebrities, and therapist to Marilyn Monroe, demanded that his patient move into a house around the block from him so she would have easier access for twice-daily sessions (as well as to run errands for his wife).
- Albert Ellis conducted weekly public therapy sessions onstage at his institute for many decades, challenging his audience: "I'll cure any fucking nut in this city for five bucks!" He would frequently attempt to do so by singing songs with them, including the standards, "Whine! Whine! Whine!" and "Maybe I'll Move My Ass."

What often separates interventions that are creative from those that are downright ridiculous, if not dangerous, is how they are received by the client. If the therapist does something innovative or experimental and the client storms out of the room or files a grievance with the licensing board, then it may not be considered creative as much as ill-advised. There is thus an evaluative judgment made *after* the behavior to determine its relative effects.

This is only one of the many neglected aspects of creative innovation that often masks or discourages the willingness of practitioners to reach beyond their comfort levels. There are other myths that are often perpetuated (Sawyer, 2006), disguising the reality that most creativity is collaborative rather than initiated by a single person. It is often improvised rather than planned and emerges unpredictably from interactions that take place between people. It is the process that *is* the creative product.

What It Takes to Be More Creative as a Therapist

Several significant themes from the stories in this book have stood out to us, and perhaps to you as well. Given the incredible diversity of training backgrounds, clinical settings, theoretical orientations, cultural differences, geographical settings, and personalities of our contributors, it is indeed challenging to find the common factors in their experiences. Yet that was our goal from the very beginning of this project—to discover and describe what is common in creative breakthroughs, regardless of differences in style and orientation.

Thousands of books and many more thousands of research studies have focused on the creative process, obviating the need to highlight the same themes that have been identified earlier. Some of the cases in this book underscore what has been known previously—that creativity is more likely to happen when professionals adopt multiple viewpoints when looking at a problem or that the most interesting breakthroughs occur during spontaneous moments that are recognized and acted on. Yet many of the themes that emerged are somewhat unique to therapeutic practice, considering the special and unique character of this relationship and goals.

Here are some of the things that struck us as most significant. In the following chapter, we look at the ways that these themes may be applied to clinical work.

Admitting That You're Lost

Before you are willing to try something new, perhaps something that you've never tried before, first you have to be willing to acknowledge that what you've already been doing isn't working. Innovation often arises from the recognition that existing options aren't sufficient to get the job done.

In the introduction to the book we discussed the idea that being/feeling lost in dealing with a case or client is not only a normal occurrence, but also a requirement in order to initiate creative breakthroughs. Unless you admit that you have exhausted what you already know, there's little incentive to delve into new territory.

This task is made all the more difficult because everyone—most of all our clients—have such high expectations that we know what is going on at all times, that we are operating with a clear, focused template, and that we have a definitive diagnosis and proven treatment plan with a series of discrete, progressive steps that are guaranteed to produce success. We aren't saying that sometimes this doesn't happen, but just as often we are operating by the seat of the pants—and this *can* be a good thing.

Over the years we have undertaken many projects that involved collecting stories of eminent therapists describing their best, most miraculous work (see Kottler & Carlson, 2003, 2006, 2007, 2008). Just as in this book, they are tales that can seem beyond the capability of mortal therapists. Yet they represent just one case out of thousands in their caseloads. Sure, they demonstrate a high degree of brilliance and creativity, as well as clinical sensitivity, but they also reinforce the idea that there are usually happy endings. Even in the one book we did about "bad therapy" and failures (Kottler & Carlson, 2002), there is still an implicit message that ultimately, even though the therapists initially felt lost, they nonetheless found their way back to solid ground.

Accumulatively, reading about success cases all the time, seeing masters on video demonstrate their wizardry, and hearing about colleagues who do such remarkable things can only make us feel more insecure and limited. It is one of the secrets of our profession that even the most confident among us have significant bouts of doubt about what we are doing and how we are doing it.

Creative breakthroughs begin once we surrender to the feeling of being lost, of not knowing, of not understanding, and teaching our clients that this is not only acceptable but also desirable in the initial phase of innovation.

Challenging Conventional Wisdom

By definition, breakthroughs take place through *un*conventional thinking. Creativity occurs when you are not limited by your preferred theory or framework but are willing to work outside of those usual bounds (Carson & Becker, 2003). This is far more likely to unfold during those times when you begin thinking outside of what is usually considered appropriate norms yet still within the boundaries of ethical practice, meaning that what we are doing is not harmful, exploitive, or disrespectful.

Alfonso Montuori (Chapter 18) talked about how creativity can be best accessed once we surrender being disciples of particular approaches and start being ourselves. He advocated for greater authenticity and genuineness in the ways we present ourselves to clients instead of fitting a mold of the way we are supposed to be. This allows us to develop a "created attitude" that gives us greater permission to color outside the lines.

Throughout the history of our field, there have been individuals who have asked themselves difficult questions, which can be summarized as follows: "Why are we doing things this way?" Jacques Lacan wondered what was so magical about the 50-minute hour and why sessions weren't scheduled according to client needs instead of therapist convenience. Likewise, Albert Ellis began experimenting with 25-minute sessions because he found that clients could work within whatever time was available. Of course, clinical experimentation must be subjected to the rigor of scientific research to test these assumptions.

It is thus a fine line we walk to stay within acceptable professional standards while also exploring new ways of operating that may not yet be considered mainstream. So many of the stories in this book involve doing things that would be viewed as more than a little unconventional. Noted figures in the field may have more latitude in this regard. They are already viewed as leaders and sometimes eccentric, so they can perhaps get away with things that might prove troublesome for others of us. More than a few times, I (Jeffrey) have returned from workshops with the likes of Virginia Satir, Albert Ellis, and other creative mavericks, only to discover that when I tried to replicate what they did with my own clients, I was laughed off my chair. We each must find our own way, our own voice, our own style, and be true to our own cherished convictions.

Entering the Zone

Creative action is more likely to take place when you join that place of curious flow (Csikszentmihalyi, 1996). Therapists who are most creative are those who can become totally engaged in the moment, losing themselves completely in the therapeutic engagement. Without conscious thought or effort, new solutions and methods emerge. That was the case with Fred Bemak's stories (Chapter 15), in which he felt totally lost about what to do and how to proceed, so he redoubled his effort to remain as present as possible and use whatever he could find to make a connection. This was also a theme for Brad Keeney (Chapter 3); when we asked him how on earth he thought to use a deer head as the vehicle to "join together" the family, he said it was the thing that was most present in the room. Laura Brown (Chapter 11), as well, paid attention to internal images that emerged when she felt stuck. Although describing herself as a rather conventional therapist, she literally thought "outside the box" to initiate a breakthrough with her client. It all began by forcing herself to remain more present with her client in order to access intuitive inspiration.

Cognitive Flexibility

In other words, creativity involves a certain willingness to consider a variety of choices in a situation rather than becoming focused on only one—perhaps the most obvious or familiar. This means approaching any situation or challenge from multiple perspectives, functioning as (1) a novelist in paying attention to details that would escape those less observant, (2) an artist in finding inspiration from ordinary stimuli that would often be ignored, and (3) a scientist in systematically testing ideas to note their effect, as well as making conceptual leaps into new domains. Berring (2008) brings these elements together in describing the way creative breakthroughs occur in experimental psychology, in which the scientist gets an idea from ordinary experience that is then empirically tested in a controlled study. In a sense, this is what we often do in therapy when events and ideas occur during daily life (or even in dreams) that spawn new interventions to try in sessions. He mentions the case of Gordon Gallup, who, in the 1970s, was shaving in front of a mirror when he accidently cut himself. He instinctively reached out to blot the blood on his face rather than on the mirror image (as most any human would) and realized in a moment of revelation that this would be an excellent way to test whether chimpanzees really do differentiate between their likeness in a mirror versus their actual self (they can!).

Mutual Trust in the Relationship

While creativity often arises from desperation, there must be a degree of trust and safety within the helping relationship such that *both* parties can experiment and take risks. There is so much talk about how important it is to help the client to trust the therapist in order to feel safe, but that works both ways. We are more likely to experiment in sessions with those we feel give us the greatest latitude to fail. If things don't work out, it's not that big a deal to try something else. Client and therapist are forgiving of disappointments when they enjoy the freedom to fail.

Judy Jordan (Chapter 9) emphasized the importance of caring and commitment in the client–therapist relationship as her main theme, but others, such as Nancy McWilliams, Sam Gladding, Bob Neimeyer, Steve Madigan, Scott Miller, and Laura Brown, also presented their creative interventions within in the context of a supportive, mutually trusting relationship.

Risk Taking and Courage

Creativity means trying something new, perhaps something that has never been attempted before in this situation. The potential for negative outcomes is high, much more so than if you stick with what is tried and true.

When pressed about how on earth she could possibly come up with such wild and unusual therapeutic interventions, Cloé Madanes just shrugged, saying casually that doing really great therapy requires a degree of courage and risk. The same was true for so many of our other contributors—Steve Lankton or Jeff Zeig or Brad Keeney, or Bill O'Hanlon. They try stuff out and see what happens; if it works out, they keep going; if it doesn't they quickly switch directions and try something out. The crucial dimension, however, as highlighted by Scott Miller (Chapter 7), is making continual adjustments in light of how clients respond to what we're doing.

In the words of painter Henri Matisse, it takes courage to be creative, to venture into the unknown. It always involves some degree of risk for us to try things that we've never done before. Yet so much of what we do is to encourage clients to take constructive risks in their lives, to get outside their comfort zones, to experiment with new behaviors that often will not work out. How can we ask our clients to do that which we are reluctant to do ourselves?

Risks involve asking a client to bring a box into the session (Laura Brown), asking a client to talk about chocolate (Fred Bemak), or making suggestions that may seem off the wall. In fact, Lankton, Zeig, Keeney, Madanes, and O'Hanlon make a point of structuring therapeutic tasks and ordeals that absolutely *don't* make sense; such an approach is seen as an important part of the cure, in that the assignments are ambiguous so that the client creates the meaning from them.

Valuing Individual Differences

Operating on autopilot makes it difficult to be very innovative, especially if you are following a template or set or procedures that are overly familiar. Creativity is more easily discovered when you are seeing a client and session as totally unique. It is also enhanced when you play to your own strengths, especially considering that innovation can be manifested in at least seven different ways, meaning that it can be expressed through verbal, aesthetic, spatial, or other forms (Gardner, 1993).

The more experience we have, the more clients we've seen, the more hours we've logged in sessions, the greater is the temptation to see any individual client or case as similar to others we have encountered. You can even hear clinicians talk about their clients in stereotypical terms: "I've got a borderline I'm seeing." "A bulimic is scheduled for 2:00 p.m." The more work we've done, the easier it is to see new clients or situations as being the same as what we've seen before. This is in contrast to the "beginner's mind," when every situation seems new and fresh.

The challenge is to view each client, and each clinical situation, with this beginner's mind-set, one that pretends that we've never encountered anything quite like what is now before us (and we haven't!). Once you go into automatic mode, kicking in your standard treatments and usual procedures for any given problem, you lose the opportunity for innovation. In many such cases, implementing proven effective strategies might simply be the best option to produce satisfactory results.

Cross-Disciplinary Synthesis

Creative innovation often arises from synthesis of existing knowledge in order to move into new domains. This doesn't mean only within the fields of counseling and therapy, but rather bringing together ideas from a variety of disciplines.

Freud was able to create a new vision for the profession of therapy by combining his vast knowledge of neurology, archaeology, and literature. Rollo May introduced existential therapy to North America by synthesizing philosophy, literature, and art into a meaning-making perspective. The same could be said for many other of our field's most creative thinkers—they borrowed and fused ideas from a range of other disciplines. Creativity is thus considered a process that is both a generalized form of original thinking and domain-specific, requiring specialized knowledge and expertise in a particular context (Lubart & Guignard, 2004).

Encouraging Expressiveness in Multiple Modalities

Traditionally speaking, from the time of Freud, psychotherapy and counseling have been labeled as "talking cures." Yet there are clearly limits to what can be done with talk alone if the goal is to inspire and support lasting change. When clients are helped to express themselves through multiple modalities, through art, movement, music, and active assignments outside of sessions, they are engaged creatively on levels that cannot be touched through verbal discussions alone (Beaulieu, 2006; Carson & Becker, 2003; Gladding, 2005, 2008; Kottler, Carlson, & Keeney, 2004; Rosenthal, 2001).

One theme that emerges from these stories is for the therapist to stop sitting there and to do something. They emphasize that if we create the space for change, clients will find what they need. As illustrated in Len Sperry's story, they involve rethinking and relabeling the so-called problem, reframing it in such a way that there is greater possibility for change. This is also a major emphasis in Steve Madigan's work, in that clients (and their therapists) are helped to "restory" the dominant narrative in more hopeful ways.

Humor and Playfulness

This often involves doing what is unexpected and surprising, attempting to shake loose the client's dysfunctional, habitual patterns. Creativity is so often about pursuing novel, unusual, and unconventional ideas, even when they might initially seem ridiculous. Many of the stories contained in this book include a level of shocking clients (think Keeney and Lankton) into new patterns of behavior by turning their predictable worlds upside down. Cloé Madanes, in particular, illustrated in several cases how being professional doesn't necessarily mean being grim and serious. Her whole approach is playful in the sense that it is designed to get people to give up what they're doing that isn't working and try something else. But that's awfully hard to do, because therapists become committed and entrenched into a system or theory, falling in love with a set of techniques and persisting in their use even when they are clearly not effective. It takes a fair degree of lightheartedness to give yourself permission to play around until a breakthrough occurs. That is one thing that Madanes described so well, how she gets people to laugh at themselves and try some very unusual strategies. That begins with not taking herself so seriously.

In so many other ways, people tend to remember things that are radically different from anything they have experienced previously. So often, therapy emphasizes predictable routines (precise time limits, repeated rituals, etc.) over variations on that theme. Just imagine how much more memorable sessions would be if each time a client arrived for an appointment, he or she would find the office arranged and decorated differently.

Embracing Mystery, Confusion, Complexity, and Paradox

As long as things make sense—or you believe they do—there is no incentive to look any deeper or further. Yet therapy encounters, as well as any other change efforts, are really so multifaceted that they defy clear explanations. In spite of the explanations we might offer, much of the time we often have no idea what made the greatest difference in a case. We might have our theories or hypotheses, but the reality is that what happens in any given session, much less in an ongoing relationship, is far too complex to ever understand completely. Once we accept, even embrace, the mystery and confusion surrounding our work, the more we are free to delve into areas that we don't fully comprehend but that nevertheless lead to new insights and growth.

With that paradox in mind, we turn to the final chapter, which tries to sort out some of the confusion and complexity that have been presented in the previous stories and offers some guidance for more creative clinical practice.

CHAPTER 20

CLINICAL APPLICATIONS

It is common in books like this to include a last chapter that provides advice on ways that professionals can become more creative in their work and lives. There is often a list included of 10, 20, or 100 things that people can (and should) do in order to apply what has been presented to infuse greater innovation in their behavior and break out of established molds. This advice is always well intended, and even solidly supported by empirical research. Readers are encouraged to follow their hearts, trust their intuition, foster curiosity, reflect on their failures, think divergently, and be more flexible—all fabulous ideas. The problem, however, is that it isn't as though we don't already know these things. When was the last time you saw such a list, nodded your head, and then promptly went out and actually followed through on the instructions? If change were really that easy, we'd do the same things in therapy—simply provide our clients a list of all the things that we think are good for them and then fully expect them to comply. Alas, it is not that easy or simple.

We could just as easily provide a list of lessons derived from the stories in this book and then tell you to go forth and apply them in your own work. We could offer practical suggestions, many of them supported by research and literature, that if you want to cultivate creativity, you have to practice the skill. That means (1) letting yourself be surprised by something *every day*, (2) surprising *someone else* every day, and (3) writing down, each day, what surprised you and how you surprised others. We're sure you'd agree this is very good advice that probably would lead to more limber creative efforts.

We *could* do that, but it seems rather futile, not to mention that it flies in the face of everything we really have learned from this project. Creativity happens most spontaneously and meaningfully not when it is treated as a muscle that is exercised, but rather as an improvised, playful collaboration *between* people who are intensely engaged in the moment.

Creativity among Mortals

Reading biographies of eminent individuals or reviewing cases of prominent practitioners such as those in this book can lead one to conclude that extraordinarily creative acts belong only to those who are among the most accomplished professionals. You have to be a genius, a superstar, a paradigm shifter, or, at the very least, infused with the qualities associated with creative innovation. Nothing could be further than the truth. In fact, *everyone* has the potential to be more creative in their work and lives—*if* they are sufficiently open to such experiences and motivated to pursue them.

The worst thing that could arise from a study of the cases we have profiled is the belief that you can obtain similar results by imitating them. It is indeed true that many of these stories illustrate the ways that the therapists were following in the footsteps of their mentors, such as Gregory Bateson, Milton Erickson, and others, but they found their own styles in which to express their work. Also keep in mind that the clinicians profiled in this book represent the most creative practitioners on the planet, those we approached specifically because of their track records of innovation. It is hardly fair to compare ourselves to the examples that illustrate the most creative behavior of the most creative people!

Although we consider ourselves to be extremely creative in the ways we work, often pushing ourselves to discover new paths, we are still a bit discouraged and confused by many of the stories in the book. They are certainly intriguing, amusing, and interesting, but the fact of the matter is that most of them are way beyond what we might ever attempt with our clients. Whereas Jon feels free to experiment with many of the strategies in his own extensive practice, soon to be described in this chapter, Jeffrey just can't picture himself putting clients in a box, asking them to hold two spoons on a beach, or having a birthday party for a deer head on the wall. We really admire that others can do this even if it just doesn't fit our own styles. We are more conventional in our practice—at least up until this point. We also share the concerns of one reviewer who believed that beginners might get the wrong idea that supervision and traditional standards of care discourage creative innovation. There is certainly a struggle between maintaining ethical guidelines and also taking creative risks that may test the limits of standardized procedures. This is what Zur (2005) describes as the difference between boundary "violations" that jeopardize client safety through irresponsible conduct and boundary "crossings" that improve therapeutic effectiveness and innovation through careful, judicious, and nonexploitive interventions that may take place outside of traditional paradigms. Clearly, the key points are staying within our own levels of competence and expertise, seeking supervision, and behaving in the most ethical manner possible.

Jeffrey Kottler: A Study of Creativity in Action

After listening to and writing these stories, how could I *not* spend a lot of time thinking about how to bring more creativity into my life?

Returning full circle to the story I shared in the first chapter, I have been doing workshops for many years, following the usual template of satisfying participant expectations. I know that people like lots of handouts, which they believe will contain some valuable information that has thus far eluded them and somehow transform their practices, if not their lives. They like PowerPoint presentations—well, maybe they don't exactly *like* them, but they *expect* them. They want the presenter to give them their money's worth by telling them stuff they don't already know, hopefully some magical technique that is going to revolutionize the way they work. Oh yeah, they also want to be entertained, because it is absolutely brutal to spend a day or two locked in a room, sitting still.

Whether you teach, give lectures, and consult, on the one hand, or work as a clinician, on the other, there is an obvious connection between the work we all do. Many of the same principles that operate in therapy sessions to promote learning and growth are also part of any good presentation or workshop—if the goal is to make the changes last. In any setting in which we are facilitating development, we try to find ways to engage participants such that they are influenced to initiate changes in their work and lives and keep the momentum going after the session ends. This is even more challenging when doing workshops, since they are essentially brief, one-shot interventions.

Ever since we began this project, I have been giving a lot of thought to how I might structure my teaching, counseling, lecturing, and supervision in more novel ways that could promote even greater, more long-lasting effects. I have considered, and rejected, many of the techniques and interventions described in this book because they just don't fit my style—or perhaps my comfort level. Yet I've felt inspired to rethink the way I do things and why I have always done them this way.

A few weeks ago I was working with a client, all the while watching our interactions as if from the position of an observer. I noticed that we had fallen into a pattern of beginning our conversation the same way, covering familiar territory each week, slipping into routines that we both found reassuring. Progress with her had been slow, steady, incremental, but hardly spectacular. In this particular session, it seemed to me that we were both a little bored, both going through the motions, and surreptitiously glancing at our watches to see how much time was left. *Dang . . . 35 minutes!*

Before exactly thinking things out, I abruptly suggested that we change settings for the rest of the session. There were loud construction noises in the neighborhood, not exactly disruptive but certainly within earshot. "Why don't we move into the courtyard out back for the rest of the session—just for a change of pace?"

My client was a little startled by the suggestion. She *liked* her favorite place on the couch, one pillow supporting her back, another on her lap. She hadn't even noticed the noises outside. But since I had already stood up, ready to make the move, she automatically followed me outside, where we completed the session. It was not that anything particularly unusual happened during the rest of this conversation—we just continued the previous discussion—but the novel context and setting made the session stand out in ways that we both remembered clearly thereafter.

In the next few meetings, we each kept referring back to the "courtyard session," and did so with a laugh. We started joking with one another that if we changed the setting for *every* session maybe each one would be more memorable. And we agreed to do just that. We exchanged chairs. We met in another room, then another time outside. Each subsequent session was branded not only by a theme, but also by a distinct location. Our work became energized in ways that neither of us had anticipated.

I realize that this small adjustment does not represent much of a creative breakthrough, but it has gotten me thinking about other ways I can play with the structure of what I do and how I do it.

Soon after this experience, I was preparing a workshop for a group of so-called master therapists. I was a little intimidated by the prospective audience and so did considerable preparation for my

PowerPoint slides, adding lots of visual and audio bells and whistles. I put together the requisite handouts, complete with bullet points, clinical applications, and all the other things that are supposed to be included. I planned each of the two days, figuring out the exercises, lectures, demonstrations, and activities I would include. I worked especially hard on my opening address, knowing that it sets the stage for everything to follow.

I've done hundreds of these workshops and have come to find them tiresome, quite literally. I put out so much energy during the day, work so hard to keep people engaged, that I am exhausted by the time it is over, even while enjoying the glow of a job well done. Perhaps even more to the point, I'm fairly bored with what I do. How on earth do actors manage to perform on stage day after day, reciting the same lines over and over?

It has taken me years, even decades, to refine my art, collect my stories, practice my craft such that I can keep audiences engaged throughout the day—and even impart a few things that might stick with them. But by and large it has always felt like workshops are an exercise in futility. Besides earning their continuing education credits, what really sticks with participants after the experience is over? Yes, they have their handouts—but a week later, once they are again fully immersed in the chaos of their lives, whatever seemed so alluring has lost its magic. The stories we shared start to fade. And whatever might have seemed so valuable or important at the time has now lost its luster. We have all been to so many workshops over the years that they seem to fade together. I was recently reviewing a file I keep of certificates from past workshops and, for the life of me, I couldn't remember having even attended most of them.

Perhaps it was the jet lag that produced the insane idea rumbling around in my head as I walked into the room to begin the workshop. Maybe I was having a flashback to the "workshop with no name" that I described in the first chapter. The chairs had been set up in a large circle according to my instructions. The projector, screen, and computer were all fired up and ready to go. The stacks of handouts were on the table as requested. I had rehearsed my opening several times and so was ready to go. With all of this in place, why was this voice inside my head telling me to start over again?

It had to be this damn book and the stories contained herein. After all these examples of testing limits, experimenting with new options, taking risks, going outside of normal boundaries, here I was about to follow business as usual. I had always thought that the best workshop I could ever go to would be one where the leader says and does a few provocative things and then gets the hell out of the way so everyone could process the experience, personalize the material, and engage with one another intimately. I had always wanted to be in a workshop where we actually got to do some work, where we weren't treated as receptacles to be filled up with stuff we would never remember. What was stopping me from actually doing that—now, with this workshop?

What if . . . ? What would happen if . . . ? That's as far as I got when an idea came to me, one that no doubt bubbled up in me as a result of these stories you've just read. What if I turned the workshop upside down, or backward, forward, or whatever? What if I started the workshop from the very beginning with the stated intent to impact the participants in some enduring way? What if I (un)structured the experience in such a way that people would never forget what happened, especially if it was quite unlike anything else?

I took a deep breath and looked around the circle, making eye contact with each person. I was stalling, asking myself one more time if I was sure I wanted to do this. My mind was clear, almost empty. I had 20 hours ahead of me with the people in this room, and now I was abandoning my agenda in favor of the great unknown. My heart was pounding.

"I'd like to thank you all for your hard work and effort as we end this workshop today on Sunday at 4:00," I said, *beginning* the workshop. "We've just spent two days together, two very full days."

I looked around the room and could see some people with very confused expressions on their faces. It was Saturday at 9:00 a.m., and I was telling them it was Sunday at 4:00 p.m. Yet I could also see some smiles on some people's faces as they seemed to get what I was doing. What *was* I doing? I wasn't yet sure.

"During the past two days that we've spent in this room together, you have had a lot of amazing experiences. In some ways your lives have changed forever."

Was this wishful thinking, or was I planting the placebo? I was certainly being wildly optimistic. I could now see that most people in the room realized I was playing with time parameters. At the very least, they would probably remember this workshop that began with the ending.

"Among all the incredible experiences we've had together, all the new things you've learned, all the new friendships you've established, all the amazing insights that were generated and the growth that has occurred for you, I'd be interested in ending our workshop by hearing you mention the one thing that stands out for you."

People were looking around the room, checking each other's reactions for a reference point about how they should respond to this very weird introduction to a workshop. Some people were openly grinning and nodding their heads, others withholding judgment—or at least showing blank faces.

"So," I continued, now on a roll, "I'd like to go around the room and have each of you share your most momentous awareness that you are taking with you. Oh, and please remind people of your names again since they may have forgotten."

There was laughter, a release of tension, and then someone jumped in right away talking in the past tense about what she had learned. Of course, the trick to this exercise, and to any other that asks people to project into the future, is to get them to declare definitive goals about what they most want to accomplish in our time together. Although this objective was clearly met when each person spoke about that they learned (meaning what they *hoped* to learn), it was the playfulness and irreverence of this task that set the tone for the rest of our time together.

I never did get around to using the PowerPoint slides I'd created, or to distributing most of the handouts. In fact, much of the content I had planned never made it into the day's events, as we were so busy processing material that emerged in the moment, just like in the best therapy. Whenever I was uncertain where we should go next, I empowered the members themselves to assist with the decision making; we ended up in places I'd never dared to go before. In fact, a whole new book was born (this happens to me a lot) following the major theme that emerged from our collective work: That Which Is Not Said. We created a community that made it safe to explore issues that were rarely spoken aloud, sometimes even to ourselves. We went deep, *way* deep, into territory that felt terribly risky, yet affirming: the ways we feel special with our "superpowers," how we learn from sessions as much as our clients, how we feel like frauds or hypocrites, not really understanding how therapy works, indulging our critical voices, not trusting what we say we believe, pretending to know more than we really do, not listening to our clients, and taking ourselves way too seriously.

Most of the work I've done these past years is as an administrator, running an academic department and a charitable foundation. Although I still teach and see a few clients, most of my time is spent facilitating systemic changes within organizations and communities. As I write these words, I am on the tail end of a monthlong visit to Nepal, where I work with two partners to provide scholarships for lower-caste girls in remote areas who would otherwise be unable to attend school because of poverty. In many cases, when the families can't afford to feed all their children, the girls are married off by age 12 or sold into slavery—some to brothels in India.

Over the past seven years, we have grown from supporting one girl to helping more than 100 in seven villages throughout the country. With modest success also comes greater responsibility and workload. It is far from easy to distribute supplies to schools that require several days of walking over Himalayan passes to get to. It is even more challenging to negotiate the complicated village politics in which elders (always male) resent the attention and benefits that are bestowed on only a few select girls who they might consider worthless. In Nepal, there are more than a dozen laws that discriminate against women, making it difficult for them to own land, receive education, or improve their conditions.

I frequently have to use my skills as a therapist—and teacher of multicultural counseling—to make sense of the dynamics that occur in a place where I have only minimal grasp of the language and customs. I am also called upon to intervene in situations, or at least lead conversations and meetings, where I have no clue what is really going on. During one such meeting among our advisory board of local community leaders, several individuals kept answering their phones and carrying on lengthy—and loud—conversations while we waited patiently (I was not so patient, quietly fuming and appalled). Should I ignore this rude behavior, or should I say something to set limits? Is this culturally appropriate in this context, and, if so, should I try to suggest alternative norms for our interactions? After all, it is difficult for us to get much work done and build collaborative relationships if every few minutes someone stops the discussion to carry on a separate conversation while we all wait. Besides, my stated role is to introduce counseling concepts to a country without such a profession and with a grand total of only 30 mental health professionals for a population of 30 million (and you think that *you* have a big caseload).

The problem that has plagued me the most recently is a dispute between two volunteers, each of whom resents the behavior of the other. I am terrified of the consequences of leaving this conflict unresolved, because it could fracture the fragile cohesion of our small group of volunteers, compromising our mission. Shyam complains that Lida is not doing her fair share of the work and that he is carrying an unfair burden. He is especially resentful that Lida has recruited a friend, Mahendra, to do a lot of the work in exchange for a small salary. In the six months that Mahendra has been working for us, he has yet to be paid, creating a further rift.

When I speak to Shyam about paying Mahendra his token salary, Shyam becomes furious. "Why should we pay him to do Lida's work? Everyone volunteers to help. He should not be different."

I see his point. Mahendra is our only paid employee at this time, even if for a meager fee for service ($5 per week). But Mahendra is very poor and could not afford to work for free. He is planning to marry soon.

When I spoke with Lida about the situation, she said she understood Shyam's point of view. She agreed that she has not been able to contribute much because of her work commitments. That's why she suggested that we hire Mahendra to help out, but this won't work if he isn't paid. "Maybe I should just resign," she added. "That will make things easier for everyone."

I studied Lida and realized she is neither pouting nor angry. She just looks sad.

"That's impossible," I said to her. "We are in this together." Then, in a moment of intuition, I ask what is really going on.

Lida confessed that her relationship with Shyam had become troubled, making her very wary and uncomfortable. That was another reason why she felt it might be better if she withdrew. But I realized that this was not really a viable option since she was a key player in what we do.

We were at an impasse. In a few more days I would return home, and unless there was a resolution agreeable to everyone, I feared the organization would collapse, taking with it the future of all the children's lives that were at stake. After all these years of raising money, building relationships, developing infrastructure, and supporting all the girls, the whole thing was falling apart.

Everyone was looking to me to do something to fix this situation. They all trusted me. As an outsider, I have leverage that can be rather persuasive. But I was also terribly frightened and overwhelmed because of the stakes involved, coupled with my ignorance of what everyone was saying—and what they really meant. I felt lost and helpless. Yet I knew I had to do something. Lest you think I was deluding myself about my central mediating role (as I also tried to let myself off the hook), several people approached me privately and said, "Jeffrey, you have to do something!"

But what could I do? This situation was way beyond anything I had confronted before. I was so far out of my element that it was as if I were in a completely foreign land, in which people spoke and acted in ways I couldn't understand. In fact, that was *exactly* where I found myself.

I reviewed the immediate options. Every time I sat with Lida and Shyam together for a conference, it quickly deteriorated into accusations and defensiveness. I tried that three times, using every mediation and couples counseling strategy I could recall. If anything, such sessions were only making things worse, as each of them was digging into an untenable position that ruled out any compromise.

I tried talking to each of them privately, helping each to share their stories in a way they felt, heard, and understood. These attempts elicited strong feelings that appeared to escalate resentments and anger. And the clock was running out. I had brought 15 other people along with me for this visit, each of whom was clamoring for attention, firing questions, wanting to know what to do. I started giggling to myself because things seemed to be spinning so far out of control.

I had to think outside the box, even outside the furthest boundaries of what I knew and understood. Since I'd never encountered a situation quite like this before, I had to assume it would require an intervention that was beyond anything I'd ever done.

A Flashback

I thought back to an Indian couple who once consulted me about marital problems. The wife wanted to get a job but the husband forbid it. When I asked them what I could do to help, the husband (who did all the talking) said he wanted me to tell them both what to do. After protesting that therapists don't usually give advice, the husband explained that this might be true in America, but where he comes from in India, experts are hired to tell their clients what they should do. "Are you not an expert in your field?" he pressed. "Did you not study for many years? Have you not helped many people? This is why we came to you."

I started to sidestep the issue once again, explaining that therapists help people to make their own decisions. I was in the midst of describing the dangers of creating dependency, when the husband politely but firmly repeated that this might be fine for American couples but not for them.

"Let me get this straight," I said in exasperation. "If I tell your wife she should not work, then she won't get a job?"

The husband steepled his hands beneath his chin and nodded with a smile.

"And if I tell you both that she can work, then you'll let her get a job?"

Again he nodded, this time very seriously.

I started to feel panic, just like I was feeling with this situation in Nepal. This couple was waiting for my verdict, as if I were a judge. What they were asking me to do, what I was about to do, was against every rule I had ever learned about how to do my work. I actually glanced over my shoulder, just checking to see if anyone was watching. I felt as though I was taking a step over into the dark side, that Darth Vader or the devil was whispering, "Go on. Do it. You know you want to do it. That's what they want, too."

I took a deep breath and said, "Okay, then. You're in America now. This is a country where women are allowed to work in jobs outside the home. You're asking me if it's okay for your wife to work." (I realized that we were speaking about her as if she were not in the room, but every time I tried to address her directly, she averted her eyes and looked to her husband to answer.)

I took another deep breath. No turning back now. "Sure," I continued. "She can work. It would be a good thing."

The husband nodded and bowed, thanked me for my time, and walked out. There were still 20 minutes left in the session, but apparently they already had what they wanted.

I was so disturbed and haunted by this encounter that I called the couple a few weeks later to find out how things were going. I had visions that my advice giving had so violated everything that was good and right about therapy that they must have imploded, gone back to India, or something far worse. The wife answered the phone and reported that things couldn't be better. She was working part time and loving it. Her husband was still getting used to the idea, but he found that his status among his American friends and colleagues had actually risen as a result. He was also feeling proud of his flexibility and adaptability to American culture. The wife couldn't thank me enough for this "half-hour cure."

Back to Nepal

I was thinking about this case as I pondered what to do with the feud now before me. Clearly, this called for creative thinking so as to not alienate one party or the other. Somehow, I had to soothe Shyam's hurt feelings, yet I also had to keep Lida happy so she didn't quit the advisory group. It was then that an idea came to me from the gods of inspiration (or from wherever such novel solutions are spawned). Even now, this plan doesn't make much sense, but at the time it felt like the right thing—make that the *only* thing—to do. If I could figure out a way for each of the three parties—Lida, Shyam, and Mahendra—to save face, then perhaps they could renegotiate among themselves a new alliance that would allow each of them to feel appreciated and respected.

I couldn't use our foundation money to pay Mahendra, because that would alienate Shyam, and I couldn't allow Mahendra to keep working without some compensation, because then Lida would quit, so I had to figure out a way to validate everyone's position.

My solution was to walk up to Mahendra and give him a "wedding present" from my own pocket, a monetary gift equivalent to his salary. This made him very happy. Lida was also happy, because her friend had been fairly compensated and would now take care of the business that she didn't have time for. And Shyam was also satisfied, because he was allowed to maintain his own dignity.

My head hurts trying make sense of all this. Maybe it wasn't the money, after all, that fixed the problem. Maybe it was the "shuttle diplomacy," or the willingness to hear each side's story. Certainly, giving the money made *me* feel better, as it gave me the sense that I was doing something constructive. It was a kind of creativity in action in which I was faced with a problem beyond my understanding and skills. I had to resort to an intervention that was also outside the usual spectrum of options. I have never before (and probably never will in the future) resort to paying a client to stop making trouble or to diffuse a conflict. But, hey, it worked!

Skeptical of Techniques

What is the moral of my story? I hope it is similar to all the stories in this book: Creativity is *not* about techniques or strategies. Don't get me wrong—I *love* techniques. I want as many of them in my bag of tricks as I can find or invent. There can never be too many. Some of the best therapy books I've ever seen are those that provide lots of practical stuff; I get so sick of reading books about theory that all seem to say the same things in different words.

My main concern is that there is an overreliance on techniques. They are just tools. I don't think it even matters so much which structures we use as long as several conditions are met: (1) The intervention is novel and attention getting; (2) the therapist believes the technique is useful and powerful; (3) the therapist can convince the client that the strategy is useful; and (4) it provides some structure for completing tasks. I agree that in many cases talk is just not enough; clients have to do things. And I become so discouraged because even the most structured therapies that produce miraculous results in a few sessions still don't necessarily lead to enduring effects.

Whether as a clinician, supervisor, or instructor, I'm really working optimally when I am creating, inventing, adapting something completely new. Therapy and teaching become stale for me when I keep repeating myself, doing and saying things I've done many times before.

At workshops or in the classroom, students and professionals are always so hungry for handouts and "proven techniques" that are guaranteed to work. The real growth in such experiences comes not from following what the presenter introduces, but rather from the ways your own creativity is tweaked and encouraged. Each of the contributors in this book has offered something unique and useful to me, yet I can't imagine myself repeating their techniques in my own sessions. I would not be inclined to ask my clients to do the things that these professionals have, but new possibilities were opened for me in terms of what I can do.

I'll mention just one example of dozens that have occurred during the writing of this book, just recently, as a matter of fact. The semester was ending and it was the last night of my graduate class on culture. I asked students to reflect on all the things we did together during the course of four months—the films they watched, the novels and text they read, the online discussions, small group work, fishbowl demonstrations, immersion experiences, class projects, lectures, and so on. What did they imagine would stick with them? If we held a reunion a year hence, what would they predict would still haunt them?

The most common response surprised me. Just as it so often happens with our clients, they are helped by things we say and do that we may not even remember.

About two months earlier, after writing up some of the wilder chapters in this book (I'll leave the candidates to your imagination), I felt encouraged to loosen up a bit more in my presentations, to be more impulsive and spontaneous. I was lecturing in a large classroom with two entrances, one on each side. As I was speaking to the class about the value of doing the unexpected, I backed out of the door on one side, ran as fast as I could to the other door, and reentered the classroom without breaking stride in my talk. There was a hesitation of 10, maybe even 20 seconds, before the shock on their faces dissipated and they began laughing. *This* is what the students mentioned they will never forget—because they'd never seen anyone do that before.

Jon Carlson: They All *Inspired Me*

I see a lot of clients each week and have been doing so for many decades. One of the ways I remain fresh in my work is by trying to always invent new ways of doing what I do. I suppose that is one reason why I wanted to be involved in this project in the first place, to hear about what the most creative people are doing in their work, hoping it would push me in new directions. Well, I never imagined!

So many of the stories in this book illustrated ideas that I had once experimented with myself, or, more often, they actually encouraged me to try new things with some of my current clients. Almost each week that we did one of our interviews, I found a way to apply something from that conversation in a session. I'd like to mention just a few as a way of demonstrating what we hope is happening with you. After reading these stories, we hope you feel inspired to try some new things in your life and work.

Showing That I Care

After we spoke to Judy Jordan (Chapter 9), I was still thinking about how much she genuinely cared—loved—her client. It got me thinking about what it means to really care for someone we are helping. I'm a really busy guy, juggling lots of different jobs at the same time—teaching, consulting, writing, making videos, being a father, husband, and grandfather—that I can barely keep up with things. My friends tell me that my communications are rather brief and pointed—in fact, Jeffrey just interrupted to tell me that this is an understatement, that my e-mails to him are sometimes a single word. Just as often, my secretary is the one who responds to people on my behalf.

Well, about a week after we talked with Judy, I received an e-mail from a client I saw 25 years ago but with whom I still remain in contact on an occasional basis. He remarked to me that he really appreciated how whenever he contacted me, I would always respond fairly promptly (if briefly). Yet he was pressing me as to why he always has to be the one to initiate the communication: Why don't I ever contact him to see how he is doing? "If you really cared about me," he said, "wouldn't you sometimes call first?"

My first impulse was to explain about professional ethics and that this wasn't how things worked with clients, or ex-clients for that matter, but he really called me on my feelings. Besides, I was still haunted by what Judy Jordan had said about what it means to care. I was hearing her voice on the one hand, and yet all the admonishments about the taboo of crossing boundaries. Isn't this what often happens when we are about to do something we've not done before, compare normative standards to our proposed actions that are outside that realm? Creativity is often about asking such questions.

In this case, I realized that there was no particular harm in validating his perception about the one-sided nature of our ongoing relationship. I also decided that he was absolutely right. Ever since then, I have been sending him an e-mail (admittedly, a short one) every week, just to check in with him, to show him that I really care.

Moving into Action

Sam Gladding's story (Chapter 4) about the boy who photographed the mailbox got me thinking about this couple I had seen for a couple of years without any significant progress. The husband was an artist, very laid back, and the wife was very talkative and controlling. If I believed in diagnosis, I might say she was narcissistic, but since I don't, I'll just say she was pretty selfish. It was no wonder that she had developed that way, considering her mother had been the same. She had learned to protect herself because nobody else would do so.

Needless to say, this was a very difficult marriage for both of them. They would come in and argue, or at least the wife would argue and her husband would refuse to respond or defend himself. Over the course of two years I tried every trick I could think of and nothing worked.

One day it occurred to me that it was time to stop talking, not unlike the conclusion that Sam Gladding reached with his resistant adolescent. I said to the husband, "You're an artist, aren't you?"

"Well," he admitted, "by training, anyway."

"That makes you an artist, doesn't it?"

"I guess so. But now all I do is teach others."

"But you still remember how to do your own art?"

The husband shrugged. "I guess so." He was looking a little nervous with all the attention on him, waiting for his wife to pounce.

"Okay, this is what I'd like you to do. I want you to make a painting or a collage that represents what your marriage is about."

The husband was becoming increasingly uncomfortable. "I don't think I can do that," he said finally.

Unwilling to accept his excuse, I insisted that he create something for our next session, which I scheduled for just the two of us. Sure enough, he came in with a package under his arm. He carefully unwrapped it to reveal a collage in which the edges had been burned all the way around. Along the right side, running all the way down the middle, were coils of barbed wire. He had drawn images of screaming people next to the wire, all of whom appeared to be in great pain, their bodies fused together. The left side of the canvas was left completely blank. It was an empty void.

I examined his artwork carefully, but wasn't sure how to respond. Letting me off the hook, he said, "You know, you might not like the way I've portrayed things in the marriage, but this is what it feels like for me."

"Have you shown this to your wife?" I asked.

"Are you kidding? She'd absolutely kill me." There was terror in his face at the very idea of such a thing.

"Well, showing her the painting might kill you. Or it might save you. Who knows?"

With a sigh of resignation, he agreed to allow his wife to join us and look at the picture. They ended up talking about it with a degree of honesty and openness that had never been present before. It really was a breakthrough for them, being able to bypass words initially and use the collage as a way to talk about the suffering that they were both experiencing. It was all possible because I finally gave up trying to do talk therapy with them.

Community Interventions

Steve Madigan described his letter-writing community intervention, and that got me thinking about a way that I could adapt that perspective. I had been seeing a woman whose infant son died when their car had been rear-ended by an elderly man who hadn't seen them. The baby had been firmly strapped into an infant seat, in the backseat, facing the correct position, and yet still had died of massive head trauma. Like the man in Madigan's story, she persisted in blaming herself, thinking that somehow she could have done something to prevent the tragedy.

Even though I'd been seeing her for several months, she had made minimal progress. People wanted her to get on with her life instead of wallowing in all the grief. Madigan's story inspired me to think outside of ordinary therapy structures, and I encouraged the woman to do something useful with her suffering. I helped her to create an organization that worked to revise the law so that drivers over the age of 70 had to take regular drivers' tests to maintain their license. Through her activism, she began to build an extensive support system of others who shared her experience. She still held her pain, but did so with loving others.

Remembering What I've Forgotten

About the freshest example I have happened very recently. So many of the stories in this book illustrate systemic interventions to alter the balance of power and level of engagement within families, Keeney and Madanes being dramatic examples. Anyway, I recently saw this woman who complained that her husband is out of town working 250 days each year, leaving her to take care of the household, the children, plus her own work. In addition, she is responsible for managing her husband's life as well—telling him when to call his mother, buying his clothes, packing his bags for the next trip.

With some of the stories in this book circulating inside my head, I suggested to the woman that perhaps she was working way too hard and that she needed to work harder at doing a lot less. She just stared at me when I said this, not sure what to make of the crazy idea. In fact, she looked like I had just reminded her of something else she absolutely had to do right away—she was about to bolt out of the room.

"Wait a minute," I said, holding out my hand, "let me explain."

She still just looked at me blankly.

"Instead of doing more and more and more, I'm saying you should do nothing."

"Nothing? How do I do nothing? If I don't get these things done, then . . ."

"Then what? Will the world end? Will your husband fall apart?"

"Well," she laughed, "maybe."

"Look, in order to have shared participation in a family, there has to be room for each member to have responsibility and be accountable. As long as you are taking care of everything, there's no space for anyone, including your husband, to do anything to help."

Of course, this is standard procedure for employing strategic, solution-focused family therapy—disrupting the system, realigning the family structure, and so on. We all learned this years ago—but that doesn't mean that we use it. Hearing the stories in this book reminded me to strive for invention and innovation, even when it means doing thing that I may have once known and "forgotten."

Here's another example. I recently saw a man who complained that he was so busy at work he had no time to spend with his kids. I told him that from now on he was to be in charge of bathing his children at night: This was his job and his alone. This was something he had never considered before because he just deferred to his wife as the parent in charge. She resented his disengagement but felt powerless to change the situation.

It's not that any of the things I'm describing are exactly revolutionary, just that they represent trying new or different things after hearing the stories in this book. Perhaps the most cogent insight I drew from this experience is that persistence pays off, to keep going with a client as long as we aren't doing the same ineffective things over and over.

Creativity for Its Own Sake

We are aware that we have romanticized the creative spirit in telling the stories within this book. In a sense we have been *selling* creativity as an anecdote for lethargy and complacency in our work, especially during times when you are functioning on autopilot, effortlessly and mindlessly nodding your head as a client is talking but not really doing much at all.

In addition to slipping into mediocrity by only doing what is familiar, there is another danger: that of initiating creative action for its own sake. There are times we are bored with ourselves, tired of hearing the same old stories we repeat over and over again. We become restless and disengaged when clients seem to be repeating the same things we've heard a dozen times before. We want to do something, *anything*, to enliven things, even to entertain ourselves in order to stay awake.

There is a temptation to launch into creative mode, not because it is what the client needs or what the situation calls for, but because it pleases us personally. Case in point: The client is discouraged and frustrated, labeling himself passive and without hope because he has always been that way. You correctly assess that this self-defeating logic is standing in the way of alternative visions in which he could redefine himself quite differently. Just like clockwork, you know just where you need to go because you have done this so many times before. Perhaps you have a story ready that is virtually guaranteed to make your point, leading to a reframing of his problem that is far more hopeful. You are confident this is the case because it has always worked in the past—without exception. Second, you know that you can help him to look for exceptions to his negative thinking by kicking in a method that you have developed and refined over years of practice.

But wait! You know exactly where this will lead and what outcome will be expected. Frankly, you are bored with where this is going. Wouldn't it be fun to try something a little different? You are doing this not because a creative intervention is called for, but rather because it would be interesting to try it.

Just One More Point before We End

Throughout this book we have been speaking about creativity as if it is a finished product, as if it is neat little package that is delivered to the client. Far more often, creativity in therapy involves a collaboration, a cocreation by both therapist and client. This is quite unlike the way creativity is discussed in the arts, in which a single individual makes some heroic product through the force of her personality and talent. By contrast, innovation in therapy represents coauthored efforts in which all parties work together to go beyond the limits of what was thought possible.

Oh yeah, just one more thing: Books like this often end with some sort of neat synthesis or summary statement that is supposed to capture the essence of all that went before. While well intended, such conclusions, with a list of important lessons, are rarely memorable. The endings that you tend to remember are outside of your usual experiences. They are novel, often incomplete, evocative, and unexpected. Sometimes, they even end without an ending. . . .

References

Beaulieu, D. (2006). *Impact techniques for therapists.* New York: Routledge.

Bering, J. (2008). What I wish every student knew. In *Quirky Little Things*, June 18. http://blogs.psychologytoday.com/blog/quirky-littlethings/200806/what-i-wish-every-student-would-know.

Carson, D. K., & Becker, K. W. (2003). *Creativity in psychotherapy.* New York: Haworth.

Csikszentmihalyi, M. (1996). *Creativity: Flow and the psychology of discovery and invention.* New York: HarperCollins.

Eberle, R. F. (1972). Developing imagination through SCAMPER. *Journal of Creative Behavior, 6*(3), 199–203.

Gardner, H. (1993). *Creating minds: An anatomy of creativity.* New York: Basic Books.

Gonzales, L. (2003). *Deep survival.* New York: W. W. Norton.

Gladding, S. T. (2005). Counseling as art: The creative arts in counseling. Alexandria, VA: American Counseling Association.

Gladding, S. T. (2008). The impact of creativity in counseling. *Journal of Creativity in Mental Health, 3*(2), 97–104.

Hill, K. (1997). *Lost person behavior.* Ottawa: National SAR.

Kottler, J. A. (1997). *Travel that can change your life.* San Francisco: Jossey-Bass.

Kottler, J. A. (2005). *On being a therapist* (3rd ed.). San Francisco, CA: Jossey-Bass.

Kottler, J. A. (2006). *Divine madness: Ten stories of creative struggle.* San Francisco: Jossey Bass.

Kottler, J. A., & Carlson, J. (2002). *Bad therapy: Master therapists share their worst failures.* New York: Routledge.

Kottler, J. A., & Carlson, J. (2003). *The mummy at the dining room table: Eminent therapists reveal their most unusual cases and what they teach us about human behavior.* San Francisco: Jossey-Bass.

Kottler, J. A., & Carlson, J. (2006). *The client who changed me: Stories of therapist personal transformation.* New York: Routledge.

Kottler, J. A., & Carlson, J. (2007). *Moved by the spirit: Discovery and transformation in the lives of leaders.* Atascadero, CA: Impact.

Kottler, J. A., & Carlson, J. (2008). *Their finest hour: Master therapists share their greatest success stories* (2nd ed.). Bethel, CT: Crown Publishing.

Kottler, J. A., Carlson, J., & Keeney, B. (2004). *An American shaman: An odyssey of ancient healing traditions.* New York: Brunner/Routledge.

Lubart, T., & Guignard, J. H. (2004). The generality-specificity of creativity: A multivariate approach. In R. J. Sternberg, E. L. Grigorenko, & J. L. Singer (Eds.), *Creativity: From potential to realization* (pp. 43–56). Washington, DC: American Psychological Association.

Ogle, R. (2007). *Smart world: Breakthrough creativity and the new science of ideas*. Boston, MA: Harvard Business School Press.

Rosenthal, H. (Ed.). (2001). *Favorite counseling and therapy homework assignments: Leading therapists share their most creative strategies.* New York: Routledge.

Sawyer, R. K. (2006). *Explaining creativity*. New York: Oxford University Press.

Simonton, D. K. (2005). Creativity in psychology: On becoming and being a great psychologist. In J. C. Kaufman & J. Baer (Eds.), *Creativity across domains* (pp. 139–152). Mahwah, NJ: Lawrence Erlbaum.

Taylor, S. E., Klein, L. C., Lewis, B. P., Gruenewald, T. L., Gurung, R., & Updegraff, J. A. (2000). Biobehavioral responses to stress in females: Tend-and-befriend, not fight-or flight. *Psychological Review, 107*(3), 411–429.